ABOUT THE AUTHOR

Paul Sweeney is an economist with SIPTU where he specialises in industrial economics and financial analysis. He regularly visits different kinds of industrial plants and enterprises and has been involved in some of the major corporate restructurings in Ireland. A former tax inspector, he is also a director of the ESB. Sweeney has written extensively on economic and financial matters in journals, books and newspapers, and is the author of *The Politics of Public Enterprise and Privatisation*. He graduated in economics and sociology from Trinity College, Dublin and also has a Master's Degree in Economics.

THE CELTIC TIGER

Ireland's Continuing Economic Miracle

Second Edition

Paul Sweeney

Oak Tree Press
Dublin

Oak Tree Press
Merrion Building
Lower Merrion Street
Dublin 2, Ireland
http://www.oaktreepress.com

A catalogue record of this book is
available from the British Library.

ISBN 1 86076 148 8   Second Edition
(ISBN 1 86076 081 3   First Edition)

The views expressed are those of the author alone and do not represent
the views of any organisation or enterprise.

Printed in the Republic of Ireland by Colour Books Ltd.

CONTENTS

TABLES AND FIGURES

Tables

Figures

ACKNOWLEDGEMENTS

I would like to thank Dr David Jacobson of Dublin City University, Dr Jimmy Stewart and Peter Connell of Trinity College, Patrick Kinsella of DCU, and a number of others for their invaluable help and for comments on drafts. I would also like to thank David Givens and his team at Oak Tree Press for invaluable comments, and many in the CSO, various government departments (including Finance), Forfás and in other state agencies who also helped with data and information. Most of all I want to thank Anne, Aimée, Ben and Julie.

PREFACE TO THE SECOND EDITION

When writing the first edition in late 1997, I was apprehensive that the Irish economic miracle would falter, or even crash, as soon as the book was published. Since then, the Asian Crisis, signalled in the book, worsened; there was a major stock market fall in late 1998 and the South American economies went into recession, led by free-fall in Brazil. Ireland's largest trading partner, Britain, hovered on recession and refused to join the Eurozone, which was a problem for its little neighbour. In spite of all this, the performance of the Irish economy improved even further, with a high growth rate, one of the highest growth rates of employment ever in 1998 and a dramatic fall in unemployment.

The economy of Ireland continues to improve substantially. Since the late 1700s, there had been two centuries of unprecedented emigration — the clearest demonstration of the failure of economic policies. Millions have been forced from the small island of Ireland to make their living in Britain, the US, Australia and other countries. There were fewer at work in Ireland in 1990 than at Independence in 1922, showing that British rule could not be blamed for everything. However, as will be demonstrated, the Irish economy entered a "virtuous circle" from 1987, and since then, the economic management of Ireland has been excellent in most areas and the players in the complex interactions of economy and society have contributed very positively to sustaining the high level of growth.

Several hundred thousand young Irish adults have only known prosperity. They are the first generation, ever, to live in a time of massive job creation and economic growth in Ireland. These are at levels seldom achieved elsewhere and for such a sustained period. On the other hand, many more Irish-born emigrants who have returned at the end of the twelve years of the boom have been amazed at the transformation of "poor old Ireland".

Yet the rapidly increasing material well-being, long sought and long deserved, has brought its own serious problems. Since the first edition only a year and a half ago, unemployment has been reduced substantially — to well below the EU average — and full employment is within reach. The very high level of long-term unemployment has fallen too. However, the other great problem, highlighted amongst the many successes, was poverty. One-quarter of the population still live in poverty. While their lot has improved, greatly assisted by job creation, the level of inequality has increased. The poor may not have got poorer, but as the rich have got much richer, they are left behind.

It is becoming clear that a sizeable proportion of the beneficiaries of the Celtic Tiger economy appear not to be interested in or, in some cases, are opposed to redistribution of income and wealth. Taxes, a main instrument of redistribution, have been reduced for the wealthy and for businesses, with some small improvements for all and for the lower paid. There appears to be a consensus among most politicians, hunting the middle ground, that taxing for redistribution is best avoided.

There are unprecedented budget surpluses, government spending as a proportion of GDP is falling rapidly, and yet infrastructure in many areas is appalling, public transport worse and schools (at the heart of the success) are often dilapidated and overcrowded. Corruption at the very highest level has been exposed, particularly amongst politicians, in the Tribunals. Many people feel that politicians are "in it for themselves", which is not true for most, but with the revelation that several powerful ones were, including a former dominating Taoiseach, Mr Charles Haughey, the public are becoming cynical.

Thus, since the first edition, the negative events in the world and at home have not halted the Irish economic boom. It appears as if there will be a slowdown, to lower, but still relatively high, levels, which are likely to continue for several years. It will be seen that the external environment is important to a small economy, yet there is much that can be done and that has been achieved with the correct domestic policies, even in this era of globalisation.

Paul Sweeney
Dublin
August 1999

Chapter One

THE IRISH ECONOMIC MIRACLE

Ireland has had the fastest growing economy in the world in the last years of the twentieth century. It has been transformed over the past dozen years. One could go so far as to say that Ireland has witnessed an economic "miracle". Since 1987, there has been a sustained and well-balanced economic boom. This remarkable performance has been in stark contrast to the very mediocre performance since the foundation of the State in 1922. The boom is transforming the country; all areas of the economy are benefiting and it is likely to be sustained well into the new century. In the words of foreign commentators, Ireland has become the "Celtic Tiger" economy of Europe, and it is leading the European Union in nearly every economic sphere.

RECENT ECONOMIC PERFORMANCE

The recent success of the Irish economy is visible almost everywhere. Irish growth rates have been the highest among the 15 European Union (EU) and the 29 OECD member states for several years in the 1990s, and have even been higher than those of the four Asian "Tigers" before their collapse in 1997/98. Growth in GDP surpassed a magnificent 11 per cent in 1995, reached almost 10 per cent in 1997 and achieved over 9 per cent in 1998. GNP growth averaged a handsome 5.2 per cent each year in the 13 years between 1986 and 1999, three times the rate of growth in the previous 13-year period. This performance is superb when a growth rate of 3 per cent is considered good for most economies.

GDP growth was higher and averaged 6.2 per cent a year in the same period. This was more than twice the European Union annual average of 2.6 per cent, and demonstrates how Ireland was catching up with the Union. In the later period, growth accelerated in the six years from 1994 to 1999; GNP grew by 8 per cent each year and GDP by 8.8 per cent. National income measured by GNP, or the size of the economy, actually doubled in real terms between 1987 and 1998.

Table 1.1 shows the excellent performance of the Irish economy compared with a sample of other countries, in terms of GDP growth, industrial production and inflation.

Table 1.1: World Economy — Growth, Industrial Production and Prices in 1998 (% Change, 1997–98)

Country	GDP	Industrial Production	Consumer Prices
Ireland	9.1	15.0	2.6
China	8.3	9.4	−1.2
Hong Kong	−5.7	−13.8	−1.1
Singapore	−0.8	2.8	−0.5
South Korea	−5.7	4.0	0.2
Taiwan	3.7	7.8	2.1
Brazil	−1.9	−3.3	2.3
Israel	1.4	4.2	7.8
Russia	−4.6	−4.9	125.6
Czech Republic	−2.9	−11.3	2.8
United Kingdom	2.7	−0.4	2.4
Germany	2.5	1.3	0.2
France	3.1	0.6	0.2
United States	3.5	1.7	1.7
Japan	−2.6	−7.5	0.2

Source: OECD (1998), *The Economist*, ESRI.

Ireland had already surpassed even the emerging economies of Asia in terms of high growth rates, industrial production and low inflation in the years prior to their collapse in 1997. In 1997, the *forecasts* for the Asian Tigers had been very positive, with, for example, projected GDP growth for 1997 of 5.3 per cent for Hong Kong, 6.5 per cent for Singapore and 5.3 per cent for South Korea; similarly, 5 per cent growth was projected for Brazil. The outcome was far lower, with negative growth rates.

As well as the Asian Tigers, Japan was in particular difficulty in 1998, with the economy shrinking by almost 3 per cent. (In comparison, Ireland had two years of "negative growth" in the lean 1980s, but of only −0.2 and −0.4 per cent in 1983 and 1986 respectively — and that felt bad!) However, 1998 was the only year of "negative growth" in the decade for Japan and the OECD forecast very low positive growth for 1999 and 2000 (see Table 3.1). Japan, not so long ago the world's leading economy in many ways, performed poorly in the 1990s, except in 1996 when growth approached 4 per cent. Russia was in deep difficulty in 1998 and the Czech Republic was not doing well. The US was doing well, but the main European economies were not. The UK was close to recession with negative industrial production and Germany and France had low industrial production.

Ireland's greatest and longest-standing problems have been high unemployment and emigration. For the first time, however, there has been a substantial growth in the number of new jobs, averaging more than 1,100 a week, each year between 1994 and 2000. This compares to a decline in total employment in the 1980s. Between 1986 and 2000, 513,000 net new jobs were created — an increase of 47 per cent — a remarkable achievement.

This is not just a far better employment performance than other European countries; it is also far better than the much-vaunted US economy's "jobs machine". Between 1980 and 1996, Irish non-agricultural employment growth, at 26 per cent, exceeded that of the EU12 with only 7 per cent and the US with 15 per cent growth (ESRI, 1997: 39). The comparison between the US, EU and Ireland in job creation is shown clearly on Figure 1.1 below.

Figure 1.1: Employment in Ireland, European Union and the US, 1982 to 2000

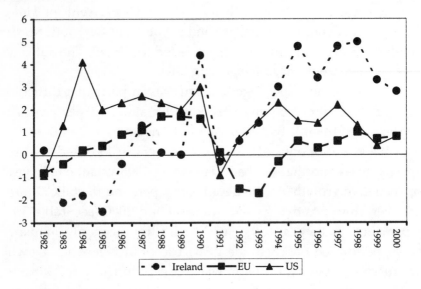

Source: OECD, 1998a

Irish unemployment has fallen in recent years to below the EU average of 10 per cent for 1998 to 6.4 per cent in November 1998. In spite of rapid job creation, Ireland still has a hard bloc of long-term unemployment. Ireland historically had a unique problem with its unemployment level: when new jobs were created, they went to new job seekers, to returning emigrants from the Irish "diaspora", or to other EU nationals, rather than to the existing pool of unemployed. However, this changed in 1994 when the growth in employment began to be matched with a fall in the rate of unemployment and even the long term unemployment level began to drop. The forecasts are for the rate of unemployment to continue to fall over the next few years. Indeed, there is a growing problem of labour shortages in some areas.

Interest rates are low and stable and are likely to remain so since Ireland joined the Eurozone in January 1999. Investment, paradoxically, appeared to fall during the boom, although a revision of the figures showed that it was at much the same level as in other European countries. Industrial production is booming, and foreign investment grew substantially, attracting in some major industries like Intel, IBM, Dell, Hewlett Packard, Xerox, Compaq, Sandoz, and financial services like Citibank, etc. Productivity increases have been among the highest in Europe, albeit slightly undermined due to transfer price-fixing by multinational companies (MNCs). Incomes rose a little in the 12 years to 1999, but because of tax reductions, average incomes rose reasonably. The income tax reductions, which amounted to a third of the increases in take-home pay, were directly as a result of the comprehensive national agreements since 1987 between the social partners. Fiscal policy has been very successful, with the country running its first surpluses for many decades in the late 1990s, reducing the national debt dramatically. Ireland met the Maastricht criteria for Monetary Union comfortably. Prices fell and remained low, as is the case in most other countries, although asset prices, in particular for housing, have soared.

Living standards have been rising rapidly. High growth occurred in the 1960s and 1970s, but was not accompanied at that time by growth in disposable income per head. The drop in the number of dependants means that Ireland's living standards will exceed those of Britain by 2000, according to forecasts, and the gap will thereafter widen, if its success is sustained. This would mean the Republic's living standards would be equivalent to the average of the European Union.

Of the consumption indicators, retail sales grew, while new car sales and registrations (of imported second-hand cars) had a spectacular boom in the mid- and late 1990s. The total number of new houses built had fallen in the mid-1980s, driven partly by a huge cut in local authority house building. The numbers of houses built increased in the 1990s and the prices of houses, which had been rising steadily, then soared from 1997 and there was overheating in the property market.

So it can be seen that Europe's fastest growing economy enjoyed a largely balanced performance, with even the old bogey of unemployment finally falling. Growth levels have been sustained at high levels since 1987, and with the dependency level falling, people finally got to enjoy the benefits of the boom in higher incomes and increased job opportunities, for themselves and for their children.

In summary, the Irish economy has never performed so well:

- A staggering 513,000 extra jobs were created between 1986 and 2000 — an increase of 47 per cent — the bulk of them since 1994;

- Every year since 1994, 60,000 net new jobs have been created;

- Unemployment dropped below the EU average of 9.5 per cent to 6.4 per cent in November 1998;

- Economic growth rates are the highest in the world, running at over 8 per cent a year in the late 1990s;

- Ireland has topped the OECD's league of the world's richest 29 countries in terms of rate of GDP growth since 1995 and is forecast to still be on top for 2000 — six years in a row;

- Inflation is low;

- Interest rates are low;

- There is a large balance of payments surplus;

- There is net immigration;

- There is a current budget surplus;

- The National Debt has been dramatically reduced to 54 per cent of GNP in 1999;

- Industrial disputes are few and conflict has been replaced by partnership in the better enterprises;

- Profits are booming;

- Workers' incomes are growing in real terms every year;

- The fall in the dependency ratio means most people are far better off;

- Irish living standards will soon equal the average in the EU;

- And the future looks good too!

But is the Miracle Real?

What have been the driving forces behind this turnaround? What lessons are there for other countries? Will the boom last? Are the growth figures telling the real story? Have the benefits of growth been well distributed? Has the rising tide lifted all?

This book will analyse the Irish "miracle" to see if it is worthy of the name. Chapter Three examines the performance of each economic indicator for the 12 years to 1999.

Twelve years is a substantial period; the Irish economy of the 1990s will be compared both to the performance in the previous decade and to the performance of other countries to see if it deserves the superlatives. Most of the earlier period, 1980 to 1987, was, in fact, an era of poor performance and so it might be said that it does not provide the best comparison. There were periods since 1960 when growth levels were nearly as high as those in the period to 1999, but these were shorter and unsustained. As the tripartite National Economic and Social Council (NESC, 1996), made up of government, employers, unions and others, said, what distinguishes the period is not its high growth levels,

> but rather the combination of good results across a number of indicators. . . . The 1987–96 period is thus unique in its harmony of high growth, improved public finances and balance of payments surplus.

But it is not just Irish commentators who laud the recent economic performance. The following are some of the comments from leading international economists and journalists.

Samuel Brittan, *Financial Times* (9 September 1997), said:

> The US investment firm Morgan Stanley coined the phrase "Irish Tiger" because Ireland has been growing as fast as the Tiger economies of south-east Asia.

Also in the *Financial Times* (11 June 1998), Richard Adams said:

> Ireland has played out one of the economic success stories
> of modern Europe, in the space of ten years transforming
> itself into a largely vibrant, modern economy.

The OECD (1999), a hard judge of economies, said of Ireland that:

> It is astonishing that a nation could have moved all the way
> from the back of the pack to a leading position within such
> a short period, not much more than a decade, in fact.

The Economist, which, in its 150 years, has generally not been kind
to Ireland, said in a cover article called "Europe's Shining Light"
(17 May 1997) that "over the past ten years, Ireland has enjoyed an
astonishing economic success". It goes on to say that:

> Ireland's transformation is so dazzling . . . one of the most
> remarkable economic transformations of recent times: from
> basket case to "emerald tiger" in ten years.

In an earlier article (27 April 1996), the same newspaper praised
the "Gaelic Boom", saying that Ireland is the only European economy "which boasts East Asian growth rates". It said that the fastest growing economy in Europe had managed to maintain low
inflation and "remarkably for a fast growing economy, Ireland
has a current account surplus".

Anthony Harris of *The Times* (13 November 1996) said:

> The Irish Republic has the fastest growth, the highest in-
> vestment, the strongest trade balance and the fastest job
> creation in the EU. Now it can add the lowest inflation and
> the tightest budget — and, not surprisingly, the strongest
> currency in the exchange-rate mechanism.

Harris continued in no uncertain tone:

> Read the figures, and swallow hard. GDP growth has aver-
> aged more than 7 per cent over the past three years. The
> visible trade surplus is nearly 20 per cent of GDP — despite
> a consumer boom and a construction boom . . .

Magnus Linklater in *Scotland on Sunday* (23 May 1999) said:

> Ireland has replaced Norway as the country Scotland would most like to be.

John Murray Brown wrote in *The Financial Times* (26 May 1995):

> Ireland has been one of the unsung success stories of the past few years. With a productivity record which would be the envy of the Germans, and a balance of payments surplus in line with Switzerland or Japan, Ireland consistently outperforms its partners in the European Union.

A year and a half later, the same paper said in an article called "Mission for Miracle Workers" (25 October 1996) that Ireland

> . . . has seen its economy grow three times as strongly as the rest of the industrialised world. The surge shows no sign of flagging.

In early 1995, *The European*, recognising the Irish boom, in an article called "Celtic Tiger treads warily — Doug Payne in Dublin wonders if Ireland's booming economy has reached peak" seemed to imply that Ireland's boom would not last, saying that there were a number of shadows hanging over it. Yet it said that "few economies boasted such strong fundamentals" (3 February 1995).

A year and a half later, the *International Herald Tribune* (1 July 1996) said:

> Ireland is enjoying a boom more characteristic of the tiger economies of East Asia than its moribund European Union partners.

Newsweek (23 December 1996) called the country the "Emerald Tiger" with a "booming economy" and said that there is

> . . . no need to search the Far East. The best answers to Europe's economic problems are much closer to home. Ireland is booming. We are talking about German style inflation, Asian style growth. Translation: an emerald tiger is at large.

THE NATURE OF THE IRISH ECONOMY

One of the wealthiest countries in the world at its Independence, Ireland[1] was to suffer a relative decline for most of the twentieth century. Living standards rose more slowly than in most other countries, particularly in Europe. The greatest economic and social failure of its new rulers was that a huge proportion of its population was forced to emigrate in order to survive.

There have been a few periods of prosperity — at times in the 1930s, 1960s and in the 1970s — but none was like the present boom. In the late 1980s, things changed remarkably.

For its first two-and-a-half decades of EEC/EU membership, from 1973, Ireland was a major beneficiary of European Union aid because its living standards were so far behind those in Europe. In the 1990s, there has been a dramatic turnabout, with phenomenal growth rates, a rapid rise in living standards and the most rapid employment growth for almost two centuries. Ireland will become a net contributor to the Union in the new century. Clearly, Ireland spent its EU money well to boost its economy.

The population of the Republic of Ireland was 3.72 million in 1999, which is just under 1 per cent of the EU's population. There had been little growth in the population for many decades until very recently. There also had been fewer people at work than at the foundation of the State, until the early 1990s. While the numbers had remained at the million mark for decades until the late 1980s, there has been a substantial growth in employment during the 1990s boom. The total numbers at work in 1999 were 1.5 million. Ireland's dependency ratio — the number of people who do not work in paid employment and are dependent on those who do — is high by European standards. However, dependency has fallen substantially recently and will continue to fall, which should benefit all.

Historically, Ireland suffered from very high net emigration, with more than 1.2 million people leaving the country since the foundation of the State (the figure for gross emigration is over 1.7

---

[1] "Ireland" describes the Republic of Ireland.

million). If they had remained, the population would be over five or six million today, assuming a continuing high birth rate over the years. This haemorrhaging began in the nineteenth century — before the Famine. Only in the 1970s was there net immigration into Ireland, but it was generated by high public spending of borrowed money. The 1990s immigration figure is the first inflow of people based on solid economic performance. For the first time ever, there were many non-Irish people seeking work in Ireland and also seeking that "quality of life" which many Irish had cited as compensation for their lower living standards in the past. This ephemeral "quality of life" — meaning the good social life, cities close to beautiful countryside, etc. — is often given as the reason for staying in a country with few opportunities for well-qualified people to change jobs.

There has been a radical structural change in employment in Ireland. Traditionally, a high proportion of the population worked in agriculture, but this has fallen rapidly from 400,000 or 37 per cent of those at work in 1960 to 8 per cent today. As in most developed countries, most people now work in services, but the numbers in industry have actually expanded slightly in recent years, against the international trend. An unusual feature of the Irish economy is the very high dependence on multinational corporations, which employ 45 per cent of those at work in industry, and they generate most output and productivity. Productivity growth has been very high, albeit from a low base.

There is a very high level of state intervention in industry, which is highly subsidised with grants, tax breaks and many other state aids. Ireland pioneered tax-free industrial zones, duty-free shopping and zero tax on export profits. It also had one of the first and possibly the most successful state agencies to encourage Foreign Direct Investment (FDI) — that is, direct investment by MNCs — the Industrial Development Authority (IDA). Ireland is very successful in attracting foreign investment. It is far less successful in building its own indigenous industry. The arguments for and against the high level of foreign industry will be analysed in Chapter Five.

The economy shows just a few signs of overheating. Inflation has remained very low, in spite of the boom. It was very high in the early 1980s, at between 10 and 20 per cent, but has averaged 2 per cent in the 1990s. The overheating occurs in two areas: house prices have rocketed, but are not included in the measurement of the Consumer Price Index; and labour shortages became apparent in 1998/99. Real disposable earnings have exceeded inflation in each year in the decade from 1987, in contrast with much of the early 1980s, and have been higher than in the UK for many years. As the analysis of performance in Chapter Three will show, Ireland also had very high growth rates of exports and a large balance of payments surplus (more exports than imports). There has been a good diversification of trade, away from the UK to the European mainland.

The public finances, which were in serious trouble for many years, are now healthy. Government borrowing and the national debt are well in check. The national debt has been dropping rapidly as a proportion of the rising GNP and the country easily met the rules for European Monetary Union.

Alongside the very strong measurable improvements in every Irish economic indicator, there also appears to be another major change in Ireland — the qualitative and positive changes in attitudes in very many spheres. There is a new confidence and an emphasis on quality and performance in many areas, which will contribute to self-sustaining growth in the future. A "can do" philosophy is becoming widespread.

Today, Ireland is a modern economy in the European mould, with a developed welfare system, highly developed education and health care systems, which mix public and private control, and large-scale state intervention in many areas.

Every economic criterion or indicator has seen a substantial improvement over the past decade. This is in contrast to many books on Ireland's economic performance which have been about the "crisis", the "Irish disease" and other titles reflecting poor performance, all of which would keep the "dismal scientists" — economists — miserable. However, this book argues that things have changed dramatically and that the performance in the period since 1987 has been good enough to force many economists to reach for their guns!

THE CELTIC TIGER VERSUS THE ASIAN TIGERS

The name "Celtic Tiger" emerged because Ireland's rates of growth in recent years have been sustained at levels close to those of the four Asian Tigers — South Korea, Taiwan, Hong Kong and Singapore. The growth rates in the Asian Tigers had been very high over three decades — averaging 8 per cent a year — although they were falling over time (before the crash in 1997/98). They had risen from a low base. For example, the average rate was over 9 per cent a year in the 1970s, but between 1990 and 1996, it had fallen to 5 per cent for Hong Kong, 8.3 per cent for Singapore, 6.3 per cent for Taiwan and 7.7 per cent for South Korea. The Asian economies crashed in 1997/98 into negative growth rates, as Table 1.2 shows. The growth forecast for the original four Tigers had been for a rate of around 5 per cent a year for the next decade, similar to Ireland's.

The Celtic Tiger outperformed the Asian Tigers in annual GDP growth even before the crash in Asia. Paul Krugman of MIT appeared to forecast this crisis in 1995, though he did not forecast the magnitude with which it occurred. His theory was that Asia's miracle is based "more on perspiration than inspiration" — that is, its growth rates were the result of high investment and cheap labour rather than productivity and efficiency. Other economists criticised Krugman, saying that his figures were wrong, being based on the dated work of another economist. When the Asian crisis emerged, people remembered Krugman's forecast; in fairness, he said that he had not been forecasting that the Asian Tigers' growth would suddenly stop and go into reverse, but that it would level out over a long period.

Table 1.2: The Celtic and Asian Tigers Compared — Real GDP Growth

Country	1995	1996	1997	1998*	1999*
Ireland	11.1	7.4	9.8	9.1	8.3
South Korea	8.9	7.1	5.5	–5.7	0.5
Singapore	8.8	7.1	5.5	–0.8	0.5
Hong Kong	4.6	4.7	5.3	–5.7	1.5
Taiwan	5.9	5.7	6.0	3.7	3.7

* = Projected

Sources: OECD (1997b, 1998), *The Economist*, ESRI

The reasons for the crisis were the weak demand for consumer electronics in the West, the rise in the dollar against the yen, to which most of the currencies were pegged, competition from China and major property speculation in some of these countries. Some of them also had weakly regulated banking systems, which borrowed abroad to lend to property speculators. Thailand, where the crisis hit hard, is one of the "new" Asian Tigers (along with Malaysia, Indonesia, China and the Philippines). The liberalisation of its banking system led to the crisis and its growth rate slowed to only 1.5 per cent in the late 1990s. The price of memory chips fell by 80 per cent in 1996, hitting Singapore and South Korea particularly hard.

There is substantial state intervention in Ireland, as in the Asian Tigers. But the similarity ends there. Some of the Asian economies, such as South Korea, have been very directive in their state intervention (Hong Kong being the exception). Most of the Asian Tigers have not been democracies for long and have harsh labour regimes. For example, in Korea, democracy really only began in 1987 and trade unions were illegal until 1993, when the OECD forced their recognition as a condition of membership. The government was slow to move on this issue and draconian labour laws caused massive rioting in early 1997. Singapore is a highly regulated society — the leader of the opposition party is not allowed to stand for election for five years because he spoke in public without a police permit. The government imposed a 15 per cent pay cut on wages, which was accepted without opposition, as the trade unions said that they were in agreement with this cut, having been consulted. There has effectively been one-party rule since Independence in 1959, with no free speech or free press. Government intervention is pervasive and the Singapore Economic Development Board's plan, "Industry 21", intends to make the country a knowledge-based economy, targeting key areas — electronics, chemicals and life sciences. Singapore and Hong Kong are really city-states that, unlike the others, have developed and properly regulated banking systems, and their per capita incomes are at western levels (though with Hong Kong's reversion to China, its future is less certain.

It is interesting to note that an Oxfam Report (1997) states that the growth in the Asian economies was partly due to investment in education and efforts to reduce poverty, particularly when compared to some African countries. The UN's Human Development Report (1997) also concluded that investment in education was the key to the Asian Tigers' success.

While Ireland modernised largely by encouraging foreign industry, countries like Korea built up massive indigenous conglomerates, the Chaebols — Samsung, Daiwa and LG — under state direction. Below these giants are tens of thousands of dependent small firms, earning Korea the description of "having the body of Arnold Schwarzenegger and the legs of Woody Allen". While Ireland's weak indigenous industry is a problem, the country has a better base to build upon, in many ways, than the Asian economies. However, there are some, like O'Hearn (1999), who argue that Ireland's economic boom is based on exaggerated growth figures and that the levels of investment are too low to sustain a real economic boom. He also argues strongly that the crises in Asia in 1997/98 serve as a warning to Ireland.

THE CELTIC TIGER VERSUS THE "DUTCH MIRACLE"

The Netherlands is a challenger for the best economic performer in Europe. Hans Tietmeyer, the governor of the Bundesbank, called it "the model country, the example for the continent", and other leading Europeans have been taken by its performance. It has been held up as a model because its economy has been re-formed while social solidarity has been maintained.

However, Holland's growth rate is well behind Ireland's at 2.5 per cent a year between 1987 and 1994, or just over 3 per cent in the five years to 1999, compared to Ireland's average GDP growth of almost 9 per cent a year in the latter period. Its GDP per capita is a little above the average for the EU, while Ireland is still at around 95 per cent of the average GNP in 1999, though its GDP per capita was the fourth highest (European Economy, 1998). Un-employment in the Netherlands was just 4 per cent in 1998 and employment grew by 25 per cent between 1985 and 1997, com-pared to just a few percentage points in Germany and the EU on average. Ireland's employment growth has been much higher, and the rate of joblessness had fallen to 6.4 per cent in 1998 and while it had been very high over the previous two decades, it was closing fast. The Dutch budget has been kept in check too, and the central bargaining system, begun 17 years ago, has maintained industrial peace, though real wages in Holland in 1997 were be-low the 1990 level — good for employers and bad for workers! A better measure of productivity is the movement in real unit labour costs, which fell by 3 per cent between 1991 and 1999, compared to a drop of 18 per cent for Ireland.

In an attack on the "Dutch Miracle" in the *Financial Times* (18 September 1997) Wolfgang Munchau and Gordon Cramb claimed that "the statistics are a mirage". They said that the employment performance is much worse than it looks for three reasons. First, part-time jobs made up nearly 40 per cent of all employment (compared to, say, 16 per cent in Germany or 12 per cent in Ire-land at that time). Second, Dutch workers work only 1,400 hours a year, compared to 1,500 even in Germany, famous for its short working year (Japan is 1,900 and Ireland 1,800). So "the economy is not producing the number of work hours the low unemployment rate suggests", they claimed.

Thirdly, there is a disproportionate number of early retirements, and more than twice as many people are on disability and on sick leave than are officially unemployed, and thus there is a low participation rate overall. The OECD put the "broad unemployment rate" in Holland at a massive 27 per cent of the working age population. This category includes those of working age who are on subsidised employment and welfare. It is clear that Holland, with its high standard of living, is expressing its social solidarity in work sharing, but its rate of increase in economic performance, even without these criticisms, is well behind that of Ireland over the past decade. Therefore, it appears as if Ireland, while below the living standards of Holland, is fast catching up, while its growth performance in most areas is unchallenged.

CONCLUSION

The success of the Irish economy in the last 12 years of the twentieth century has been unsurpassed in its history and by international standards it has also been excellent. The performance since the late 1980s has been superb, and this is demonstrated by virtually every economic indicator. Ireland has sustained such high levels of economic growth that it has jumped from being one of the poorer EU member states to the middle range of European economies in a short time, against all forecasts. The boom has been evenly spread; it has lasted over 12 years; there is no sign of overheating; and it is likely to continue.

Economic growth (GNP) in the six years to 1999 averaged 8 per cent a year — a stunning performance. Non-agricultural employment has grown by almost a half a million additional jobs since 1987, from a base of just over one million. Many of the new jobs are high-skill, high-wage, and are being filled by young educated people.

For the first time, in 1997, the government set out its plans for medium-term development, forecasting that the Irish economic boom would continue to the end of the century, albeit at lower levels of growth. The forecasts for growth, and indeed most other indicators, have erred on the side of caution. The Irish economy was twice as large in 1998 than it was twelve years earlier.

There will also be continued strong employment growth, low inflation, strong export growth, high investment and good fiscal performance with a steadily reducing debt and low borrowing by governments for the next few years, in spite of problems else-where. The OECD had forecast growth for all its member econo-mies in 1997 — the first time since 1985 — and it also forecast that Eastern European countries would enjoy growth too. More im-portantly, it also forecast that the next few years could see the most broadly based period of economic growth since the early part of this century. It was wrong. The Asian crisis changed the overall growth figures. In its 1998 Outlook Report, the OECD re-vised its world forecast down a little, from 3 per cent to 2.25 per cent for that year and to 1.7 per cent and 2.3 per cent for the fol-lowing two years. As a trade-dependent economy, the fortunes of other economies, especially its main trading partners, the UK, Germany, the US, France, the Benelux countries, Japan and Italy (for exports in 1998) are important to Ireland. These countries are forecast to see some growth in 1999 and 2000.

The Irish miracle appears to have established a solid modern foundation on which a lasting edifice can be built. This foundation consists of reasonably good infrastructure; investment in that im-portant capital, human beings; and a healthy demographic struc-ture. This should leave the country far better placed than most for the foreseeable future. The new approach in many areas, includ-ing the new forms of work organisation, where more people are empowered at every level of the economy and society, has the potential to make Ireland one of the world's leading economies.

There are huge challenges remaining for the Irish people. The first major challenge is the high level of poverty, with one-quarter of the population classified as poor. The second is that the level long-term unemployment remains too high. Unemployment is, of course, related to poverty. The third problem is the failure to modernise infrastructure, and its poor level in many areas is exacerbated by the growth; without investment, this growth will be undermined. The fourth is the soaring house prices, which have placed home ownership, the big ambition of most Irish people, well beyond the reach of average workers.

An important lesson to be learned from the Irish economic success story, therefore, is that its rewards are not evenly distributed. Low price rises, a healthy balance of payments and other economic indicators are secondary economic objectives. The three primary objectives in any economy are sustainable high growth, full employment and an acceptable distribution of income and wealth. Ireland has been superbly successful in the first objective in recent years, moderately so at the second and poor at addressing distribution. Thus, the success is tarnished.

Since 1987, the consensus between the social partners at national level ensured that welfare was not dismantled, as was happening in some countries, but instead rates were increased faster than inflation. However, little radical economic policy was implemented in areas such as redistributive taxation or tackling long-term unemployment, in order to eliminate the high level of poverty. For Ireland to be truly successful, the next phase of economic development must address unemployment and poverty.

While material growth is clearly a major ambition for most people, there is now strong recognition that it must be sustainable. The pursuit of endless growth and material goods appears to be an almost universal goal, but it appears at odds with the aim of sustainability. The Irish people have long lagged behind other European countries in material well-being, demonstrated most clearly by mass emigration for two centuries. As Ireland reaches European average living standards, it clearly will lose other attributes. It already has lost some of them. The economic boom has not been evenly shared and many beneficiaries are against sharing. The unfinished business of the miracle will be analysed in Chapter Seven.

All of the issues raised in this chapter will be examined in detail in later chapters. A historical perspective is essential to give the complete picture. In the next chapter, Ireland's economic history is examined, from 1800 to the mid-1980s; in this context, it will be seen that the recent changes are even more remarkable.

Chapter Two

A BLEAK HISTORY

The economic history of Ireland over the past two centuries is a sad tale for many Irish people. But the tale has a happy ending, as the country enters the twenty-first century in very good shape, with a reasonably well-balanced economy, which should benefit most people. The last two centuries were characterised by population decline and some de-industrialisation. Irish economic history reveals much on how Ireland became the type of country it is today — why it was so poor and so socially and economically conservative. Economic history gives a sense of perspective, but is neglected by many economists, who are often blind to either the long-term perspective or lateral, as opposed to direct, linkages, and are more impressive as technicians than as thinkers, according to Lee (1989).

In 1801, the Act of Union tied Ireland to Britain in the United Kingdom. Walking around Dublin's magnificent Georgian streets, which were built before this time, and which were to see little development until the brash 1960s, one could believe that economic progress stopped with the Act of Union. It appeared as if all the leading citizens left the city for the capital, London, and there were few new buildings after the Union. Dublin had been the second city of the Empire.

However, the Act of Union did not actually have an immediate effect, and even its long-term effect has been exaggerated, according to economic historian, Cormac Ó Gráda (1995). The economy did grow in the early part of the nineteenth century. The population of four to five million in 1801 (there were no censuses then) rapidly expanded to almost seven million by 1821 and to

over eight million by 1841. Emigration predated the Famine, because between 1815 and 1840, over 1.5 million emigrated, one-
third to Britain; of those who went west, half went to Canada and
half to the US.

However, most people worked on the land, and the growth in
population led to such a level of subdivision that many farms became economically unviable. Rents rose but were often spent
abroad by landlords. British capitalists preferred to invest on the
mainland — the "core" — and few industries were established in
Ireland.

The view of the dominant centre was put forward by Crotty
(1979) who argued the "core-periphery" case, where the dominant
centre pulls in most development at the expense of the periphery.
Crotty argued that the growth of huge industrial centres in Britain
raised the demand for cattle over other agricultural products,
which made cattle farming very attractive. This in turn reduced
the price of more labour-intensive agricultural sectors such as tillage.

The early part of the nineteenth century witnessed de-
industrialisation in Ireland. A depression in 1825/26 closed down
many Irish woollen and cotton mills, especially in Leinster and
Munster, and imports of woollen products from large British factories grew rapidly. However, these large factories also wiped out
smaller industries in towns and villages such as Norwich in Britain, according to Cullen (1972). Concentration and scale became
more important and cotton production became concentrated in
Lancashire and Glasgow.

The Famine of 1845–48 led to the death and emigration of over
one million people. The population was to decline to 6.5 million in
1851 and to 5.5 million by 1871. The Famine hit the poor hardest.
The number of agricultural labourers fell from 700,000 in 1845 to
300,000 in the early twentieth century, the number of small farmers (5–15 acres) was halved, and the cottier class was almost
wiped out.

After the Famine, fertility fell dramatically as a result of a reduced marriage rate and a trend in later marriages. Of the five

million people who emigrated between 1851 and 1921, most were single adults. The strong farmers left the farm to the eldest son and sent many of their other offspring abroad and so preserved the integrity of their farms. People had far fewer children and those who had land became hard in their attitude to inheritance.

The famine had a major psychological impact on the Irish people, which remained for a long time. In its immediate aftermath, the numbers of marriages fell dramatically, the age of marriage was delayed, there was a large growth in celibacy, fertility declined and there was greater female emigration in the nineteenth century. "The Great Famine set off a population decline unmatched in any other European country in the nineteenth century, a decline that lasted in Ireland as a whole until the 1900s and that has continued in some rural areas until this day" (Ó Gráda, 1995: 213). Emigration and these changes in fertility allowed for increased incomes for those who remained.

In spite of the growing dichotomy between the north-east and the rest of Ireland, Lee (1973) concluded that "southern Ireland modernised probably as quickly as any other country during this period (1848–1918)". While Ireland was much poorer than Britain (the latter was the richest and most advanced country in the world at the time), Irish living standards on a per capita basis were only a little below the average for Western Europe by 1913. Using various sets of figures, Kennedy et al. (1989) found that Ireland's "relative standards were surprisingly high for a country commonly thought of as very poor and undeveloped" (p. 15). However, it will be seen that Ireland had "developed" in a perverse way. There was a massive decline in population, but for those who stayed, there was growth in average incomes.

BRITISH MISRULE OR *LAISSEZ-FAIRE* ECONOMICS?

The key question in examining nineteenth century Irish economic history is whether the very poor performance of the economy, evidenced by de-industrialisation and population decline, when most of Europe was growing, was due to British misrule or to purely economic factors. There was little state intervention and the policies of *laissez-faire* economics were of such vigour that even famine relief was seen as "interfering in the market".

There was a great belief in the power of tariffs and many were to argue (mainly retrospectively) that, had there been an independent state, it would have imposed high tariffs and Ireland would have prospered. The nationalist perspective purported that if Ireland was independent, it could have raised tariffs against the cheaper British goods, allowing Irish products to develop. For example, James Connolly, writer, historian, and a leader of the Easter Rising, saw the Irish capitalist class as a problem, as it would not join with the people to demand an independent state where

> . . . popular suffrage would undoubtedly have sought to save Irish industry while it was yet time with a stringent system of protection . . . with a tax heavy enough to neutralise the advantage to the foreigner from his coal supply, and such a system might have averted the decline which was otherwise inevitable (Connolly, 1973: 32).

There are two different schools of thought in Irish economic history: the nationalists and the revisionists. George O'Brien, a very influential economic historian at the turn of the century, belonged to the nationalist school and blamed many of the ills on the British. He cites Britain's role as impeding the growth of Irish industry. Certain laws obviously did impede Irish trade — for example, the Navigation Acts in the seventeenth century and the Act of 1699 which prohibited the export of Irish wool. O'Brien claimed that Ulster's success was due to the "Ulster Custom", which gave tenants better rights on their holdings and more security, which in turn led to greater prosperity and some innovation. He also argued that it was the Huguenot immigrants who created the linen industry, Ulster's largest industry. Cullen (1968), a revisionist, disputed the importance of the Ulster Custom and stated that such property rights in the rest of the country were no less secure.

Modern economic historians see a more complex picture than O'Brien's. It is possible that tariffs would have given some measure of protection to, say, cotton and woollens, and this would have allowed them to survive a little longer. However, Britain was the leading industrial country in the world and, due to economies of scale, its goods were so cheaply produced that they would have knocked down most tariff barriers.

Virtually all of Ireland's exports went to Britain and thus severe tariffs, had they been imposed by Ireland, would have attracted tariffs on the other side of the water.

Cullen attributes the decline of industry to the growth of large-scale production in Britain. Ireland's

> . . . proximity to the leader of the Industrial Revolution and the dramatic reductions in transport costs in the nineteenth century in conjunction left Ireland's small-scale and domestic industries vulnerable in a more fiercely competitive age (Cullen, 1968).

In an article on the decline of industry in Ireland in the nineteenth century, O'Malley (1983) also agreed that the key to Ireland's failure to industrialise was the existence of large-scale British organisations and centralised production from the very early stages of mechanisation, and their proximity to large markets. He sees the north-east of Ireland as being more closely integrated with Britain and, for the rest of Ireland, the "competitive advantage lay mainly in agriculture . . . and indeed a type of agriculture which required diminishing input of labour". This meant continued emigration and population decline. He concluded, "free market forces can by no means be relied on to generate industrial development . . . in a late developing economy".

Cullen, O'Malley, Foster and other modern historians have argued that the very poor performance of Ireland in the nineteenth century had less to do with British policy, especially policy hostile to Ireland, than with the sheer size, dominance and economic power of British products. Irish industry could not develop, except in some urban centres, particularly Belfast.

Ireland's comparative advantage was in agriculture, especially in pasture rather than tillage, which was less labour-intensive.

Ireland's wet weather was good for grass growing — thus for beef, which was in greater demand in Britain, where incomes were rising as a result of industrialisation. The Irish farmer responded to the signals of the market by shifting to cattle production. His children, other than the first born, joined the priesthood, married other farmers, or emigrated. Farm labourers also emigrated. The Irish farmer had learned the lesson of the Great Famine — don't divide up the land, and fill it with cattle — even if he lost his children. Hard economics!

The landlords were being bought out, particularly after the Wyndham Act of 1903. This provided landlords with prices a little above the market price, and it gave tenants the land they so long coveted and felt should be theirs. This Act resolved the land wars, and by 1920 over nine million acres were sold and another two million were in the process of being sold (Lyons, 1976: 219). This Act removed the potential for rural radicalism, which had begun with the founding of the Land League by Michael Davitt in 1879, and which had grown rapidly. Davitt was a radical, unlike Parnell who, while radical on the Home Rule question, was conservative on economic issues. After the Wyndham Act, the peasantry became the owners of small businesses.

Assessing the Performance in the Nineteenth Century

By 1913, in spite of the depopulation and de-industrialisation of the nineteenth century, Ireland's per capita income was "not widely different from the European average" according to estimates by Kennedy et al. (1989). They placed Ireland at twelfth place among 23 countries; another estimate (Barioch, 1981) put Ireland at tenth of the 23 countries (see Table 2.1) — almost 60 per cent higher than Eastern Europe as a whole, higher than Italy, Norway and Finland, and close to France, Austria and Sweden. Ó Gráda's analysis of income growth places Ireland a little behind other estimates (Ó Gráda, 1995: 382). This was still a very good performance for a country which, a few generations previously, had endured a Famine and had seen its population decimated.

Table 2.1: Real Product Per Capita in Europe and Elsewhere Relative to the UK, 1830, 1913 and 1985

Country	1830 (UK = 100)	1913 (UK = 100)	1985 (UK = 100)
United Kingdom	100	100	100
Switzerland	65	84	123
Denmark	61	83	113
Belgium	65	76	98
Germany	65	72	111
Netherlands	73	69	104
Sweden	64	66	116
Austria	65[a]	65	99
France	74	63	107
Ireland	40[b]	61	62
Norway	61	57	128
Finland	51	49	105
Italy	65	43	99
Spain	54	37	70
Hungary	—	35	67
Soviet Union	49	32	72
Greece	39[a]	31	55
Portugal	68	31	51
Yugoslavia	38[a]	28	58
United States	65	126	152
Australia	97[a]	102	108
New Zealand	70[a]	75	93
Japan	49	29	108

Notes: a = 1860, b = 1841.

Source: Adapted from Kennedy et al. (1989).

Average incomes grew faster in Ireland than in many European countries. There were several reasons for this. The first was that the relatively rapid increase in *per capita* income, from a very low base, was achieved by the rapid decline in population, particularly by the virtual elimination of the poorest, thereby boosting average incomes. As populations in most European countries were increasing, even with economic growth, their *average per capita* incomes were rising slowly. Finally, agricultural prices almost doubled between 1850 and 1910.

As Kennedy et al. (1989) have said, this improvement is similar to what happened after the Black Death in Europe. With the same amount of land divided between fewer people, living standards rose for the survivors, even without technological advances. So Ireland had a standard of living that, while far below Britain's, was comparable to the rest of Europe on a per capita basis.

So after the Famine, things improved for most of those who remained in Ireland, though there was little innovation, enterprise, or growth in output. There was also a large degree of deindustrialisation. These factors meant that Ireland became a very conservative society economically.

THE EARLY TWENTIETH CENTURY

The relative prosperity helped underpin the "Celtic Revival" at the end of the nineteenth century, best illustrated in the literary revival (Yeats, O'Casey, Synge, Joyce, Shaw, Russell (AE)), and the emergence of the Gaelic Athletic Association (GAA), which acted as the intellectual background for Irish nationalism and which was to culminate in the 1916 Rising.

On the social side, however, there was great urban poverty. Much employment in Dublin was casual, with few large industries. The main employment areas were processing, transporting and servicing of agricultural products. The great Georgian houses of the eighteenth century were now tenements packed with slum dwellers, whose lives contrasted sharply with the bourgeoisie in the south suburbs.

> Living conditions were horrific by contemporary standards; the surveys before 1914 show 25 per cent of Dublin

families living in one-room tenements occupied by more than four people, with at least 16,000 people living below the poverty line (Foster, 1989: 437).

The city burghers were mainly interested in nationalist themes and ignored social issues. One of them, Alderman Meade, bought several houses in Henrietta Street, once the most fashionable of all Dublin streets, ripped out the staircases and fireplaces and sold them in London (Craig, 1969: 103) before making them into tenements.

Trade unions were weak and usually part of British unions, but this situation was to change in 1913. The tramdrivers' "Lockout of 1913" was supported by the Irish Transport and General Workers Union, the new trade union of James Larkin and James Connolly. It failed, however, because there were too many workers chasing too few casual jobs and they could not bring any big industry to a halt. But the lockout marked a seachange in workers' attitudes and the union was to grow very rapidly afterwards.

The First World War benefited the Irish economy. Not alone had 150,000 Irishmen joined up with the British army by April 1916, sending back "the King's Shilling", but the scarcity of food in Britain boosted prices and farmers did exceptionally well (Lyons, 1976: 359).

INDEPENDENCE IN 1922

The new Cumann na nGaedheal government in 1922 did not change policy radically. Partition cut the new state off from the most industrialised part of Ireland. The government did not view industry as important enough, believing that agriculture was the mainstay of the economy. Half the workforce was involved in agriculture; food and drink made up most exports and there was a huge market "next door". There was no thought of an industrial policy, in spite of the continuing decline in agricultural employment. Patrick Hogan, the Minister for Agriculture, said that economic policy should aim to maximise farmers' incomes, and that this policy should take precedence over self-sufficiency and reducing unemployment (Kennedy et al., 1989). James Connolly and Arthur Griffith, the leader of Sinn Féin, the leading party before Independence, who might have supported an industrial policy of self-sufficiency, were both dead by this time. For the first decade, the new government introduced only very limited protectionism. It adhered to the existing free trade policy, very much the dominant policy at that time.

In the run-up to Independence, the unionist fear of the power of tariffs was one of the key drivers behind the economic outlook that was so important in laying the foundation for the partition of Ireland. Those in powerful positions, and many who worked in the booming industries in the north-east, feared that the new government of an independent Ireland would immediately introduce tariffs in order to develop its own indigenous industries. Therefore, they fought hard to have the north-east excluded from the new state. Their reasons were very logical at the time, though the new state actually maintained free trade for a decade, only moving to protectionism later.

The population of Ireland at Independence in 1922 was 4.4 million, of which 3 million were in the 26 counties. This was around half of the 8.2 million in the early 1840s. In the 1840s, the population had been half that of England and Wales combined, whereas it had fallen to only one-ninth by 1922.

The new government had a good inheritance. There was a good banking system in place, most farmers were already owners of their own land before Independence (which was different to the situation in most eastern European countries), and the new State had many educational, social and political advantages and infrastructures (Lee, 1989). It was the Cumann na nGaedheal party, formed in April 1923 when the original Sinn Féin split over the Treaty, which accepted the partition of Ireland. The other wing, the opponents of partition, were to become Fianna Fáil. There was also a small Labour Party and a small Farmers' Party.

Cautious and conservative, the Cumann na nGaedheal government did not favour a large public sector. It was imbued with the *laissez-faire* politics dominant in Britain and wanted to reduce taxes, which it did on income by 1927, though there were few income tax payers at the time. Most taxes were on property and customs and excise. The old age pension was cut by a shilling in 1924 by Ernest Blythe, Cumann na nGaedheal Finance Minister, and while it was extremely unpopular with the people, there was an abstentionist "opposition".

In 1928, Sean Lemass of the opposition Fianna Fáil party attacked the Tariff Commission for not going far enough or fast enough in erecting tariffs, saying that:

> Ireland can be made a self-contained unit, providing all the basic necessities of living in adequate quantities for the people residing in this island at the moment and probably for a much larger number (quoted in Lyons, 1976: 610).

Yet 166,751 people were to emigrate in the decade to 1936. Only the Depression was to halt this outflow.

In the late 1920s and early 1930s, Fianna Fáil stressed the need for setting up native industries and moving agriculture from cattle to tillage to create more jobs. Yet employment in agriculture continued to fall. Ireland had a free trade policy until 1932 when Fianna Fáil came to power under de Valera. From 1932 until the late 1950s, it introduced a high level of protection; many of these policies were contradictory and subject to political (rather than economic) influence.

Fianna Fáil would not be so harsh as to cut the pension, and while the increases in welfare proposed by them were modest, they were to become the party of the working class after 1932. De Valera tried to introduce a "Social Justice" policy in 1932, which was to be paid for by cutting civil service salaries. He was not successful!

There had been some progress in clearing some of the dreadful slums in Dublin at the beginning of the twentieth century, but the Cumann na nGaedheal government only built between 1,500 and 3,000 houses a year with state aid. There was a massive housing programme in the 1930s to try to clear out the city slums, with new housing estates built in Crumlin and Cabra in Dublin and

Gurranabrahar in Cork. Fianna Fáil increased the number of state-aided houses to around 14,000 a year in the mid-1930s (Ó Gráda, 1995: 440).

FIANNA FÁIL AND PROTECTIONISM

One of de Valera's first actions after stepping into government in 1932 was to declare that the land annuity payments (for land bought by tenants from landlords) by the "Free State", as it was called, to Britain were not legitimate. He was wrong; these payments had been excluded from the 1925 "absolution" of Ireland from British debt, but it had been one of Fianna Fáil's main election promises. Britain retaliated with high tariffs, particularly on cattle (as high as 80 per cent) and quotas. This hit Ireland hard, as 96 per cent of exports went to Britain. The value of agricultural exports was to fall by two-thirds.

The decision to withhold the annuities did reduce the impact of the economic war, but as Irish exports depended so much on Britain, all areas of the Irish economy suffered. The deadlock was mitigated in 1935 with a coal-for-cattle pact and it was finally settled in 1938. The annuities were cancelled for £10 million — much less than the £90 million (including interest) owed — and some Irish ports were returned. De Valera regarded the return of the "Treaty ports" as his "greatest political achievement" according to Foster (1989). The public backed de Valera's policies, which made the introduction of protectionism easier. Lemass, the "chief architect of the 1930s tariffs", according to Ó Gráda, believed that "it didn't matter who started the 'economic war'; the main thing is we won it" (Ó Gráda, 1995: 432). Ireland suffered much under this "war", and it is highly debatable whether it "won" it.

Protectionism was, however, being introduced elsewhere in response to the Depression. The Control of Manufactures Act of 1932 was designed to keep Irish manufacturing in Irish ownership. Irish people had to control 51 per cent of the voting shares in manufacturing firms. In essence, it was an anti-foreign ownership investment strategy, which was not to be reversed until 1958.

During this period, the volume of industrial production grew rapidly — by almost 50 per cent between 1931 and 1938 — and employment grew from 110,000 to 166,000. Given the Depression, these appeared to be good achievements, greatly helped by protectionism.

However, all the figures were based on the domestic market; productivity actually declined a little in manufacturing, given the rapid rise in output which should have boosted it. Unemployment without the "safety valve" of emigration rose fivefold to 14 per cent of the labour force in 1935.

A number of foreign manufacturers were allowed to ignore the Control of Manufactures Act and set up plants here. They did not export and some firms were forbidden to do so. Thus protection prolonged the life of many firms that would have failed in unprotected markets. This was to lead to the shake-out of indigenous industry after the 1960s, when they were no longer protected.

While Cumann na nGaedheal had pursued a free trade policy, it was not a pure one. Some of its members were close to Fianna Fáil thinking in seeking protectionism; in November 1927, President Cosgrave boasted of high tariffs on non-agricultural imports. There was a

> . . . drift to greater protection in the years 1927–1932 in response to changing external circumstances and growing internal pressures from an aggressive opposition and increasingly vociferous interest groups (Daly, 1992).

Ó Gráda agrees, saying that had Cumann na nGaedheal remained in power in the 1930s, it is likely they too would have become far more protectionist, following the world pattern (Ó Gráda, 1995: 387). But Fianna Fáil pursued the policy with great conviction.

Was the policy of protectionism a success? It boosted employment in the 1930s, and by 1950 employment in manufacturing was double the level of 20 years earlier, albeit from a low base. It was, however, to stagnate in the 1950s. Irish manufacturing, protected from competition, often produced poor quality and expensive goods in the small home market. Productivity was low, so there was insufficient surplus to boost jobs in services. So manufacturing jobs were supported by long-suffering and relatively poor Irish consumers. The biggest indictment of the policy of protectionism, with the benefit of hindsight, was that no firms were encouraged to develop export markets. It has been seen that some foreign-owned firms were even forbidden to export. This left Irish industry uncompetitive and weak when competition did arrive in the 1960s.

Exports as a proportion of output fell substantially in the protectionist period. Policy-makers in the 1930s might be excused because the Depression and the War book-ended the decade; but once the War had ended, and in the face of stagnation and deficits, outward-looking policies should have been the immediate priority.

Ó Gráda says that the policies of protectionism were not as irrational as some commentators have claimed. There was a logic to such policies when the world was in severe depression and then at war. What was irrational was "the determination of both Fianna Fáil in 1945 and the Coalition Government in 1948 to continue them in the altered post-war circumstances. Their limitations would have been obvious by then," he concludes (Ó Gráda, 1995: 433).

The Second World War saw Ireland's national income stagnate, rising by a mere 14 per cent between 1938 and 1947, compared to 47 per cent in the UK and even more in Northern Ireland in the same period. Exports had fallen by half; industrial output and employment also fell. GNP stagnated during the War but living standards fell, with less goods available. During the War, the supposedly self-sufficient nation now exported everything — that is, 99 per cent of total exports — to Britain! Emigration rose to 36,000 a year, twice the level of the previous decade, with most going to Britain. Imports fell, however, and external reserves were built up.

DIRECT STATE INTERVENTION

Patrick McGilligan, the Cumann na nGaedheal Minister for Industry and Commerce, appeared to have strong views on state intervention. He said: "it is not a function of the Government to provide work for anyone . . . people may have to die in this country and die through starvation" (Lee, 1989: 127).

Yet it was McGilligan who was to establish the first state-owned commercial company, the ESB, which would build the very ambitious Shannon hydro-electricity scheme. It first came before the Dáil in 1924 and proved very controversial, mainly because the State was involved. Work began in 1925 and was completed in 1929 (Sweeney, 1990: 17–22).

In 1927, two other commercial enterprises were set up by the Cosgrave government. The Dairy Disposal Company was set up to buy private creameries where there was wasteful competition. It was intended to sell it on to the co-ops, but this did not happen until 1972! The Agricultural Credit Corporation was set up in 1927 to offer credit to farmers on reasonable terms. It was to be sold to the public but because of a poor response, it remained a state company. The Cumann na nGaedheal party, re-elected in 1927, did not establish any more state-owned companies.

Fianna Fáil established the Irish Sugar Company in 1933 by nationalising a private company in difficulty, in spite of large subsidies since 1926. At one time the company had up to 20 plants (Sweeney, 1990: 22). They also set up a small bank in 1933, the Industrial Credit Corporation, to supply credit to business. In 1937, the national airline, Aer Lingus, was established, then as a subsidiary of Aer Rianta, the airport company. In 1939, the Irish Life Assurance Company was set up through the nationalisation of five subsidiaries of UK companies. Several other commercial state companies were established in the 1940s, including Irish Shipping, Irish Steel, CIE and some smaller ones. Most of these companies still exist; some are now private and some are fairly large.

According to Sean Lemass, these companies were "set up only where considerations of national policy were involved or where the projects were beyond the scope of, or unlikely to be undertaken by, private enterprise" (quoted in Sweeney, 1990: 3). So much for ideology, or radical attempts to nationalise the "commanding height of the economy", as was the Labour Party's ambition in the UK. Yet the commercial state companies were to play an important role in the economy's development. At their peak in 1987, they contributed more than 10 per cent to GNP, over 18 per cent to gross capital formation and employed over 6 per cent of those at work, or nearly 70,000 people.

THE STAGNANT FIFTIES

The problems of the 1950s were exacerbated by a balance of payments crisis, as the surpluses that had been built up during the War were wiped out between 1947 and 1956. In 1955, a Capital Advisory Committee, appointed to examine public investment, recommended that a programme for economic development be prepared. This was an important and historic recommendation.

The Secretary of the Department of Finance, T.K. Whitaker, was given this task. "Economic Development" was published in 1958. It was an indictment of the previous 40 years of unproductive agriculture, population decline and emigration, lack of industry, risk-averse Irish capitalists, and wasteful public investment.

Its recommendations were aimed primarily at aiding agriculture. But the main recommendation from the point of view of industry was that foreign capital was to be enticed in with tax concessions and other incentives. The report stated that "it must now be recognised that protection can no longer be relied upon" and "in the case of new industries, to confine the grant of tariff protection to cases in which it is clear that the industry will, after a short period, be able to survive without protection".

The "Programme for Economic Expansion" was an indicative economic plan, but it was not called a plan! As well as the tax breaks for foreign investors, it recommended an integrated development programme to try to stop emigration. It worked well for industry but not in agriculture, with only a 1 per cent increase in net agricultural output between 1957 and 1963, whereas industrial production rose by 47 per cent in the same period (Lyons, 1976: 630). The eradication of bovine TB was one of the objectives. Sadly, this remains to be achieved, despite spending hundreds of millions of pounds of taxpayers' money.

One of the first industrial policy reports in the early 1960s, by the Committee on Industrial Organisation, was to provide a very good assessment of industry and set out plans to strengthen firms. It was, however, largely ignored. Many of the weaknesses outlined were to remain with us for many decades — small-scale, short-run production, lack of R&D, poor marketing, poor quality and design, etc.

Table 2.2: Net Emigration from Ireland, 1850–1998

1850s*	800,000
1860s*	697,000
1870s	502,000
1880s	597,000
1890s	396,000
1900s	262,000
1910s	116,000
1920s**	136,000
1930s	101,000
1940s	250,000
1950s	409,000
1960s	135,000
1970s	(104,000)
1980s	208,000
1990–98	(20,000)

* Gross outflows
** Estimate

Note: The figures from 1852 to 1921 are from returns to the Registrar General and are persons who have been identified as leaving Ireland permanently with the intention of not returning by the police at the ports. The figures are for all the island of Ireland until 1924, after which they are for the Republic of Ireland. The figures for the 1970s and the 1990s show net inflows.

Sources: NESC (1991) and CSO.

Table 2.2 shows the numbers of people who left Ireland in each decade since the Famine ended in 1848, giving a staggering gross total of over 5 million in 150 years, with the net figure being over 4.5 million people. In the context of a population of 5 million for the whole island today, there is no comparable level of emigration from any country in modern times. Emigration in the 1950s was extraordinarily high as a proportion of a population of less than 3 million, compared to 6.5 million in the 1850s.

A total of 1.1 million (net) emigrated from the Republic since Independence. The biggest decade of emigration was the infamous 1950s, with 409,000 emigrating between 1951 and 1961, bringing the population down to only 2.8 million.

For all its ideology of independence and self-sufficiency, the new State was still tied closely to Britain where most of the exports — and emigrants —were still destined. Cattle and beef had risen to 70 per cent of exports by 1961, up from 51 per cent in 1938.

The 1950s were stifling, culturally, intellectually, and economically. However, some new thinking was going on behind the scenes, even if it was to take a long time to emerge into practice. The Coalition Government of 1954–57 began to talk to the World Bank and IMF. Politicians and others began to wake up to what was happening elsewhere. The first three decades of independent rule had seen the government attempt to balance the books. It was only in 1956–57 that Keynesian expansionism became acceptable. Ireland had received nearly £150 million in aid under the Marshall Plan by 1950 (Foster, 1989: 577). In spite of the fierce debate going on behind the scenes between de Valera and Lemass and within Fine Gael and Labour, the country had taken foreign money!

Sean Lemass was the most influential figure in the Irish economy in the twentieth century. This was partly because he was around so long — he was in the GPO in 1916 and became the Minister for Industry and Commerce when Fianna Fáil come to power in 1932. He held this ministry in every Fianna Fáil government until 1959 (except two years as the still important Minister for Supplies during the Second World War), when he became Taoiseach, succeeding de Valera. He was Taoiseach until 1966.

It was he who staunchly defended and introduced protectionism in the 1930s and it was he who was to abandon it with great vigour in the 1960s. Farrell (1983: 27) says that:

> Lemass was already envisaging a far more interventionist role by the State. He saw protection as part of a co-ordinated set of policies designed not in the interests of the mercantile class but in the interest of the community as a whole.

And that was partly "to break the strong tradition of investing abroad among the Irish capitalist class" (Farrell, 1983: 29).

It was William Norton of Labour who, as Minister for Industry and Commerce, first opened up to foreign investment, travelling to the US in 1956 to seek investment; he also accepted a proposal for an oil refinery in Cork Harbour. De Valera was against Norton's attitude to foreign investment, and Lemass backed his leader, attacking foreign companies. Even in 1956, he was ambiguous in his statements on foreign investment, though he was to come out in favour shortly after.

Lemass played both sides on the foreign investment debate, according to Bew and Patterson (1982). In 1945 he was not so determined in his opposition to foreign investment, but he opposed the establishment of the Industrial Development Authority in 1949 and the Coalition's pursuit of foreign capital in 1956, while in opposition. Yet he had pursued foreign investment in 1953 — demonstrating some ambiguity or hypocrisy. Perhaps he was having difficulty in getting through to de Valera on the issue. Lemass and Whitaker were not a partnership. Whitaker was very orthodox and hostile to all impediments to the free workings of the market, whereas Lemass had a more Keynesian view (Bew and Patterson, 1982: 194).

In January 1957, Lemass said that exports could not be developed "without linking up with external firms with ample financial and technical resources and established connections in the world's markets". So "the architect of protectionism" in the 1930s was preparing to ditch the now defunct policies, just prior to the 1957 election — which Fianna Fáil won.

OPENING UP TO THE FOREIGNERS

This delay in coming to terms with the failure of the protectionist experiment was to give Ireland the late starter status again. O'Malley (1989) pointed out the difficulties for Ireland as the late-comer to industrialisation in the nineteenth century; he also pointed to the disadvantages in the country's "late-comer" status to modern industry this century. Had Ireland opened up ten years earlier, it would have joined in the post-war boom, which lifted Europe into the most sustained period of economic growth ever, and which was to last until the early 1970s.

Ireland had actually applied for membership of the EEC in 1961 with Britain, but was turned down and was finally admitted in 1973. The first steps to free trade were taken with the signing of the Anglo-Irish Free Trade Agreement in 1965. Foreign firms be-gan to invest in Ireland and the first ever growth in population since the Famine was recorded in 1966.

While it was realised that opening up to free trade would prove difficult for indigenous Irish firms, the effect was far worse than anticipated. The firms in the sectors sheltered from competi-tion were not too badly hit; but those sectors that were forced to compete saw employment fall massively by a quarter. The largest firms (over 500 employees) were worst hit, with almost half of all jobs being lost between 1973 and 1980 (O'Malley, 1989).

Import penetration grew as the share of imports rose dramati-cally. There was a wider choice to Irish consumers, the quality was better and prices cheaper. All sectors were affected, especially clothing, textiles, footwear and chemicals. Car assembly was wiped out (ironically, the car components industry employs more today than in the heyday of assembly).

THE BOOMING 1960S AND THE 1970S

The other side of the coin was a rapid growth in exports; by the end of the 1960s, Ireland had changed from an agricultural country to an industrial one. Yet even agriculture, which had hardly increased its output since the First World War, rapidly grew, thanks to large subsidies granted under the first two Programmes of Economic Expansion, higher world prices and easier access to Britain under the new trade regime. Tourism also boomed until the Northern conflict began in 1969. The population rose for the first time since the Famine.

The 1960s saw economic growth reach its highest levels ever, averaging 4.4 per cent a year between 1960 and 1973 — only surpassed recently. These figures were well above British rates and in line with Europe. The reasons for the growth were exports, improving terms of trade, fiscal expansion, rises in real wages due to real productivity gains and a booming European economy. As the growth rate was from a low base, it was still low when compared to other poorer countries, in both Western and Eastern Europe.

The fiscal expansion in the capital side was not confined to productive investment, as "Economic Development" had advocated. High social spending was maintained, but the high level of exports and the favourable economic climate allowed the policy to be pursued. There was a broad consensus on the new direction in policy, on foreign investment and the importance of industry. A tripartite body, the National Industrial and Economic Council (NIEC), facilitated this consensus.

Economic planning also helped in building consensus. The first Programme for Economic Expansion (1959–63) was quite successful. The Second Programme (1964–70) set out targets for each sector. It was abandoned in 1966, partly because it was based on the assumption that Ireland would join the EEC. A Third Programme was launched in 1969 for 1969–72, but its targets were not achieved, especially on employment.

Before the current boom, the 1960s were long hailed as having been the best period in the economy — and they were good. They appeared even better when contrasted with the 1950s. Alongside the economic growth, there was the advent of television and the cultural changes it helped to bring. It culminated in the "Gentle Revolution" in 1968, an expression of the confidence of students and their willingness to challenge authority. The other major feature of the late 1960s was major industrial unrest, with over a million person-days lost in 1969 and 1970.

In 1972, manufactured exports finally equalled agricultural exports, whereas they had only made up one-quarter of exports in 1958. There were also more people employed in industry. The greatest disappointment was that unemployment was rising in the 1970s, along with labour force growth. The rate of unemployment was still only around 7 per cent, less than 100,000 people. Even in 1980 it was 91,000, but it was to soar in the 1980s, peaking at 232,000 (ILO-type measurement) in 1987. Only 8 per cent of women were in the labour force in 1971.

It was surprising that indigenous industry seemed unable to respond to the many incentives that were attracting foreign industry. Even as early as 1974, 60 per cent of manufacturing output was generated by those foreign firms attracted by tax breaks and other incentives. Over half of all investment was financed by the State, either directly or in aid to the private sector. Kennedy et al. (1989: 72) say that "there was no tendency in business towards greater self-reliance". Inflation took off, as in most other countries, rising from 2.7 per cent in 1961 to 8.2 per cent in 1970, then rose into double digits, peaking at 20.9 per cent in 1975 (annual average), falling and rising again to a peak of 20.4 per cent in 1981, and falling below double digits from 1984. The oil crises of 1973 and 1979 exacerbated inflation and damaged other economic activity.

After the 1973 oil crisis, all OECD countries suffered declines in growth compared to the post-war situation. Ireland did not suffer as much as other countries until the second crisis in 1979. Ireland had been helped by public spending and favourable demand abroad. Membership of the EEC in 1973 brought immediate benefits to agriculture. There was a boom to 1978. Farmers were so confident that they ran up large debts. From 1978 they saw the biggest drop in income, with real income per person falling by one-third by 1980.

ASSESSING GROWTH — 1915–1985

Ireland's growth rate in the 70 years to 1985 was below that of every European country except Britain, according to Kennedy et al. (1989). They point out that, even with the lowest population growth, Ireland still remained near the bottom of the European league table of per capita growth, just above Britain.

In the period from 1973–85, Ireland had one of the fastest GDP growth rates; this was partly because rates slowed everywhere else. Yet growth per capita was below the rise elsewhere, because Ireland's population was growing when it was falling elsewhere, and because of outflows of profits which distorted these particular figures. The new foreign companies were contributing much to the economy and the problems of indigenous industry were not seriously addressed. This continuing problem will be examined in Chapter Five.

Importantly, the growth from 1977 was based on massive public spending, financed by borrowing. This spending spree, promised by Fianna Fáil to win the 1977 election, was to be one of the great mistakes of Irish economic policy in the twentieth century. It took a long time to get the public finances back on track.

Ireland's trade was mainly with Britain this century. It did not fall below 50 per cent of total exports until the mid-1970s. As Britain was in relative decline, Ireland was tied to its faltering performance. It was still growing, but slowly, and so too was Ireland. It is significant that the eventual shift in trade to other countries was to help set the basis for the economic miracle of the late 1980s and 1990s.

Independence did not give Ireland its hoped-for boost — it remained tied to Britain, which had declined relative to most other European countries. In Kennedy's words, its performance was "very mediocre" (Kennedy et al., 1989). He points out that the rise in real product per capita in the 70 years since the First World War was much the same as in the preceding 70 years or so.

CONCLUSION

The key question now asked of nineteenth century Ireland was: Did British rule mean that Ireland was held back? Ireland, like other parts of the United Kingdom, did not suffer discrimination under law, but it did suffer because its industries, such as they were, could not compete with superior British factory products.

Britain had the advantage of an early start, as well as large markets, coal and iron and other attributes, especially early concentration of industries and economies of scale. Northern Ireland was caught up in the first wave of the Industrial Revolution, particularly in the textiles industry. It was able to diversify into related products, which was the basis for its industrialisation. Irish industry, on the other hand, was wiped out, except in the north-east and some urban centres, where industry did grow.

The increase in demand for beef shifted agriculture from more labour-intensive tillage to pasture, which was not conducive to employment and population growth. It is possible that tariffs would have slowed down the elimination of Irish industry, but it is unlikely to have grown with the aid of such taxes. More was needed and there was little evidence of it happening, except in the north-east.

Ireland saw its population growing rapidly from four or five million in 1800 to 8.2 million in 1841, the eve of the Famine, even though another 1.5 million emigrated in this period. The extensive subdivisions of parcels of land and subsistence living could not be sustained. The Famine caused a seachange in attitudes to reproduction and inheritance, which was to have a real material affect on the development of Irish society. The population fell dramatically in the second half of the century, while it was growing everywhere else, and it did not expand until the 1960s.

Those who survived to live in Ireland saw their incomes grow at much the same rates as in many other countries, even though there was little innovation. With the exception of the north-east, Ireland was an agricultural country at Independence. Most people in the north-east, fearful of the potentially devastating effect of high tariffs if introduced by the new government, wanted to remain in the Union with the United Kingdom. Their wishes were granted and Ireland was partitioned.

The new State followed the ruling orthodoxy of *laissez-faire* economics and relative free trade. When Fianna Fáil came to power in 1932, they introduced protection and started an "economic war" with Britain. Ireland did not benefit from this war, except that it gained a write-off of most of the debt and regained the "Treaty ports". The country suffered during the Second World War and in the 1950s it stagnated, while the rest of Europe boomed.

Finally, policy-makers woke up and revoked the out-of-date protectionist policies and engaged in economic planning. They began to dismantle protection and to encourage foreign investment. This led to unprecedented growth in the 1960s. The 1970s were a period of growth too, but with the oil crises and huge public spending at the end of the decade, the economy was not in good shape. The 1980s were lean and hungry with a big drop in industrial employment and with falls in national income in some years.

To conclude, there were five major policy decisions made since Independence which damaged the Irish economy:

- The first was to provoke the "Economic War" with Britain, which Ireland largely lost (even if it made some feel good).

- The second was the experiment in protectionism in general, which was greatly flawed. Its tariffs were inconsistent and it discouraged firms from exporting, so they were very weak when tariffs were dismantled. Of course, de Valera truly believed in self-sufficiency and in "frugal living". The Irish people had different ideas.

- The third was the delay of a decade in changing the policies of protection and self-sufficiency to outward-looking trade policies, which was the only way forward for a small economy, especially when it was so obvious that the rest of Europe was booming.

- The fourth was that the policy recommendations of the various reports, including the Committee on Industrial Organisation, were not followed immediately and vigorously to address the problems of indigenous industry.

- The fifth major policy mistake was the 1977 spending-spree, which was to seriously set the country back for a long while.

Things were to change by 1987, as we will see in the next chapter, where we take a look at the Celtic Tiger economy today.

Chapter Three

THE IRISH ECONOMY TODAY

This chapter assesses the recent performance of the Irish economy. Government ministers had been full of the good news for several years, but it was not until 1997 that the economic boom finally became widely recognised in the Irish media and in the popular psyche. But is it real, or are the traffic jams in urban centres and huge rises in house prices just reflections of a consumer-led, easy-credit boom? Is it an illusion, like the "Thatcher Boom" in late 1980s Britain, which was caused by easy credit and which burst, leaving hundreds of thousands with homes worth far less than they had paid for them? Is the performance real?

The best way to check this out is not to count the number of cars per thousand people, or shopping sprees, though this will be done, but to take each of what economists call the main "economic indicators" and to subject them to scrutiny. These will be analysed, compared with earlier periods and with the performance of other countries for the period from 1987 to 1999, where the data is available. It will be seen that for almost every indicator, Ireland scores exceptionally well. Indeed, the economic performance has been excellent.

THE ECONOMIC INDICATORS

The economic indicators that will be examined are growth rates, employment and unemployment, trade, balance of payments, investment, interest rates, productivity and output, incomes, prices, consumption indicators and fiscal performance. In addition, the level of growth will be questioned, as well as the distribution of that growth.

GROWTH — GNP AND GDP

It has been seen that in the 12 years to 1999, Ireland enjoyed an annual average GNP growth rate of over 5 per cent,[1] or over 6 per cent for GDP. This is extremely high, especially over such a long period of time. This was almost treble that achieved in the previous ten years. In the six years to 1999 the rate of GDP growth is forecast to average 8.8 per cent each year.

Compared to other countries, Ireland's recent growth rate has been very high — far higher than that of the EU and the OECD in the 1990s. In the 1980s, it had been marginally higher than the EU and the US. But at around 3 per cent a year in the previous 30 years, it was just a little below that of other EU countries. As its main trading partners were in recession for several of its best growth years, Irish growth rates are even more remarkable, indicating a growing share of markets that were in recession.

Table 3.1: Real GDP Growth in Major Industrial Countries and Ireland, 1996–2000

Country	1996	1997	1998	1999*	2000*
United Kingdom	2.6	3.5	2.7	0.8	1.5
Germany	1.3	2.2	2.5	2.2	2.5
France	1.6	3.0	3.1	2.4	2.6
Italy	2.6	3.5	2.7	0.8	1.5
Ireland	7.4	9.8	9.1	8.3	7.3
Total EU	1.8	2.7	2.8	2.2	2.5
United States	3.4	3.9	3.5	1.5	2.2
Japan	3.9	0.8	–2.6	0.2	0.7
Total OECD	2.0	2.5	2.5	1.7	2.3

* Forecast

Sources: OECD, 1998, Review and Outlook, Central Bank and ESRI Quarterly.

---

[1] Most figures are rounded. Most figures are from the government's Central Statistics Office (CSO), or the OECD, or from reputable bodies like the ESRI, NESC or Eurostat (the EU statistics office).

Table 3.1 shows the excellent growth rates in Ireland in the five years to 2000, compared to the EU, to the total OECD countries and to some of the leading industrialised countries in the world. Indeed, some estimates for Ireland's growth are even higher than those given in the table. Slow growth in the EU allowed Irish GNP to close and it was around 95 per cent of the average in 1999. The 1995–96 figures were above the Asian Tiger performances before their fall, and while the Irish GNP figure is lower than GDP, both are nonetheless impressive. They are multiples (over three times) of the average of the 15 EU member states and of the 29 OECD members, and well above the US and Japan.

The good news finally hit home in October 1997 when the government announced that it had taken in £500 million more in taxes than it had expected for the first three quarters of 1997. One mandarin in the Department of Finance, Michael Tutty, embarrassed by the riches, was inspired to remark that "things just keep getting better and better". The editorial of the *Irish Times* on that day (3 October 1997) said that the figures were "nothing less than sensational". Also on the same day, unemployment fell below a quarter of a million on the Live Register for the first time since 1990. The forecast for economic growth for 1997 was also revised upwards by Mr Tutty to 7 or 8 per cent for GNP, and it was followed by similar growth in 1998. This compared to less than 3 per cent for the EU, Germany, France and Italy, Japan, and most countries with the OECD, US, and UK at 3 per cent plus for 1997, as the table shows. In December 1997, the government had forecast a deficit of £89 million for 1998. The outturn was a surplus of £747 million. The first quarter results for 1999 indicated that there would be a surplus of over £1 billion for the year, which showed that there was no sign of a slowdown.

MEASURING IRISH GROWTH

There are two problems with growth statistics. First, Irish growth figures, particularly Gross Domestic Product (GDP), were exaggerated for many years, but are now more accurate because of changes in how national income statistics are compiled. The reason for the figures being overstated was that multinationals were engaging in transfer price fixing. When the cause of the problem — the repatriation of vast amounts of profits — became obvious and even foreign commentators were beginning to voice scepticism about the growth figures, government agencies had to amend them. Therefore, the growth figures used in this book are the revised ones. Even with the downward revisions, the Irish growth figures are very impressive.

The second problem with the growth figures is a general one: orthodox measurements of economic growth in all countries have their faults. Economic growth figures are the main measurement of an economy's performance. Therefore, had Ireland's figures of over 5 per cent a year, each year since 1987 been exaggerated, the economy would not be a Celtic Tiger but a "Celtic Tortoise"!

The Irish Republic does have an unusual and specific problem when its rate of growth is examined. Unlike most countries, there is a large divergence between Gross National Product (GNP) and Gross Domestic Product (GDP). The difference between GNP and GDP is called "Net Factor Flows". In 1999, the gross outflow for Ireland amounts to a massive £17.3 billion, from which inflows of £8.5 billion must be deducted. Repatriated profits and royalties amounted to £7.7 billion in 1999 — or a substantial 7 per cent of GNP. A further £2 billion in "reinvested earnings" might be added to this, which are profits made by multinationals but not yet repatriated. There were interest payments on the national debt too. And just to make it even more confusing, leading Irish companies are now major investors abroad and repatriate profits, but to Ireland. The bottom line is that net factor flows (or payments) amounted to £8.7 billion in 1999 and this, deducted from GDP of £60 billion, gives GNP of £51.3 billion, which is the unique Irish difference.

This is both good news and bad news. The multinationals are making vast amounts of money in Ireland, but they are sending it home. But are they really making loads of money here? They are doing very well in Ireland, but the low rate of company tax (nominally 10 per cent compared to 30–40 per cent elsewhere)

does induce them to declare additional profits in
they do not really make here. This inflates GDP a
land look richer than it really is. Thus, earnings
nationals can seriously distort the key economic indicator of a
small economy.

Transfer Price-Fixing

"Transfer price-fixing" is basically a method of fiddling the books,
and most multinationals do it. They depress the price of raw materials from, say, the US for the Irish operation, and this gives the
Irish plant very large profits. As the tax rate is only 10 per cent
here, little tax is paid compared to what might be due in the US.
For the MNC as a whole, this does not matter because they produce group accounts, with all the internal prices balancing out. A
very large proportion of MNC transactions do not take place in
the market, but are internal corporate arrangements where
"prices" are determined by factors such as tax rates, political
situations, boosting market share and other corporate objectives.
Intra-firm trading of multinationals is a huge and growing factor
in world trade, making up one-third of all trade.

By locating the profits in Ireland, MNCs are paying a level of
company tax that would not otherwise be received, and thus they
are helping the Irish Exchequer (artificially). For example, it has
been estimated, by analysis of the Irish trade figures for "other
food ingredients", that Coca-Cola, which has a plant in Drogheda
with around 200 employees, may make profits as high as £400
million each year in Ireland. With a nominal tax rate of 10 per
cent, this could mean tax for the Irish Exchequer of up to £40 million a year. This low rate applies to both manufacturing and exported services. It would be a foolish person who believed that
the 200 "super-workers" in the Drogheda plant were really generating this amount of wealth. Cola essence may be a valuable
commodity today, but is it more valuable than gold?

Another big success in tax revenue, if not in jobs, is the export-
driven International Financial Services Centre (IFSC) in Dublin's
Docklands. In 1998, it brought in £240 million in taxes. There were

ɔ,100 jobs (the target was 7,000). The taxes fluctuate in response to tax changes in other countries and to changes in the financial markets. While the IFSC is based on artificial incentives, it appears that it will become embedded in the economy even after the tax incentives lose their attractiveness. It is a success for three reasons: taxes, highly paid jobs (even if below target) and the skills learnt in the arcane world of derivatives, swaps and other non-productive but rewarding transactions in the global financial economy!

The Left had long been critical of transfer price-fixing by MNCs in Ireland as a distortion of the figures since the early 1970s. Stewart (1977) was one of the first economists to analyse the problem and this work was developed by O'Leary, Foley, NESC (December 1992) and others.

Antoin Murphy of Trinity College named the outflow as "the Black Hole" in the 1980s. "The Black Hole" was the massive out-flow of profits and royalties from MNCs which the trade and na-tional income statistics had ignored. Murphy focused on what he called the "three Cs" — computers, cola concentrates and chemi-cals, including pharmaceuticals.

In 1990, MNCs manufacturing these goods were producing 52 per cent of all manufactured exports, generating £4.1 billion with just 24,000 workers. Irish manufacturers, employing 106,000, pro-duced a net output of £2.8 billion. So Irish manufacturers were producing only two-thirds of the net output of the "three Cs" with a workforce four-and-a-half times larger. Even taking account of the capital intensity of the three Cs sectors, turnover per employee was far too high. It had to be accounted for by exaggerated sales, due to transfer price-fixing. Murphy argued that "tax factors en-courage many MNCs to attribute to their Irish operations the out-put of other divisions, most notably those involved in R&D lo-cated elsewhere" (Murphy, 1994).

As policy-makers base much of their policy on key statistics like GNP and GDP, their assumptions could therefore be wrong. For example, the EU bases most of its analysis and decisions on funding, etc. on GDP. The Maastricht criteria for Monetary Union, which include the debt-to-GDP ratio, would be over-optimistic for Ireland. GDP per head of population would be exaggerated and any other ratio (to GDP) used by economists would be incorrect. It also has the effect of understating the importance of Britain to the Irish economy, because Irish companies are more labour-intensive and trade more with Britain than MNCs.

Arriving at Accurate Growth Figures

There is yet another complicating factor in measuring Ireland's national income, which is that there has been a regular fall in the terms of trade in recent years. A very high 90 per cent of Ireland's GNP is represented by merchandise exports, particularly computers and electronics. The prices of these products are falling all the time. Therefore, as the prices of Ireland's exports are rising at a slower rate than those of imports, the terms of trade are hit, which reduces Ireland's overall disposable income by about 1 per cent a year below the GNP figure. To make it even more complex, the fall in EU funds reduces disposable national income by about 0.5 per cent a year. Thus, disposable national income, which is income available for spending by the public, has risen by about 2 per cent less than GNP did in the 1990s. In spite of these qualifications, the figure for disposable income has still grown strongly each year.

As we have seen, a large number of MNCs in a small economy can distort the national figures. To correct this, the CSO issued statistics in the middle of 1995, revised back to 1989. In particular, the 1993 GNP growth figure was reduced substantially. This revision of the National Income data dealt with the problem sufficiently to accept that the statistics are a reasonable record of reality. The best figure to use for Ireland is the more modest GNP rather than GDP (which most countries and world bodies use), because the MNC profit adjustment has been made. Even with the revisions, there are still some like O'Hearn (1999) who are sceptical of the revised figures, though his critique is largely that the "southern Irish state" has not had the sustained growth rates for as long as the Asian Tigers, that it is over-dependent on multinationals and therefore it cannot really be called a "Tiger economy".

Distortions can still remain. For example, one company has never distributed dividends from its profitable Irish operation. Instead, it lends large sums to the parent company which amount to what a company would typically remit in dividends to its shareholder. The parent only pays a paltry amount of interest on these cumulative loans. The effect is that the Irish subsidiary is not getting a fair return on its "loans". If interest were paid at the market rate, the Irish company's profits would be higher. This leads to a slight understatement of national income, but grossed up for all companies that may be operating in this manner, it may be distorting.

There are other problems in measuring growth in any country. Take three examples. First, there is usually no attempt to measure work done in the home — mainly by women. Second, food grown for home consumption is not measured, and the consequent lack of purchase reduces national income measured in this way. Third, if there is a massive road accident, with many deaths and injuries, the orthodox measurement records an increase in "national well-being", in spite of cars written off, talented people dead or in hospital, grief and time lost by relatives, etc. This is because it stimulates car sales, insurance markets, medical costs, funeral costs and many other measurable costs, adding to GNP. Similarly, environmental disasters subtract from national well-being, but boost national income on the statistics. An oil spill will stimulate economic activity — rental of boats, insurance claims, etc. Accounts record the depreciation of man-made capital, but not of natural capital. But how is the ozone layer valued?

Those who compile national accounts are aware of their shortcomings. As they adhere to common international practices in order to give consistent and comparable measurements, they are slow to change. (An exception was the revision in Irish national income accounts to take account of transfer pricing — Ireland is ahead of other countries in this area.) Statisticians have not agreed on how to measure resource depletion and environmental pollution, but they know that there are problems and are working on them. For example, a World Bank study has argued that it is the people travelling in a polluting bus rather than the bus company who should be described as the polluters.

In conclusion, for some time the Irish growth figures had been distorted. There was a big Black Hole in the national accounts in the past caused by repatriation of MNCs' profits. Ireland's growth was exaggerated. However, in 1995 the CSO revised the figures downwards. Most international economists use GDP, but in Ireland it is better to use GNP — while it is lower, it is more accurate than GDP. Whatever figure is used, however, the performance is still very impressive. Ireland is still a Celtic Tiger, slower than at first glance, but still moving fast.

LIVING STANDARDS

In spite of the good economic figures, people did not feel that things were improving. The "feel-good factor" was very slow to materialise, because much of the growth went to redress the huge national debt; there was a shift in the division of the share of national income from employees to profits for companies; the terms of trade were not so good; and finally there was a fall in EU transfers. Thus, household income did not rise as fast as GNP. There was little growth in jobs until 1990, when there was an increase of 46,000 net new jobs, a massive increase in one year. The new workers added to taxes and there were reduced welfare costs as unemployment fell and people began to feel more prosperous.

There had already been good progress on living standards for those *at work*; this had been reaching European standards in the late 1980s. The importance in stressing "at work" is illustrated in these figures: Irish GNP per capita was £13,800 in 1999 compared to the very substantial £34,200 on average per person at work. However, this gap has closed in recent years, reflecting the drop in dependency. The growth of the economy and the fall in the dependency ratio meant that, in the 1990s, average living standards in Ireland began to close on the EU far faster than anyone had anticipated and may reach the EU average in 2000.

Irish living standards reached the same level as those in Northern Ireland by 1997. Northern Ireland had been highly industrialised at the turn of the nineteenth century, with one of the most successful regional economies in the world, whereas the rest of Ireland, with the exception of Dublin, was a relatively backward agricultural country. Not alone did Ireland also catch up with the UK by the end of 1997, but forecasts are that it will continue to rise above it within the following years.

In 1999, Ireland's GDP per person was the fourth highest in the EU, which is a dramatic improvement — higher than in Germany and Sweden. This would be fine if GDP were an acceptable measure for Ireland, but it is more accurate to use GNP for Ireland. With GNP per capita around 95 per cent of the European average in 1999, Ireland falls down from fourth to thirteenth position, just behind Sweden and the UK. This more accurate measure of GNP is, of course, why Ireland was able to secure a further tranch of €645 billion in EU funds in 1999, for the period 2000–2005.

Living standards are generally measured by income per person. There are difficulties with this measurement, as we have seen, with the difference between those at work and those who are not, the distribution of income and between GDP and GNP. However, this is a consistent measurement and therefore the very rapid closing of the gap between the Republic and the EU is impressive, no matter what criticism is levelled at the methods of measurement. It had been 59 per cent of the EU average in 1973, when Ireland joined the EEC, compared to the UK at 103 per cent. It hardly moved in the 1970s. However, by 1999, Ireland had risen to 111 per cent of the EU average (which itself had continued to rise) and the UK had fallen to 99 per cent (having fallen as low as 94 per cent in 1991).

Figure 3.1 illustrates this dramatic rise in GDP per capita for Ireland, by far the most rapid in the Union. This is the key reason for the catching up by Ireland on the average and it is worth noting that most of this gain was achieved in the period under review.

Figure 3.1: GDP per Capita Change Relative to EU Average, 1973–1999

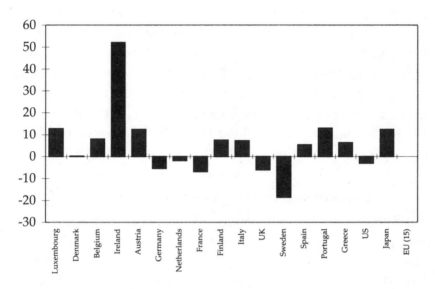

Source: European Economy, No. 66, Table 9

At the rate Ireland is growing, it is catching up fast and it is generally accepted that it will become a net contributor to the Union's lower income states after 2005. There can be little argument with that. In essence, most economic activity is about living standards. People have come to expect that their living standards will be higher than those of their parents, and this was spectacularly true in the US and most of Europe after the Second World War. It was far less so in Ireland, where standards did improve, but slowly.

Indicators of living standards for international comparisons show that Ireland still has a long way to go to catch up with the US, where the number of televisions per capita in 1994 was 816 per 1,000 people compared to Ireland's 301. It is, of course, debatable whether the number of TVs is an indication of economic well-being.

If telephones are chosen as a measure, then the US had 602 telephones per 1,000 people to Ireland's 350 (in 1994). In 1999, Ireland was in the top 20 countries for mobile phone penetration. If we look at cars, the US had 565 per 1,000 people compared to

Ireland's 264 (1994). With the rapid rise in car sales reflected in urban congestion in Ireland, we may be closer to the US today, but the US has twice as much land per person than Ireland!

Growth rates *per capita* rose by three per cent a year between 1987 and 1996, which was very good; when compared to the stagnation of the previous decade, it is particularly impressive and it has accelerated since. It was not just economic factors that caused growth per capita to rise. The important social contributor was the fall in dependency. This helped boost the impressive rise in income per person at work.

Dependency and the New-Style Emigration

The fall in dependency began in 1980 — the year after the Pope's visit to Ireland! In that year, the birth rate fell dramatically. It has stayed low ever since. Irish people embraced contraception in 1979. In this way, the people themselves addressed the serious economic problem of a high growth rate in the labour market, which had dogged Ireland since the early 1800s, forcing millions to emigrate over two centuries.

Since 1950, there has been net emigration of 628,000 people, after deducting immigration. This is the "Irish Diaspora". It has been estimated that there are 20 million people of Irish descent, of which 3.6 million (in 1996) are Irish citizens, 1.2 million are Irish-born and the rest are descendants, with many qualifying to play on the Irish soccer team!

The total numbers who emigrated averaged 34,200 a year in the 1990s to 1998 inclusive (with the higher number of 36,500 returning each year), giving a net figure of net in-migration in the eight years to 1998 of 20,000. There was high out-migration and low in-migration in the early 1990s, and this was reversed from 1996 to 1998, with over 127,000 immigrating (gross) in these three years. These emigrants are far different from the "Paddies" of the 1950s who looked for "the start" in English building sites. Many are well educated. While 44 per cent left to find work abroad (most of whom had been out of work for less than a year), another one-fifth left jobs in Ireland to take up employment overseas, and 10 per cent to complete their education. Around half of graduates who emigrate return, with experience. Such migration adds to the stock of human capital.

This type of emigration is a total change to Ireland's previous history. Those who were emigrating were finally doing so by choice and when they returned, as many did, they were bringing back skills and experience with them. Those who stayed away could come home with ease because of improved travel and cheap air fares. In 1996, Ireland had the highest immigration in the EU, with the equivalent of 1.6 per cent of its population entering the country. However, 69 per cent of these were nationals returning (Employment in Europe, 1999). These immigrants generally bring skills to the economy.

PUBLIC SERVICES

While public spending was reduced as a proportion of GNP, it still grew slightly each year. Indeed, the opposition and many economists would generally say it grew too much. Public spending on health, education and social services adds to living standards (unless, of course, the money is poorly spent).

Social spending rose substantially between 1989 and 1996, by almost 5 per cent a year *in real terms*. The increase was larger for certain areas like health (over 6 per cent) and education (over 5 per cent) but there was a fall in spending on housing, which is dealt with below, and subsidies (NESC, 1996: 80). The general rise, however, is in sharp contrast to the fall in the preceding years. NESC sees this as "one component in the social partnership approach". It ensured that all, and particularly the less well-off, did share in the boom to some extent. However, the rise in social spending was lower than the growth in real disposable income of workers. The numbers employed in the public services between 1988 and 1998 grew by a mere 5,000 to 300,000.

EMPLOYMENT

Ireland has had a historical problem with unemployment, as has been seen in Chapter Two. It still has a long-term joblessness problem, yet its performance in job creation has been remarkable, especially in recent years. Ireland has outperformed even the US in job creation. The US has been seen as the miracle job-producing economy, and proponents of deregulation of the labour market cite it as the model to follow. At its crudest, their philosophy for the unemployed is "work or starve". Ireland's performance sets out a challenge to this crude approach.

Table 3.2: Employment Growth in Ireland, 1987–2000

Year	Total at Work	Change	Change in Non-Agricultural
1987	1,090,000	+9,000	+13,000
1988	1,090,000	0	−1,000
1989	1,088,000	−2,000	+1,000
1990	1,134,000	+46,000	+39,000
1991	1,134,000	0	+14,000
1992	1,145,000	+11,000	+10,000
1993	1,152,000	+7,000	+17,000
1994	1,188,000	+36,000	+38,000
1995	1,248,000	+60,000	+59,000
1996	1,297,000	+49,000	+54,000
Change 1986–96	–	**+216,000**	**+244,000**
1997	1,338,000	+41,000	+45,000
1998	1,427,000	+89,000	+96,000
1999*	1,496,000	+69,000	+71,000
2000*	1,551,000	+55,000	+57,000
Change 1986–2000	–	**+461,000** **+42%**	**+513,000** **+47%**

Notes: Figures show year to April; Principal Economic Classification. * Estimate.

Source: CSO, ESRI Quarterly.

Table 3.2 shows that the increase in jobs in the whole economy between 1987 and 1996 was a very substantial 216,000. Ireland still has a structural problem with unemployment, particularly in agriculture — a large number continue to leave the land each year. When the measure of job creation excludes agriculture, the growth in jobs is even higher, at 244,000 net new jobs in the decade. The estimate for the increase in total non-agricultural employment in the economy to 2000 is likely to be a massive 513,000 or a 47 per cent increase in only 14 years (change on the base year of 1986).

According to the OECD (1997a: 25–6), Ireland created more non-agricultural jobs than the US between 1986 and 1996. Total employment rose by 26 per cent in Ireland, compared to only 7 per cent for the EU or even 15 per cent for the US. This increase has been almost all in the private sector, as public sector employment growth has been negligible. And the trend has continued with Ireland's rate being much higher than the US since 1994, as Figure 1.1 demonstrated.

The Irish jobs machine has been performing at a phenomenal rate since then and is likely to continue, and as stated in Chapter One, the new jobs are generally better than those lost in the 1980s. Between 1994 and 2000, 420,000 extra non-agricultural jobs will have been created in just seven years — a staggering performance, particularly when contrasted to zero jobs in the first 70 years since Independence. It is an increase of over one-third in seven years or an annual average increase of 60,000. With the traditional job losses in agriculture, the key figure is non-agricultural job creation. In the period under review — the period of Ireland's transformation since 1987 — over half a million extra jobs will have been created in the economy, an increase of almost 50 per cent or one extra new job for every two that existed before.

Contrary to popular myth, most of the jobs have not been "McJobs". They have not been low-skill, nor have many people been forced to accept part-time work when they would prefer to work full-time. What kind of jobs have therefore been created? The real picture is surprisingly good, except for the unskilled. While a growing proportion *are* part-time — this more than doubled from less than 7 per cent of total employment in 1983 to over

17 per cent in 1998 — the incidence of under-employment (those who *would like* a full-time job) fell substantially to 13 per cent in 1997, showing that most of those working part-time wish to do so. Nonetheless, there has also been a growth in low-paying jobs and in part-time work (Quarterly National Household Survey, Last Quarter, 1998).

The numbers employed in agriculture continued their downward fall, as has been seen, from 17 per cent in 1983 to 8.4 per cent in 1999. Manufacturing, which had severe job losses in the 1980s, especially with a shakeout of uncompetitive indigenous industries, enjoyed a substantial increase of around 3 per cent growth a year in the 1990s, against the international trend of decline in manufacturing jobs. But the biggest increase in jobs was in services and there has been a "significant upgrading of the occupational structure" according to O'Connell (1998), as Table 3.3 shows.

Table 3.3: Numbers Employed in Main Occupational Groups, 1981 and 1995

Sector	1981 (000s)	Per cent	1995 (000s)	Per cent
Agricultural	177	16.0	135	11.0
Managers, Proprietors	95	8.3	124	10.1
Professional etc.	156	13.7	224	18.2
Clerical	158	13.9	170	13.8
Service Occupations	92	8.1	127	10.3
Sales	74	6.5	98	8.0
Skilled Manual	214	18.8	205	16.7
Semi- and unskilled	172	15.1	145	11.8
Total	**1,138**	**100.0**	**1,228**	**100.0**

Source: Duggan, Hughes and Sexton, 1997.

"Over the 1981–1997 period the strongest growth took place among professional, technical and managerial occupations, but also in clerical and sales occupations", according to O'Connell.

"Expansion at the upper-end of the occupational structure was accompanied by a decline in the demand for semi-skilled and un-skilled manual workers, although there has been some growth in employment in these categories in the 1990s", he found. The decline has been in both skilled and unskilled manual and, of course, agricultural workers. Within services, public sector employment, including the civil service, defence and state companies, have barely grown in the 1990s, having also been held still in the 1980s. The trend towards upgrading of jobs in the labour market is more than "a shift from manual to non-manual activities" in Ireland, according to O'Connell. This is following a similar pattern in other countries. New jobs require qualifications, skills and flexibility that are considerably different from those required in traditional employment.

Women's participation in work increased dramatically, though from a low base of 32 per cent in 1986 to 44 per cent by mid-1998 (CSO, 1999). In contrast, men's participation has moved in the opposite direction, falling from over 76 per cent in 1981 to 69 per cent in 1998. This left the overall participation rate almost unchanged in the 1980s at around 53 per cent, though it has risen to 57 per cent in 1998. By the middle of 1999, labour shortages were evident in some areas. There has also been a substantial rise in the numbers participating in education — up from 200,000 in 1981 to 340,000 in 1996 and rising.

There appears to be little change in self-employment, but when agriculture, which has been in decline, is excluded, there has been substantial growth, with numbers up from 90,000 in 1981 to 150,000 in 1996.

UNEMPLOYMENT

Unemployment has fallen substantially from a peak of almost 18 per cent in 1987 to 6.4 per cent in late 1998. There is still a core of long-term unemployment because of new labour market entrants, returned emigrants and new immigrants snapping up job vacancies, often due to better experience and qualifications and because of the poor education and skills of the long-term unemployed.

The numbers on the live register had also fallen from a peak of over 294,000 in 1993 to fewer than 200,000 in 1999. However, the live register has not been accepted as an accurate measure of un-employment in Ireland since the mid-1980s. There were several reasons for this. By international standards, many on the Irish live register would not qualify as unemployed. For example, a quarter were no longer economically active and most of these were not looking for work. There was also widespread abuse of the social welfare system. Eleven per cent of those registered were working, with three-quarters of those in full-time jobs, and 28 per cent did not live at the addresses given, according to the controversial CSO study of 1996! The 1985 Social Welfare Act, which required equal treatment of men and women, encouraged women working in the home to register, and they are classified as unemployed. They could be described as discouraged workers who want jobs. Women account for over 85 per cent of the increase in registered unemployment over the last decade. The question of discouraged workers — both those who, because of their age, feel that they cannot or should not get work, and those working in the home — is also controversial. The growth in the number of jobs will help to lessen the problem.

In spite of the excellent performance in job creation outside ag-riculture, there are a number of other problems with Ireland's unemployment. The most serious is the proportion of long-term unemployed (over one year). However, this has fallen at last, dropping from 129,000 in 1993 to 51,000 in 1999. But it is still too high, and a major blot on the economic and social landscape. The unemployment problem will be analysed in detail in Chapter Seven.

TRADE AND BALANCE OF PAYMENTS

Ireland exports far more than it imports. At first sight, Ireland's success in exports appears to be phenomenal. Not alone were staggering rates of growth in exports recorded every year for many years, but the composition of that trade and its destination have improved substantially. However, behind this great success there is the serious problem of the outflow of funds — largely the repatriation of profits by multinationals, as discussed earlier. The role of multinationals in the Irish economy and the problem of measuring growth will be examined in Chapter Six.

Ireland is one of the "great trading nations of the world", with exports and imports amounting to around 180 per cent of GDP in 1999. However, most small countries have a high level of trade, while for large countries like the US, trade only amounted to about 25 per cent of GDP; Japan's trade only amounted to 21 per cent in 1999, with exports being only 12 per cent of GDP.

From the foundation of the State until 1985, Ireland imported more than it exported. In 1985, for the first time, exports exceeded imports. For many years the imbalance in trade had been made up by "emigrants' remittances" or money sent home by emigrants.

By 1999, exports of goods amounted to £58 billion, compared to imports of £50 billion. Therefore merchandise exports exceeded imports by £8 billion, or a good 16 per cent of GNP. Exports have grown at an annual average rate of over 20 per cent a year in the 13 years to 1999 and by 27 per cent in 1998. Compared to the growth in the EU or even other small countries like Denmark or Belgium, this is real success.

Another important positive development is that Ireland's trade has diversified substantially in recent decades. From a great dependency on Britain, where 90 per cent of exports went in the 1930s, this was ever so slowly reduced to 77 per cent by 1958. It had fallen to 22 per cent by 1998 (including Northern Ireland). A high proportion — close to half — of the exports of indigenous firms go to the UK. Britain's decision not to join European Monetary Union did not present problems for Irish exporters in the first half of 1999 because of the strength of sterling. However, Ireland as a member of the Eurozone has a very high proportion of trade outside the zone (60 per cent).

Trade with the rest of the European Union grew, and Germany became the second largest export destination with 15 per cent of exports in the late 1990s, up from 2 per cent in 1958 and under 10 per cent in 1983. France was next (in the Union) with 8 per cent, having been a mere 1 per cent in 1958. The US is the third largest destination for Irish exports, just behind Germany.

On the import front, the UK is the largest partner with 33 per cent in 1998, down substantially from the past. The US is the second largest source of imports, a large proportion of which are capital goods for finishing in US factories in Ireland.

The third positive event on the export performance is that, while the total growth of exports was faster than that from indigenous manufacturing, the performance of indigenous industry grew strongly from the end of the 1980s. This indicated that domestic industry, which is now exposed to full global competition, is well able to survive and even grow.

Capital goods, raw materials and components accounted for 17 per cent of imports in 1995, a healthy sign.

TOURISM

Tourism has contributed substantially to the Irish economic success in recent years. While export tourism — that is, foreign travel by Irish residents — is high, the numbers of foreign visitors and spending came to over 5.5 million visitors, with an estimated £2.3 billion in foreign earnings in 1998. This was up from 2.2 million visitors spending £731 million in 1987. With this growth, Ireland has bucked the trend in Europe, where tourism has not grown.

The government, recognising that tourism had some particular problems, implemented most of the 1992 recommendations of the Tourism Task Force, with some success. While many other factors played their part, policy implementation helped in this growth.

To a small open economy, trade and tourism are extremely important. Almost half of all Irish jobs are supported by exports, according to a Trade Board report (Bacon and Walsh, 1996), up from one-third in 1985. Employment, direct and indirect, grew from 64,000 in 1989 to 110,000 in 1997. Pay is low in the sector and it is already seeing Irish workers replaced by immigrants as the Irish abandon it for higher paying jobs in other sectors.

INTEREST RATES

Irish nominal interest rates, once high and occasionally volatile, are now low and stable. In December 1986, Irish rates were almost 14 per cent, compared to just over 5 per cent in Germany. The gap began to close from early 1993. Irish interest rates were low by the end of 1998, prior to the establishment of the Eurozone on 1 January 1999, and then converged. This means that the cost of capital is low, which should encourage investment. Irish interest rates are now the same as in Europe and are likely to remain low. The problem with membership of the Eurozone is that when house prices are soaring in Ireland, the Central Bank cannot move to dampen demand by raising interest rates.

INVESTMENT

Investment is crucial in creating wealth and income, and in modernising an economy. The State is traditionally the largest investor and this is still the case in Ireland in the 1990s, but there are two major external sources that contribute substantially — the European Union and multinational investment.

The EU investment was the equivalent of a Keynesian boost, and it worked well in the case of Ireland. The remarkable success in investing the EU transfers paradoxically means that these funds will be substantially smaller in the early years of the Third Millennium.

Investment had been higher in Ireland than in the UK and the EU between 1960 and 1987. As it began from a low base, this was necessary to catch up. However, since then, in the boom decade to 1996, it seemed not to have risen by much and appeared to be below the levels of other countries. This was is in spite of the unprecedented funding from the EU and large-scale foreign investment.

The average growth in investment between 1986 and 1996 was only 2.7 per cent a year and in several years (1991, 1992 and 1993), this fell. However, in late 1997, after some detailed analysis, the figures were revised upwards and the level of investment was found not to be out of line. As investment underpins growth, and especially the economic boom, this sorted out an apparent paradox. It is possible that sectors of the modern economy, such as export services, do not require high capital (as opposed to human capital) investment. The ESRI (*ESRI Quarterly*, July 1997) revised its investment figures for 1996 and 1997 upwards substantially.

Investment rose by around 13 per cent in 1998 compared to an average of 5 in the Union and 4 in the OECD as a whole. Investment was particularly strong in construction, but investment in machinery was also historically high in the late 1990s.

INDUSTRY, PRODUCTIVITY AND OUTPUT

The amount of goods produced by Irish industry doubled between 1987 and 1998. It had increased by 56 per cent in the previous decade, but there had actually been two *falls* in the volume of industrial output, in 1980 and 1982, in that decade. However, behind this increase, there was a huge growth in productivity in modern manufacturing, with output quadrupling. This was in stark contrast to only a relatively small increase of 50 per cent in "traditional" or Irish-owned industry.

The growth in domestic demand doubled, rising from 2.4 per cent a year on average between 1987 and 1993 to around 6 per cent between 1994 and 1999. This boosted the labour-intensive indigenous industries. It is worth noting that the rate of growth of the government component of demand was very low in the 1990s.

Productivity has grown rapidly in Ireland. Between 1991 and 1999, real unit labour costs in Ireland fell by 18 per cent, almost the same as in Finland, as Table 3.4 shows. This compared to a small rise in both the US and Japan, a small fall of 3.4 per cent in the UK, or a fall of 6.9 per cent in the EU (14 states) (*European Economy*, 1998). Indeed, Ireland was top of a long list of countries in the National Competitiveness Council's Report (1999: 179), just ahead of Finland, and second for low nominal unit cost growth between 1992 and 1998. While Ireland's fall was from a lower base than other countries, it was still impressive. The problem is that in the traditional, indigenously owned sector, the rate of unit costs, while falling, was doing so at a much slower rate than the foreign-owned sector was.

Table 3.4: Percentage Change in Real Unit Labour Costs, 1991–1999 (Total Economy)

Finland	−18.4
Ireland	−17.7
Italy	−14.4
Austria	−8.5
Spain	-7.5
Germany	-7.4
Portugal	−5.7
Belgium	−4.5
Sweden	−3.8
United Kingdom	−3.4
France	−3.3
Netherlands	−3.2
Denmark	−2.5
Greece	−1.9
EU (14)	−6.9
United States	+1.3
Japan	+1.2

Source: European Economy, No. 66 (1998).

It has been seen that employment in industry had fallen between 1980 and 1987, but that it recovered and grew in the period to 1999. This was in contrast to declines in other countries. The number of redundancies did not fall by much in the latter decade in comparison with the decade to 1986, but this indicates that, while there was still a rapid turnover of jobs, the redundant jobs were being replaced more rapidly with newer modern ones.

There was a large fall in industrial disputes and in days lost due to them in the period from 1987, with a substantial drop on

the level of the previous decade, illustrating the power of the negotiated partnership process.

While there may be an over-dependency on foreign industry,
which has had low linkages with the Irish economy, recent studies found that these linkages had improved.

Finally, Ireland won some of the most prestigious high-tech
foreign investment industries in the 1990s. These include Intel,
Xerox, IBM, Hewlett Packard and others, listed in the Appendix.
In short, there was an unprecedented and excellent performance
by industry in the decade to 1996. (An analysis and an assessment
of industrial policy follows in Chapter Five.)

INCOMES

Incomes rose relatively slowly in the period to 1999. However,
real after-tax incomes rose substantially in the 12 years under review, which coincided with the first 12 years of the national
agreements. So workers did share in the fruits of the boom. However, profits rose far more sharply, with the result that their share
of national income rose substantially (see Figure 7.1).

In the "free-for-all" prior to the nationally negotiated pay
deals, 1980–86, the take-home pay of workers remained stable —
they did not rise or fall. But as taxes were rising, real disposable
incomes fell. Net pay had risen by a high 10 per cent in 1978 and
1979, but fell sharply in 1980, and the take-home pay packet of the
average single industrial worker actually *fell* by 7 per cent between 1980 and 1987 inclusive. It also fell for married workers, but
by a smaller amount. In contrast, average take-home pay increased by around 2 per cent a year between 1988 and 1996 inclusive. Under Partnership 2000 (1997–2000), the average married
worker will see a gain of 19 per cent on gross income or 13 per
cent in disposable income after inflation by 2000. The national
agreements included provision for after-tax pay. With the high
level of growth and employment, the government could easily
afford to cut taxes. So employers have enjoyed low wage increases, while workers enjoyed reasonable take-home pay increases, thanks to tax cuts.

PRICES

The fall in inflation has been an international phenomenon. Irish prices are no exception, having fallen to low levels in the period to 1999, and they look set to remain low. Inflation fell progressively from under 6 per cent in 1990 to 1.5 per cent in 1996 and 1997, rose to 2.4 per cent in 1998 and around 2 per cent in 1999. The modest wage settlements have contributed to this positive development. Inflation had averaged 14 per cent a year in the 1970s, compared to 11 per cent in Europe, and also in the 1980s, Irish inflation at 7 per cent was slightly higher than the average for the EU. Irish inflation is a little higher than the European average at the end of the 1990s.

The huge rise in house prices is not reflected in the consumer price index. Asset prices began to rise substantially in 1995. House prices rose by a staggering 25 per cent in the two years to September 1996. This rise continued and by quarter three in 1998, Dublin second-hand house prices had risen by 42 per cent in the year, up by 37 per cent nationally, with new house prices up by a lower but still very high 20 per cent. Farm land rose even more, to 43 per cent in the third quarter of 1998, a very surprising high, considering the weak farm incomes in 1998, with a drop of 5 per cent in income. There may be a case for some revision of the consumer price index measurement and even the conservative Central Bank has suggested such consideration.

FISCAL POLICY

Ireland had a severe fiscal crisis in the late 1980s, when the national debt reached 125 per cent of GNP. Borrowings were running at 8 per cent of GNP between 1980 and 1987 and the servicing of the debt was taking the equivalent of all income tax receipts in interest payments.

Government debt began to rise after the 1973 oil crisis and the subsequent rise in unemployment. Government spending soared after the 1977 election. Current government spending rose by a huge 24 per cent in one year (1978), peaking at 29 per cent in 1982.

The Public Sector Borrowing Requirement (all government borrowing) peaked at 20.1 per cent of GNP in 1981 and remained in double digits until 1987, when it was substantially reduced to 3.7 per cent the following year, and it remained at just 2 or 3 per cent until surpluses were generated in the late 1990s, demonstrating successful management of the public finances. As stated elsewhere, all parties and the trade unions agreed with this strategy of cutting public spending as a percentage of GNP — or put another way, reducing the rise in spending. This was easy in a time of high growth.

Fiscal policy saw lower levels of spending, borrowing and taxation after 1987 than in the previous 10 to 15 years. Government spending as a proportion of GDP fell dramatically in the 1990s, having peaked at 52 per cent in both 1981 and 1982. In 1999, total government expenditure as a percentage of GDP was only 29.9 per cent, the lowest in the EU, and even lower than in the US and Japan. This compared to an average of 49 per cent in Ireland in the 1980s and it was low compared to the EU average of 45 per cent, a figure which had been relatively stable since the early 1980s, but which fell in the late 1990s. On the other side of the coin, total government receipts of the Irish government as a percentage of GDP were also the lowest in the Union in 1999 at 33 per cent, compared to an average of over 46 percent. Even taking account of the difference between Irish GNP and GDP, these figures for Ireland are low (*European Economy*, 1998).

The current budget deficit averaged 6.5 per cent of GDP between 1979 and 1987, and it was cut to 1.7 per cent in 1987. It was only 1.1 per cent in 1995 and turned into a surplus from 1996, with a substantial current budget surplus of £2 billion in 1998 or 1.8 per cent of GDP, rising to 2.2 per cent in 1999. The national debt, once dangerously high, is to fall to around 40 per cent of GDP in 2000, the lowest in the Union (bar Luxembourg, which does not borrow).

Ireland was able to adhere to the Maastricht criteria, established in 1992, without pain. Again, this was largely because of the high rates of growth.

CONSUMPTION INDICATORS

Other indicators of economic performance and particularly economic well-being are consumption and construction, especially of houses. These are lagging indicators, because they usually come after the performance in the main indicators. People generally do not buy houses, cars or spend freely in shops unless they feel that they are doing well.

However, the words "generally" and "usually" are important. This is because people do not always behave rationally, or their behaviour can be influenced by policy or mood. The classic example was the Thatcherite "consumer boom" in the late 1980s in the UK, where cheap credit caused people to spend so much that when the artificial boom eventually burst, it left many worse off than they would have been if it had never happened, including some with homes worth far less than they had paid.

New car sales fell in 1987 by 8 per cent, and rose afterwards, but fell by a substantial 18 per cent in 1991 and were lower in the following two years. From 1994 they soared, reflecting the "feel-good factor", with a growth rate of 34 per cent in 1994 and a smaller rise in 1995. If new and second-hand cars registered are examined, in 1993 the total was 87,352 and it more than doubled in the five years to 1998! Retail sales were slow to move in the early years of the 1990s, expanding rapidly from 1996 (Table 3.5).

House completions had fallen to a historic low of under 16,000 in 1988 from an average of 24,000 to 26,000 in the mid-1970s. A key reason was the massive cut in local authority or public housing. The number of local authority or social houses had been dramatically cut in the late 1980s (from 7,000 in 1984 to one-tenth that in 1989), but numbers were again increased from 1994. The number of houses built in 1998 reached a historically high level of 43,000. With the boom, rises in real incomes, the growth in population and in those at work, demand for housing will continue.

Table 3.5: Consumption Indicators

Year	New and Second-Hand Car Registrations	Retail Sales Value (1990 = 100)	Retail Sales Volume (1990 = 100)
1990	105,849	100	100
1991	89,589	101.5	99.5
1992	85,492	105.9	102.0
1993	87,352	109.0	103.4
1994	116,636	118.0	109.3
1995	124,595	123.7	112.4
1996	153,833	134.0	119.4
1997	167,000	145.0	128.4
1998	178,104	159.6	139.8

Source: CSO.

A housing crisis arose in the late 1990s, with few social houses being built and the widest disparity between incomes and house prices ever. In the first quarter of 1999, the average price of a new house in Ireland was £111,000 and £142,000 in Dublin. Average earnings in industry were £15,500. This means that buying a house for the average person had become very difficult. The government's decision in 1996 to abolish the property tax on expensive houses fuelled the house price inflation. Ireland is one of the few countries without taxes on property, but few politicians have the courage to even raise the issue. Housing will be discussed in more depth in Chapter Seven.

Prices vary in different parts of the world. A humorous study of purchasing power parities has been done on the working time needed to buy a Big Mac hamburger, as well as some staple goods, in selected cities. It attempts to show how much time it takes to work to pay for different things. Union Bank of Switzerland compiled comparative tables for 56 cities around the world in the second quarter of 1997, taking 12 sample occupations as the basis for average income (see Table 3.6).

Table 3.6: Working Time Needed to Buy Various Goods

City	"Big Mac"	Kilo of Bread	Kilo of Rice
Average Time (minutes)	37	24	24
Amsterdam	19	13	14
Athens	15	12	22
Bangkok	39	33	22
Berlin	18	12	24
Brussels	21	13	19
Caracas	117	36	34
Dublin	19	11	20
Geneva	15	10	8
Hong Kong	11	14	8
Houston	9	11	9
Jakarta	103	39	18
London	20	9	13
New York	12	12	8
Singapore	24	41	12
Taipei	20	14	13

Note: Figures represent minutes for 12 selected occupations.
Source: UBS (1997).

In this table, it took less time in Dublin to buy any of the three items than the average. The average working time across the 56 cities needed to buy a Big Mac was 37 minutes on net earnings of 12 occupations. The average in the US was 11 minutes. To buy a kilo of bread took an average of 24 minutes; the figure for Dublin was less than half of this. The average for a kilo of rice was the same at 24 minutes, with Dublin being 20 minutes. Being the staple diet in Asia, it averaged 22 minutes, but took a lot more time in some cities. The countries with the highest productivity generally find it easiest to pay for goods, with local variations based on consumption patterns. Dublin fares well by this ranking.

There are other factors, such as the huge numbers of holidays and flights (especially from Dublin), which indicate increases in economic welfare. In general, personal disposable income growth averaged around seven per cent a year between 1996 and 1999.

DISTRIBUTING THE GROWTH

The benefits of the excellent economic performance in Ireland have been enjoyed by many, as the consumption indicators of retail sales, car sales and house sales show. The growth in the economy is not something "out there" which people see others enjoying, but most people have felt their living standards rising, have experienced higher disposable income, and have seen their children get jobs in Ireland, or come home regularly.

There are far more people at work and paying tax, so taxes can be reduced for the ordinary worker. At the same time, interest rates are low. The numbers on the dole have fallen at last, and prices have not risen much. Public spending on education, health and services is growing modestly, providing more services and so adding to the quality of life. Things have never been so good in the Emerald Isle.

Tens of thousands of Irish people are returning each year, setting up home and families. They are coming back to Ireland because they expect to enjoy a standard of living equal to the European average. And for many of those at work, it would be a better material standard of living than in Britain.

Indeed, Britain has been wonderfully hospitable to millions of Irish over the past two centuries, and thousands of British-born people, some married to Irish people or with Irish connections, are now beginning to settle here too. It is highly likely that tens of thousands of Europeans will settle in Ireland in the future, as the higher living standards attracts more immigration. This is already happening. In the 1990s, there was net immigration of 20,000 people into the country (by the end of 1998), bringing their skills and education, and finding work.

The long-term unemployed still find it difficult to get work in Ireland. And there is still a high proportion of long-term unemployed in Ireland. The benefits of the boom are being unequally shared.

The NESC (1996) report had much to say on consensus and shared understandings, on interdependence between public and private, between trading and non-trading sectors of the economy, but it said that a major aim has not been met: the elimination of unemployment and poverty.

In an unprecedented economic boom, it should be easier to deal with poverty and one of its key causes, unemployment. Ireland has now been successful in dealing with unemployment at last and this, in turn, has had some impact on poverty, which is an interlinked problem. The long-term unemployed, a marginalised segment of the working class — 51,000 people in early 1999 — .who are on the fringe of Irish society, have been officially neglected in the boom. In addition, as a result of the decline in agricultural employment, there are pockets of rural poverty in too many parts of Ireland, hidden away from tourists and urban weekenders.

Chapter Seven will examine the extent of this problem, of the failures of Irish policy which spoil the long overdue success now enjoyed by the majority of the Irish in their own country — but first, let's take a look at the key reasons behind Ireland's amazing economic turnaround.

Chapter Four

THE REASONS FOR SUCCESS

There is no single reason for the Irish economic success. Many factors came together at the same time to create a benign conjuncture that facilitated the transformation of the economy. Of those that are most important, it is worth categorising them as *external* — those over which the government and people had little or no influence — and *internal* — those over which people and policy-makers did have a measure of control. Part 1 of this chapter deals with the key external reasons for Ireland's economic turnaround, and Part 2 deals with the internal factors over which Irish policy-makers had control or influence.

The reasons for the sustained growth of the Irish economy are complex, yet several key factors stand out. The social consensus agreed in 1987 is generally highlighted by many as important; the substantial foreign investment in growing industries, a tighter fiscal regime, a stable macroeconomic climate, good all-round competitiveness, EU transfers, the Single Market in Europe and timing were other factors which helped develop the boom. It began in 1987. The Irish economy and society had performed particularly poorly in the previous seven years, making the contrast of recovery in the next 12 appear even more remarkable.

The success was helped greatly by a very favourable global trading environment, which was to end in 1990/91. The real test of the Irish experience was to see if the boom would continue when recessions hit its main trading partners. It did. In fact, the following years saw even greater progress. This was partly due to an increase in domestic demand, which was of greater benefit to domestic firms, and because they are more employment-intensive than foreign firms are, this helped boost employment in the years after 1994.

The OECD, which compiles regular reports on each of its 29 member countries — the richest in the world — noticed the improvement in the Irish economy early, in its 1988/89 report. In its 1991 report, it gave the reasons for the improvement, saying "this good performance owes much to the broadly-based consensus which has allowed macroeconomic policies to focus on the medium term". It said that the 1987 Programme for National Recovery's policy commitments had been carried out, "with marked beneficial effects on interest rates and business confidence". It listed improvements in investment, productivity, profits, low inflation and growth at almost 5 per cent for the previous two years.

The 1997 OECD report said that Ireland had enjoyed strong expansion, with activity being boosted by a quarter in just three years. It said that Ireland has had "an outstanding performance . . . associated with sound macroeconomic management . . . and sustained foreign investment". The country's "22 per cent increase in GNP was more than three times faster than that seen in both the European Union and North America, and on par with countries in the Pacific region". Its 1998 *Economic Outlook* report said government should aim to retain the consensus-based approach to wage formulation. It also warned of overheating, "especially in the labour market". Its 1999 country report called Ireland's economic performance "stunning" and "astonishing". This powerful, conservative body usually finds plenty to criticise, but its recent reports on Ireland could become collectors' items, such is their praise!

Other commentators also gave reasons for Ireland's success. Anthony Harris of *The Times* (13 November 1996), quoted already in Chapter One, was critical of the role of the conventional free market view of economics in building the Irish boom:

> This is an Irish miracle. But an example to us all? An uncomfortable one, if you share the conventional Euro-wisdom. The Irish miracle owes nothing to tax cuts, deregulation or privatisation. Until recently, taxes have been

raised, not cut. The economy is still riddled with subsidies, so revenue is wasted. Yet the national debt has been reduced by a third, measured against GDP, without what the European Commission calls "Treasury transactions". The main utilities are still publicly owned. Cost inflation has been controlled not by competition or tight money, but by a successful incomes policy.

The *International Herald Tribune* (1 July 1996) said that Ireland is "enjoying a boom more characteristic of the Tiger economies of East Asia" and it believed that the reason was that "cuts in public spending revived a sick economy".

The *Economist* (27 April 1996) asked "which West European country can boast East Asian growth rates?" and found that the reasons for Ireland's success included a well-managed economy, by all parties, since 1987, a greater effort to maintain the Irish pound's value in the ERM and thirdly, the national agreements "to hold wage increases down".

Neil A. Martin of Barron's (1 March 1999) commented that:

> . . .the Irish tiger economy does not seem doomed to follow Asia's path. Ireland is now second only to the US as a software exporter, and supplies 33 per cent of Europe's personal computers.

In a major article on Ireland, *Newsweek* (23 December 1996) held that it is "the canny use of EU funds, not their huge scale" together with prudent public spending, a lower birth-rate and the fact that "foreign corporations looking for a low-cost, English-speaking home in the EU are enchanted" which made Ireland the "Emerald Tiger".

John Murray Brown, the *Financial Times'* Ireland correspondent (25 October 1996), believed that there were a number of reasons for the Irish boom:

> Where a few years ago, the growth performance was driven largely by the export sector, led by the foreign-owned high technology companies, today there is a more balanced growth picture, with exports complemented by a

booming domestic economy, house prices rising and car sales reaching record levels.

He went on:

> The achievement has been helped by sound fiscal and monetary policy, partly determined by the strait-jacket imposed by Ireland's adherence to the narrow band exchange rate mechanism, but helped by a labour policy that has kept wage increases to below inflation for the past two years.

According to *The Economist* (17 May 1997):

> The visible hand, this time in the form of industrial policy, went to work again . . . successive governments have sought, with increasingly impressive results, to attract foreign investment. . . . Something else Ireland has in common with your Asiatic Tiger: its experience supports different, contradictory views of what makes countries grow.

In this author's view, many elements came together to create a benign conjuncture to allow the Irish economic transformation to take root. It has long been argued that Ireland has suffered a vicious cycle of economic development for many decades, as Chapter Two has shown. For once, there was a coming together of many factors that reinforced each other and combined to boost most economic indicators.

PART 1: THE EXTERNAL FACTORS

The main external factors that contributed are now analysed.

❖ The External Economic Environment

The contribution of the external economic environment is of vital importance to any economy in this era of globalisation, trade and interdependence, but it is especially important to a small open economy like Ireland. The level of trade, where exports and imports add up to more than GNP, is the determining factor on living standards in small economies. Yet, for several of Ireland's boom years, the European economy was in recession, with low rates of growth, and there was even a fall in national income for the 15 member states in 1993.

The Trading Partners

Ireland trades mainly with the EU, where two-thirds of its exports went in 1998 (but from which it gets 54 per cent of imports). However, its main trading partner is the UK, where 22 per cent of exports went (34 per cent of imports), followed by Germany at 15 per cent (6 per cent of imports) and the US with over 14 per cent of exports (16 per cent of imports) in 1998. Each of these economies went into recession in the early 1990s. Germany, the second largest destination for Irish exports, suffered after reunification in 1990. There was low growth in Germany after 1991 and there was even a *fall* in national income in 1993. The largest trading partner, the UK, was in recession between 1989 and 1993, with an actual *fall* in national income in 1991 and no growth in 1992.

The 1991 OECD report on Ireland warned that tough times were coming. The boost given by strong external markets was beginning to slacken, with Ireland's major trading partner, the United Kingdom, and also the United States, in recession, and there was pressure on interest rates because of the demand for credit to finance the rebuilding of Eastern Europe. The tough times came with the external downturn for a few years, but the performance of the Irish economy did not slacken.

Boom in the Gloom

So what happened to allow Ireland to boom when most of its trading partners were in recession? It has been seen that domestic demand picked up, and this was important. However, the key driver in the success was that most Irish exports were in the fastest growing sectors, where goods and services were bought in spite of recession. There was continuing diversification of trade with rapid expansion in exports of computers (Hewlett Packard, Apple, IBM), pharmaceuticals (Bristol Myers Squibb and Smith-

Kline Beecham) and chemicals (Sandoz). Ireland boomed while the rest of Europe and the US did not.

The external environment is very important for a small open economy, but the level of overall growth in foreign markets was less important in generating the Irish boom. There was still adequate demand in these economies and it was especially high for the type of products exported from Ireland. In short, Ireland's leading export goods and services were recession-proof. After 1993, the UK and US economies picked up and later most of the EU states began to expand again, helping Ireland's other exports.

Ireland's exports grew faster than markets expanded in most years, both when there were international recessions and when there were not. Its export growth was substantially faster than the growth in the export markets, and as Ireland is not an exporter of raw materials, this was due to expansion of manufactures. For example, there was virtually no growth in international export markets in 1991 and 1992, but Ireland's exports grew by 5 and 14 per cent respectively and when there was growth of around three per cent in the international markets in 1994 and 1995, Irish exports grew by almost 14 per cent, indicating the increased penetration by Irish exports of its markets (Forfás, 1996: 72–73).

The main export growth in the period under review has been in industrial goods, especially computer-related goods and chemicals. In 1998, computer-related products made up a very high 22 per cent of Irish exports, far more than the level of food and live animals, which were then at only 9 per cent. Computer-related exports soared in recent years, as did pharmaceuticals. Computer equipment rose to £4.8 billion (as Table 4.1 shows), or a rise of 29 per cent in 1998. Organic chemicals rose a staggering 92 per cent to £7.8 billion or 17 per cent of the total in the year. Exports to the US greatly increased by 54 per cent in the years and there was also a large increase in exports to Germany and Benelux, more than making up for the fall in Asian markets.

It can be seen from Table 4.1 that there was slow growth of Ireland's once key exports, food and live animals, but a staggering ninefold increase in pharmaceuticals to over 7 per cent of exports in 1999, and a four and half times increase in computer equipment, or near to a quarter of exports.

Table 4.1: Composition of Exports, 1988 and 1998

	1988 (£m)	1998 (£m)	Per cent
Food and live animals	2,899	3,955	8.9
Beverages and food	251	569	1.3
Crude materials (not fuel)	551	582	1.3
Fuels, lubricants, etc.	65	119	0.3
Animal and vegetable oils	12	39	0.1
Chemicals	1,613	14,206	31.7
of which: Pharmaceuticals	*368*	*3,322*	*(7.4)*
Manufactured goods	1,035	1,413	3.2
Machinery and transport goods	3,838	16,414	36.7
of which: Office equipment (computers, etc.)	*2,262*	*10,045*	*(22.4)*
Miscellaneous manufactured arts.	1,606	5,261	11.8
Other	429	2,211	4.9
Total	*12,300*	*44,777*	*100*

Source: CSO, 1999.

❖ EU Funds

The EU has given structural and cohesion funds to the less developed regions, particularly the poorer states: Portugal, Greece, Spain and Ireland. The reason for the cohesion funds was the recognition that with the establishment of the Single Market in the European Union, poor and peripheral areas could lose out. The funds were designed to help countries catch up.

These funds were substantial and were invested in infrastructure, such as ports, roads, airports, telecommunications, universities and other areas. Most of these investments were capital-intensive and had a large import content (they suck in imports like machinery, plant, etc.), but they did have a multiplier effect on the economy; that is, they generated economic activity elsewhere. They also added to the modernisation of infrastructure. In addition, large sums were invested in human capital, largely in training.

The amounts of cohesion and structural funds were to be largely determined by the EU on the basis of objective criteria of needs. They were, however, open to negotiation. The Irish government, in promoting a "yes" vote for Maastricht in the 1992 referendum, was promised far more money than was to be received. The government had hoped for and was promised over £8 billion, but received only £6 billion. This lesser sum was nonetheless sufficient to help get Ireland up and running. It still got more per capita than the other "cohesion countries", Greece, Portugal and Spain, and this helped too.

While there have been question marks from the EU's Court of Auditors over the effectiveness of spending in Portugal and Greece, Ireland was the model country in spending probity and effectiveness (with some exceptions in CAP spending).

> One senior Commission official puts it: "Ireland is the success story on Cohesion, the miracle economy" (*Financial Times*, 24 June 1996).

Adds to Growth . . .

The ESRI (1993) had estimated that the first tranche of structural funds (1989–93) would add as much as 3.5 per cent to Ireland's GNP in 1992 and 1993. Both first and second (1994–99) tranches have raised the level of Ireland's GNP by between 2 and 3 per cent cumulative above what it would have been without them in the long run (Barry, Bradley and Hannan estimated it at 3 to 4 per cent of GNP in the late 1990s (Barry et al., 1999)).

While the figure may seem small, the funds came at a crucial time. In 1989, Ireland's debt was just past its peak, and a chorus of economists were singing for massive public expenditure cuts. Public capital spending had been savaged by a massive 19 per cent the previous year, so the cuts chorus was a big hit with the government.

Bottlenecks Cleared . . .

Had the structural funds failed to come when they did, Ireland would never have built the infrastructure and other investments which both helped to generate and sustain the prolonged economic boom which it still enjoys. The EU funds also ended the stop-go investment policies of Irish governments (which were typified by a new stretch of road, followed by many rusting barrels, with completion on hold, awaiting the following year's money). It also forced them to adopt long-term planning, which has been of immense benefit to the people. It prevented many bottlenecks from emerging, though the current boom is producing others, such as a shortage of skilled workers and Dublin's traffic congestion. On balance, the country's productive capital is far better now, thanks to the EU funds.

The Single Market is More Important than the Funds . . .

The ESRI argues that the Single Market is more important to Ireland than the EU funds. Bradley et al. (1992) forecast that the Single Market would allow Irish trade to grow substantially and, while there would be downsides in the rationalisation of enterprises, they found that Ireland's GNP would be around five per cent higher in 2000 than it would have been without it. The EU's Cecchini report had made the ex-ante study, but it excluded the effects of the Single Market on smaller countries. Another EU Commission study of its effects, after the Single Market was introduced, found that Ireland was a net beneficiary of the Single Market, particularly in its manufacturing sector. Therefore, the effects of both the Single Market and the funds did help Ireland significantly.

The CAP Fits . . .

Ireland had been, and still is, a major beneficiary of the EU's Common Agricultural Policy (CAP). However, the CAP is regressive, benefiting mainly larger farmers and agribusiness. For each pound spent, the CAP has a smaller economic impact on the Irish economy than a pound invested through the structural funds. Yet around half of the total EU Budget goes on the CAP and Ireland gets its share of this vast spending.

The CAP pays out in two ways — through the EU Budget and in guaranteed high prices (often double the average world market price) to farmers at the expense of consumers. There is a net gain to the economy, but at the expense of EU taxpayers and consumers!

In Summary . . .

The EU structural and cohesion funds amounted to a mini-Marshall plan to help the Irish economy out of recession. The funds did help, and help a lot! According to the ESRI, the Single Market played a more important role than all the European funds between 1989 and 1999. It follows that the third, smaller, post-2000 tranche is even less important. The significance of this is that the funds will dry up in the early years of the 21st century, but the Single Market is likely to remain. Another point is that the structural funds have declined in relative importance to the economy over the five years to 1999 and the economy still boomed.

If Ireland managed to successfully exploit the Single Market in its first years, the most difficult time, then it should do very well in the long term. Chapter Two showed how Irish industry found it very difficult to adjust to membership of the EEC after 1973. With easier access to huge new markets in the Single European Market, and with funds and the CAP, Ireland's membership of the European Union was of great benefit in the 1990s.

Ireland has used the European money so well that it has helped to bring its living standards close to the EU average. The Commission's Agenda 2000 (1997) said that enlargement with Central and Eastern European countries and Cyprus will add 500 million people but "barely 5 per cent" to EU GDP, which indicates their relative poverty and the importance of agriculture to them. With the planned admission to the EU of the more agricultural and poorer Eastern European countries, Ireland will have a chance to reciprocate the largesse it received and which helped its economy.

❖ Foreign Direct Investment

The flow of foreign direct investment (FDI) is ultimately determined in the boardrooms of multinational companies (MNCs), but it can be strongly influenced by the Irish government's industrial policy and, in this sense, it is subject to some domestic influence.

Ireland has benefited greatly from a high level of foreign direct investment, particularly from the largest foreign investing country, the USA. The level of US FDI in Europe grew substantially since the 1992 Single Market began and there was a large increase in Ireland's share of this rise. In 1995, Ireland replaced the UK as the favourite site for US electronic hardware overseas investment, securing 30 per cent of new projects in the EU against 19 per cent in the UK (according to KPMG, *Financial Times*, 13 December 1996). Ireland attracted 37 per cent of all US investment in the EU, just behind the UK, but also received 31 per cent of UK investment in the EU between 1992 and 1996 (*European Union Direct Investment Yearbook*, 1997). One-quarter of all manufacturing jobs are in US-owned firms.

The problem with foreign investment is that it is mobile — in other words, it can pull out and locate elsewhere. This happened in 1996 with Continental's Irish subsidiary, Semperit, a tyre manufacturer, and GM's auto components Irish subsidiary, Packard Electric, both large employers in west Dublin. In spite of its turnaround and the excellence of its own plant in Cork, Apple decided to transfer 450 of its 1,000 jobs to a sub-supplier, LG, in Wales in early 1999.

The 1,137 firms in the foreign sector made up 47 per cent of all manufacturing jobs, 71 per cent of exports, and paid corporation tax of over £700 million in 1998, according to the IDA. There will be an examination of the debate on the "over-dependence" of the Irish economy on foreign multinationals in Chapter Five.

❖ The Revolution in Communications

The revolution in communications has contributed to the boom. This revolution has been a technological one, and is still underway. It could not have come at a better time for Ireland. Ireland had long seen itself as disadvantaged by its "peripherality" — its status as "an island, off an island, off Europe". It was far away, poor and disadvantaged. It had an appalling telephone system, shipping links with other countries were reasonable but not excellent, and airfares were very high.

The government invested massively in a state-of-the-art telephone system in the late 1970s and early 1980s. The dramatic reduction in the cost of, and the improvements in, telecommunications gave most people in Ireland instant, reliable and reasonably priced communication. More needs to be done in modernising the former state telecommunications company, Telecom Éireann (Eircom) which is to restructure and was privatised in June 1999.

There was increased competition in air routes and telecommunications and importantly, because of technological change, competition became possible in areas where there had once been natural monopolies. There was acceptance of competition, once it was seen to be fair and when the transition to it was also seen to be fair. The Competition Authority was established and began to take effect.

The investment in ports and airports, in modern airplanes and general improvements in transport logistics have also been beneficial. For example, the price of a unit of sea freight has dropped 70 per cent in real terms between 1970 and 1996. Airfares have fallen dramatically internationally and the number of passengers using Dublin Airport more than doubled in six years to 13 million people in 1999. Aer Rianta recently invested £120 million in Dublin and Shannon Airports. However, the modernisation of inland transport infrastructure is seriously behind the requirements of the economy.

A computer-literate population and the development of the Internet and e-mail also helped. Many telesales companies have located in Ireland. The nature of much modern industry, such as computers, with high-cost, low-weight products, means that air-freighting to anywhere, which was once a problem, is now cheap and easy.

Conclusion on External Factors

The external factors that contributed to the Irish economic transformation that took place between 1987 and the time of writing, mid-1999, are amongst the most important economic factors. There was strong interaction between these factors — for example, between the level of foreign investment and government policy to attract such investment. This policy includes long-term strategies such as investment in education many years ago, current tax breaks, the fiscal management of the economy and the social consensus. There was a domestic policy influence in some of the external factors. For example, the spending of the EU funds, while under EU guidelines, was controlled internally; and the high level of foreign investment in booming industries was won over by policies such as improvements in the quality of the workforce, attitudes to foreign investment, a stable economic environment, cost and quality of local inputs, etc. Similarly, investment in telecommunications helped to bring Ireland closer to the rest of the world and in attracting FDI. Thus, the role of policy has been extremely important, a point which will be developed later.

It has also been stressed that each factor came into play approximately at the same time, developing a benign conjuncture, with positive developments reinforcing others. This is in stark contrast to the "vicious circle" in which Irish economic development occurred over the past two centuries, as has been examined in Chapter Two.

The rest of this chapter will analyse the domestic factors that have contributed to the economic performance of the country.

PART 2: THE INTERNAL REASONS FOR SUCCESS

This section examines those reasons for the Irish success that have been influenced by the Irish themselves, as politicians, policy-makers or citizens. It is argued that much of the economic success may be attributed to domestic factors, over which policy-makers had influence. It will be seen, however, that many of these policies took a long time to bear fruit.

❖ Fiscal Reform and a Stable Economic Environment

Ireland had a very serious fiscal crisis for most of the 1980s. The government had spent far more than it was earning in taxes. The national debt reached an extraordinarily high 125 per cent of GNP in 1987, eating up vast amounts of money in interest. Typically, 40 per cent of the interest payments were flowing abroad to foreign banks, which were enjoying the benefits of secure loans, paid for ultimately by ordinary Irish workers. While the other 60 per cent was going to Irish lenders, the process was generally regressive and most importantly, the taxes were not building the economy nor going to those who needed money. For a number of years, the equivalent of all income tax was going to repay the national debt.

There was widespread recognition in all sectors, political parties and lobbies, thanks to hard experience, that "tax and spend" policies did not work. While the Left traditionally wants to spend more on welfare, health and education and has a greater propensity (though not sole ownership of the idea) for investment in failing companies to "save" jobs, it and all other groups were chastened by the extent of the failure of the Fianna Fáil government's 1977 election programme. It eliminated most taxes on property (rates on domestic dwellings) and car tax and engaged in a large spending programme. Cutting taxes and increasing spending at the same time led to a major and prolonged fiscal crisis. The lesson was that public spending and tax cuts do not lead to growth — they cost a fortune in taxes later and can be regressive. In particular, this undermined local democracy by abolishing rates and the local property tax, which, while faulty, was politically almost impossible to replace.

A reform programme was begun by the coalition government in the 1980s, but it was really implemented by a chastened Fianna Fáil government in 1987, when a reduction in public spending was made by Ray McSharry, who had already been Minister for Finance in a short-lived Fianna Fáil government in 1982. It was the largest "cut" ever made. In fact, gross current spending by government rose by 1 per cent to £9,684 million in 1988 over the previous year, though this was a reduction of 1.1 per cent in real terms. In this sense it was a cut, but it was a crucial step in a different direction and marked a radical change. It was supported by the opposition parties under what became known as the "Tallaght Strategy".

The later "cuts" were really reductions in the *rate of increase* in borrowing, rather than cuts in spending. Total borrowing had been running at a very high 12 to 15 per cent of GNP in the 1980s, and while it had been reduced to a still high 9.4 per cent in 1987, it was cut deeply to only 3.1 per cent in the following year. Exchequer borrowing for current spending was reduced from 6.2 per cent of GNP in 1987 to 1.6 per cent in 1988. Borrowing was reduced to less than 2 per cent by 1990 and was close to that for subsequent years.

It has been argued that "the shock therapy of cutting public expenditure played a key role in the successful stabilisation of the economy in the 1980s" (Leddin and Walsh, 1997). Public spending was cut, but only once — in 1987 — and it was a small reduction in real terms. The current budget deficit and borrowing were cut very substantially in 1988. While the amount of public spending did not rise sharply in the following years, it did rise. What was important was that the continuous rises were halted. It did not really constitute a "shock" to the economic body. With growth, these adjustments were not difficult.

By 1994, current spending had broken even and surpluses were actually recorded in 1996 and 1997, a fairly unusual occurrence. The year 1998 saw an unexpected surplus, and 1999 will see a huge surplus, boosted by the capital receipts from the privatisation of Telecom Éireann. The huge debt, while still rising in nominal terms until 1994, fell from the peak of 125 per cent in 1987 to only 48 per cent of GDP in 1999, the lowest in the EU (excluding Luxembourg which does not borrow), and to a projected 40 per cent in 2000. There had also been a devaluation in 1986, though it was largely a reversal of an appreciation in the Irish pound.

This was an excellent performance, and one that was not anticipated by most economists or other commentators. The key was economic growth, which made prudent management easier. The "cuts" were minor, but the change in direction was vital in 1987. A stable economic environment was achieved with the social consensus, which is dealt with below. Since 1987, the country has enjoyed low inflation, low government deficits, which became surpluses in the late 1990s, and also surpluses on the balance of payments account. Strong growth and a relatively good balance of macroeconomic policies allowed the government to manage the economy with reasonable ease. The commitment to the strict EU Maastricht Treaty criteria did add to macroeconomic stability, but with high growth, such adherence was not difficult.

❖ A Structural Revolution in the Economy

From 1960 onwards, there has been a revolution in the structure of the Irish economy. It may have reached a crucial phase in the years leading up to the take-off. In the 1980s shakeout of industry, those who lost their jobs were often poorly educated, middle-aged and predominantly male. They were replaced by young, well-educated and more adaptable people. This was part of the rapid step-change from a low-skill, low-pay economy to a high-skill, high-pay one.

Another change in the structure of the Irish economy is that the number of hours worked fell by a substantial 2.5 hours a week between 1983 and 1995 (*Employment in Europe*, 1997). Of this, 40 minutes can be attributed to the growth of part-time work, and an hour (in industry, but less when grossed up for the whole economy) to the reduction in the 40-hour week to 39 hours under the national agreement. Most of the change reflects the move to service employment.

Agriculture employed 36 per cent of the workforce in 1961. This was to fall to only 8 per cent by 2000. This was a drop of more than a quarter of a million people to 122,000 in agriculture, fishing and forestry. While it is sad to see people having to leave the land, it does demonstrate a phenomenal rise in agricultural productivity, as output actually rose substantially in the period. Far fewer farmers were producing far more.

Table 4.2: Numbers Employed in Main Economic Sectors ('000s)

Sector	1961	1981	2000*	% of 2000 Total
Agriculture	379	196	125	8
Industry	259	363	483	31
Services	415	587	943	61
Total at Work	*1,053*	*1,146*	*1,551*	*100*

Source: CSO, ESRI Quarterly.
* Forecast.

Agriculture — Less Produce More

Ireland is still known, incorrectly, as an agricultural country. In 1999, agricultural products made up less than 6 per cent of exported goods and when tourism and services are included, it made up less than 5 per cent of all exports. Industry now dominates. The main products exported from Ireland are computers, pharmaceuticals, chemicals and soft drinks.

With modern farming methods and the Common Agricultural Policy (CAP) reform, still fewer people will be required on the land. Even with the big drop in numbers, they are still high compared to other countries.

The only option here is a radical reform of the CAP, with incentives to move to more organic, environmentally friendly, but less productive, farming. This may be the future as the BSE and other food and environmental crises have made people aware of the necessity for change. Agriculture is one of the major sources of pollution in Ireland today, with incentives provided by the CAP intensive system.

The CAP was to be further reformed in 1999, especially as the Union is to be enlarged. However, the member states baulked at reform. The Union can no longer afford the generous price supports and subsidies, which still take up half its budget, especially in ways that are often regressive and that cost consumers dearly. This reform will have to occur at the next review in 2002, before the predominantly agricultural countries of Eastern Europe become members.

Industry Modernises

Manufacturing in Ireland, dominated by MNCs, has defied trends elsewhere, where numbers have fallen dramatically, as productivity grew. Here it has actually grown in size as a sector, while productivity has simultaneously soared. After large job losses in the 1980s, numbers grew again from 1989. Thirdly, there was a big shakeout in the 1980s.

For industry as a whole (which includes manufacturing, construction and energy production), the numbers employed in 1987 were 300,000, down on the peak of 363,000 in 1981. By 1999, the numbers have risen again to a new peak of 456,000, or 30 per cent of those at work. Industry had largely modernised and the shakeout of most of the weaker firms had occurred in the 1980s. By the late 1990s, there was little "old" industry left.

Productivity in manufacturing grew so much that it was worthy of several studies (e.g. NESC, 1992). The answer was already known: transfer pricing by MNCs exaggerated the figures. But even with this stripped out, productivity was still impressive. This was largely, but not solely, in the foreign sector. Domestic industry's productivity has picked up too.

Productivity growth in Irish industry has been high for over 30 years, (at around 4.4 per cent a year from a low base, compared to 1.5 per cent for the other smaller industrialised countries) but it was particularly high in this period. Stronger indigenous industry, world class foreign industry and new forms of working all combined to help generate the boom.

Services — The Job Generators

Jobs in industry have grown, but it is the service sector where the bulk of the jobs are being generated. In Ireland, the services sector is still somewhat smaller than in several other industrialised countries, but it is growing rapidly, making up 61 per cent of those at work. While some of the new jobs in services include hamburger flippers, many are skilled, as has been seen in the previous chapter.

From Table 4.3, it can be seen that employment will continue to increase, that services will supply most of the jobs and that utilities, which are publicly owned, will shrink, as will transport and communications. Other economists have forecast a higher population in 2010, with Connell and Stewart (1997) estimating it as high as 4 million in 2011. The 1998 Fourth Quarterly National Household Survey showed that the rate of unemployment had fallen to 6.4 per cent in 1998, already well below the projection for 2010. Also, the labour force has risen to 1.651 million, the total numbers at work were 1.545 million and the population was 3.721 million in 1999, all ahead of what had been expected only a few years before. In its 1998 Employment Survey, Forfás found total industrial employment had already risen to 306,000, which was close to its 1996 forecast for the year 2005.

Table 4.3: Employment Projections, 1995–2010 ('000s)

	1995	2010
Agriculture	139	100
Manufacturing	247	295
Construction	82	170
Services:	765	1,355
Utilities	13	10
Transport and communication	76	95
Public administration	72	85
Other services	604	1,165
Total Employment	*1,231*	*1,920*
Unemployment	192	90
Labour Force	1,423	2,010
Unemployment rate	13.5%	4.5%
Population	3,575	4,100
Dependency ratio	1.90	1.10

Source: CSO and Estimates.

Lower dependency (see below) and consequent increases in average living standards, and increased numbers at work, means that there is greater demand for services. There has been growth in foreign export services, especially in engineering and financial services. There was also a substantial growth in the use of Irish services by MNCs. Finally, there was a growth in the quality and choice of services in Ireland, from tourism to finance.

These structural changes in the main sectors show that the Irish economy is quite similar to other "industrialised" (or rather post-industrialised) societies today. While the decline in agriculture will continue, the numbers in that sector are now so small that its employment decline will no longer stifle growth elsewhere. Indeed, as has been mentioned elsewhere, non-agricultural employment growth in Ireland has exceeded that in Europe and the US since 1986.

❖ The Demographic Dividend

By 1999, it was clear that all demographic forecasts would have to be substantially revised upwards. A forecast for a labour force of just under 2 million and a fall in unemployment to around 3 per cent is realistic. This is a remarkable change from a labour force of only 1.2 million for many decades. In 1998, NCB forecast a labour force of 1,694,000 by 2001 and 1,889,000 by 2006, just shading two million by 2010. ESRI (1999) forecast a labour force of 1,868,000 by 2010 and unemployment of under 4 per cent, implying around 1,800,000 at work. In conclusion, the forecasts are for continued strong growth in employment.

The fall in the dependency ratio — the number of people in an economy who are dependent on those who are at work — is very significant. "Dependants" include the elderly, children, students and the unemployed. The fact that they are not employed in the conventional economy does not mean that they are not engaged in extremely useful work and/or activities in society. With a large young population and high unemployment, Ireland had a high dependency ratio in the 1980s. Irish family size decreased substantially from 1980 on.

While it has been seen that per capita income of *those at work* has fast converged with the EU, the average income *per head of population* gives a better picture of overall living standards. The difference depends on the number of dependants for every worker in the country. In 1960, there were 170 dependants for every 100 persons at work, well above the then European average, imposing a big burden on workers to pay for the health care, education, etc., of those not at work. The high dependency continued for almost 30 years. It peaked at a very high 230 dependants per 100 persons at work in 1985, which is a higher level than the feared "greying" of the population that many EU countries are facing in the future. A burden on those at work, it was especially so in an economy where the tax system was not equitable, skewed in favour of companies in the effort to attract mobile investment. The gap between income per worker and per head of population widened in the mid-1980s because of this dependency and because pre-tax incomes of workers were rising.

The ratio has fallen and will continue to fall even more rapidly in the next 10 to 20 years. The forecast for 2010 — not too far away — was only 125 dependants per 100 workers, according to the ESRI (1997), but it looks as if it will be lower than that. There will also be a small decline in the numbers of elderly, in contrast to other European states. This reduction in dependency will greatly improve Ireland's average living standards. It was the people themselves who, around 1980, reduced the dependency by embracing contraception — with a passion — and having far less children.

Even in the early 1990s, forecasts for the rise of Irish per capita income were that it would still be well below that of the EU average by 2000. Now it looks as if it will reach the European average by then, well ahead of all expectations.

❖ Consensus — Altogether Now!

As mentioned elsewhere, a crucial ingredient to the success has been the social consensus, which began in 1987 with the first of the new comprehensive national agreements. According to

O'Donnell and O'Reardon (1996), "the social partnership approach produced the much-needed recovery from the disastrous early and mid-1980s and has underpinned a sustained period of growth since then".

National or Macro-Consensus

Globalisation demands stability and social cohesion, which a consensus approach to economic and social problems can facilitate. The national agreements allowed the social partners to have a say on take-home pay — that is, on the level of income tax. This shifted the emphasis from the illusory gross wage to take-home pay and, if there were tax reductions, a lower gross could therefore be acceptable. This actually happened — gross pay increases were moderated,[1] but tax cuts ensured that take home pay of workers increased in real terms.

The trade unions had a say on tax matters and on many other aspects of the economy and society, including fiscal policy, and their views on exchange rate policy were, at least, noted. It is important to realise that these agreements were far more than mere incomes policies. Incomes were part of the deals, but they were only a small part of them. They were the headline figures, but the Irish unions knew that in a high tax (on incomes) country, after-tax income was the key variable.

The unions ensured that public spending cuts would not include welfare and that tax would be cut on incomes. Thus they got some tax cuts and also got increases in social welfare payments in return. Winning the unions' agreement on a tight fiscal policy, on debt reduction and on exchange rate policy was a considerable help to government policy implementation.

The first consensus deal was the appropriately named, and ultimately successful, Programme for National Recovery (PNR) 1988–90, agreed between a Fianna Fáil government and the social partners in 1987. It was based on the "Strategy for Development"

---

[1] "Moderate" is a subjective term. Here it means a real increase (above inflation) of around 1 per cent.

of the National Economic and Social Council (NESC, 1986), the tripartite think-tank of the social partners, where policy is analysed and consensus formed. This deal achieved trade union support for a radical correction of the public finances. The National Debt had peaked in that year. The then Minister for Finance, Ray McSharry, later a successful European Commissioner for Competition, decided to tackle the growing fiscal crisis. This had been started by Fianna Fáil's own high spend and tax cuts election promises, exactly a decade earlier, which had ultimately driven debt up.

A hard currency policy was supported by the unions in spite of the currency crisis of 1992–93. In response to appreciation of the Irish pound, there was a 10 per cent realignment of the currency in the ERM in 1993, which translated into a 5 per cent decline in the average value of the effective exchange rate. This devaluation worked well for the economy, and Ireland did achieve low inflation and low interest rates.

The "Programme for Economic and Social Progress" (PESP), 1991–93, and the "Programme for Competitiveness and Work" (PCW), 1994–97, were both similar to the PNR, with agreed pay increases and agreements on many policy areas, such as tax reform and social equality. The increases for average workers, after tax, were 8 per cent (1987–1990), 6 per cent (1990–1993) and 5.6 per cent (1993–1995) (SIPTU, 1996a). The trade unions saw the PCW as very restrictive on pay and it seemed possible that it might be the last such tripartite agreement. Profits were booming, with increases averaging 27.8 per cent for all firms in the three years 1993–95, compared to employees' nominal increases of only 5.4 per cent in manufacturing. Many individual firms doubled their profits in the five years to 1995 (SIPTU, 1996b) and the trend of high rates of profitability continued to 1999 (OECD, 1998).

However, in 1997, the fourth programme, designed to take Ireland into the new century, "Partnership 2000" (P2K), was agreed by all the interest groups, including voluntary groups. It covered a wide area, setting out targets and agreed strategies. Partnership at enterprise level was a key part of P2K, which represents major challenges and culture changes for many enterprises, and while there were already major partnership deals in some plants, there is still a long way to go to deepen the process.

Under Partnership 2000 (1997–2000) the rate of increases in pay were moderate but were accompanied by promises of tax reductions which were exceeded, thanks to the performance of the economy. Thus, the average married worker was due to receive an increase of 8 per cent after inflation, but in fact his or her take-home pay rose by 19 per cent. This was a real increase of 13 per cent after inflation of 6 per cent, ending up with £16,400 per annum (SIPTU Report, 1999).

Neo-Corporatism

It has been argued by Teague (1995) that the Irish social partnership experiment has been an agreement by a trade union elite to tough measures being introduced to allow the economy to adjust to the fiscal crisis and to further European integration. He also argues that social partnership at national level is weakly represented in the workplace. Roche (1994) and others have argued that the trend in social and health spending and progress on employment legislation have contradicted this. NESC has said that, while the share of public spending as a proportion of GDP has fallen dramatically, the volume of such spending has increased, especially in health, education and social welfare. This is "one component of the partnership approach", it concludes.

The other critics of Irish social partnership have been conservative economists who object to unions having a role as "insiders" and blamed the then high level of unemployment on the agreements (e.g. Lee, 1994). They would have had difficulty in explaining the subsequent increase in the number of jobs, or how the 1980–87 free collective bargaining did nothing to help Ireland's dismal economic performance. That recession was particularly bad for employees, with average take-home pay dropping by 7 per cent for single workers (over 5 per cent for married) between 1980 and 1987.

A surprising critic of social partnership was former Labour Court Chairman, John Horgan, who claimed that the exceptional economic growth rates of recent years were not due in any significant measure to social partnership or "sacrifices of trade unions". He argued that inflation, wage demands and industrial unrest had all been curbed during the period of the "free for all" between 1984 and 1987. "In other words, social partnership did not bring low inflation or wage moderation or industrial peace. These all arrived before we started national partnership" (*Irish Times*, 14 May 1999). It may be that he was particularly hostile to the introduction of a minimum wage and a form of trade union recognition that was agreed under the aegis of Partnership 2000. His argument is flawed, because trade unions and workers are usually most militant in times of prosperity (such as the time he was speaking) which only began to develop at the time of the first partnership agreement in 1987. Partnership developed and deepened after then.

In the absence of such agreements, income determination would have been more fractious, with more strikes and higher pay settlements for the most powerful groups. Yet there would still be a large number of collective agreements within particular sectors, some covering tens of thousands of workers. This would occur in most areas, but especially in the public sector, and would be adopted by the large swathe of private sector employers who almost automatically follow the public sector deals. But wage setting or leadership would begin in industries where workers are strongest. It would be unlikely to translate into similar increases for most other workers. Thus, free collective bargaining is not really free — it is the strongest organised workers who set the trends and gain most.

Finally, it would be naive to believe that there is anything "free" about the negotiations on the price of labour in late twentieth-century Ireland. The national deals shifted the already structured and institutionalised system of wage bargaining onto a higher plane, where there is greater information, consultation and sharing of perspectives and where the parameters are greatly extended.

With the exception of the 1990 Industrial Relations Act, which constrained trade union activity, there has been good progress on employment legislation from the employees' perspective, though some perceive Ireland as a country with low labour regulation (Koedijk and Kremers, 1996).

Micro or Enterprise Partnerships

Teague (1995) was correct on the lack of progress on partnership at enterprise level, initially, but this has altered substantially, with agreements to revolutionary changes, especially when compared to the old adversarial industrial relations. The major change is that virtually all collective agreements under Partnership 2000 agree that partnership is the way forward. The trade unions have largely accepted partnership and it is official policy of the largest union, SIPTU. While it is clear that there are very different understandings of what partnership should mean, the fact that both employers and unions have embraced it is quite a radical change in attitude.

Roche and Geary (1998) found that there was team-working in 57 per cent of Irish workplaces; direct employee participation in one-third of them; and that worker participation is quite widely practised in Ireland in comparison to other countries. Where there was team-working, half of the workplaces had seen a reduction in the number of supervisors. Ireland is in the top league for employee participation, but they were critical of "the conceit of Ireland as an exceptional instance" because "only 19 per cent of workplaces introduced new work practices" in the three years before their survey in 1996/7. Yet this seems quite a lot *at that time*, when it was really only beginning. In half of the companies, team members controlled their own time-keeping and in one-third of them, they controlled attendance. In some other areas, they found that employees do not have much direction in their work.

While the level of progress may appear small in terms of numbers of enterprises at 19 per cent in 1996/97, it is surprisingly deep in some plants; there has been substantial progress since; the verbal commitment of both employers and unions to it; and the success of the new process where it is in place, all mean that any turning back will be temporary. Global competition has forced rapid adaptation to new forms of working (see below and Chapter Six) in modern manufacturing and services which demand partnership, or at least greater co-operation and trust, between workers and management. On the other side, workers are far better educated and wish to be involved in having control over their own working lives and to have an interest in their company and job.

There have been fewer strikes and far fewer days lost to strikes in recent years. The numbers of strikes fell substantially under the new partnership approach at national level. In the eight years to 1987, the number of strike days lost averaged 316,000 a year, whereas in the twelve years to 1998, under the national deals, the annual average had fallen to 103,000 a year, with 75,500 in 1997 and 37,400 in 1998. In the first quarter of 1999, there were only 2,033 days lost, compared to a low 13,629 in the comparable period of 1998.

Irish social partnership has passed the experimental stage and is now rooted in society. It had lagged behind other European countries, but in many areas it has now surpassed them, and this was achieved in a short period of 13 years. It was an idea whose time had come, and it was an important part of the benign conjuncture. Increased competitiveness, recognised by the unions in most local bargaining agreements, made partnership essential for the country to progress and prosper. New demands from the market and new forms of working made trust and agreement essential to achieve quality and competitive output. The Irish trade union movement and the Irish Left, which once looked to the Swedish model for inspiration, now found themselves the subject of foreign study tours!

The Limits of Public Spending

An important aspect in building the consensus was that the parties of the Irish Left — Labour, the Workers' Party/Democratic Left (most of the members of the Workers' Party formed Democratic Left in 1992 and it merged with Labour in January 1999) — and the trade unions did not believe that more public spending was the solution to problems, unlike the Left in the UK and elsewhere. Most would stoutly defend social spending, but are aware that public spending does not define one's socialist credentials, and some had argued strongly that much public spending can be regressive.

There was fairly widespread recognition of the spectacular failure of the Fianna Fáil experiment after 1977, where current or "day-to-day" public spending was supposed to boost the private sector.

The politics of Ireland, where political parties have not been strongly aligned to the right or left, make it difficult to see if the policies pursued are a triumph for Right or Left. The crucial change was the growth of consensus and whether this was a victory for Left or Right is difficult to gauge. Within the unions, it is the Left that is leading the move to participation.

❖ **Competitiveness**

The recognition of the importance of competitiveness by all the social partners and a common definition of the term is a vital component of the success. The recognition, at enterprise level and at national policy level, of the multitude of factors that combine to make a firm competitive has been important.

It is not long ago that competitiveness was defined by economists, employers and government as the rise in average manufacturing earnings, irrespective of their base level, of how they stood compared to other countries, or of exchange rate movements.

Competitiveness is a loosely used term. It is made up of a large number of factors at the level of the firm. These include unit costs, quality, reliability, innovation, etc. At national level, the quality of banking, services, transport infrastructure and political stability, etc. are also important ingredients. Indeed, the other factors of the Irish success story all demonstrate aspects of competitiveness. In a way, this component (competitiveness) is superfluous to the others, being a symptom of them, but its importance makes it worthy of consideration as a separate factor. The role of competitiveness is so important that it will be examined in greater detail in a separate section in Chapter Six.

❖ Public Enterprise — Commercialised and De-Regulated in Partnership

Ireland did not achieve its economic transformation by following the prescriptions of neo-classical economists, which include privatisation, cuts in public spending and shrinking the state and its services. In many ways, it took the opposite direction. It has social partnership, not "free" determination of labour costs, and there was little privatisation, though this is changing, albeit in agreement with the unions. Yet it would be wrong to assume that the commercial (and many non-commercial) publicly owned enterprises did not radically adjust in the period under review.

In Ireland, state-owned companies, including the monopolies, have been commercialised and largely de-regulated. Several of them had been unprofitable, poorly managed, and some had made poor investments. All shifted into a far more commercial mode in the period under review. Most are now profitable, as Table 4.4 shows. Most of these companies are planning continuous improvement through innovative partnership programmes, e.g. Aer Rianta, Bord na Mona and the Electricity Supply Board (ESB).

In 1986, domestic electricity prices were about 8 per cent above the European average, but from 1989 they were reduced steadily and by 1996 were almost 29 per cent below the EU average. For industrial users, prices were reduced from around 25 per cent above the European average to between 5 and 10 per cent below it in the 1990s (UNIPEDE, 1997). Prices of natural gas and telecommunications have fallen too and at the end of 1997, Telecom

Éireann began to restructure and to bring the benefits of this to its customers. Its unions, long opposed to privatisation, agreed to it, winning very generous and valuable shares for the employees, whetting the appetite of workers in other state companies for shares and forms of privatisation. The State, which had already sold 20 per cent to KPN/Telia, reduced its stake to zero in June 1999 with the flotation.

Table 4.4: Performance of Commercial Public Enterprise (net profitability, £m)

Company	1987	1997
Aer Lingus	24.3	53.7**
Aer Rianta	17.5	41.7
Bord Gáis Éireann	(35.4)	78.5
Bord na Mona	(15.9)	4.9
Coillte	(0.3)*	14.3
ESB	(5.0)	160.0
INPC	(3.7)	(6.9)
IFI	(15.6)***	7.1
An Post	2.8	6.3
RTE	8.9	6.1
Telecom Éireann	(8.0)	154.6
ACCBank	(14.9)	11.8
ICC	2.6	11.0

* 1988 results — year Coillte was established.
** 1998 results.
*** NET (precursor of IFI) results for 1987.
Figures in brackets represent net losses.

These companies accounted for around one-tenth of the economy in the 1980s, and most of them adapted to competition in the decade. The above results show the improved performance of most state companies in the period. Overall, the aggregate net profits improved from losses of £43 million in 1987 to profits of £543 million in 1997.

The biggest driver to increased competition in the country has been EU rules on competition — Articles 85 and 86 of the Treaty of Rome and its rules on state aid and its implementation. What were once seen as natural monopolies, such as Telecom Éireann and the ESB, now have competition. The flag carrier, Aer Lingus, which underwent a major restructuring in 1992, necessitating one of the first EU "state aid" examinations, is now reasonably profitable and is joining the oneworld alliance with BA/AA.

Two companies, Aer Lingus and Irish Steel, got what the EU calls "state aid" as opposed to "equity investment" from its shareholder, the state. It is generally agreed that this was most likely the last tranche of such subsidies. In the Aer Lingus case, this was allowed by the European Commission, partly because of under-investment by the shareholder in the first place. This is a problem which several state companies have had. Some of them, like the ESB, RTE, Aer Rianta and Bord na Mona (up until recently), had no equity and were totally funded out of retained earnings and borrowings. All, especially the unions, have long recognised that the days of the state subsidising ailing industries, public or private, are gone.

Trade unions have been long opposed to privatisation, mainly because their main objective was to preserve job security. This concern was greatly eased with the job creation success, and sweetened with generous share options. They also recognised the increasingly anti-entrepreneurial shareholder/governing State departments, which would not invest in successful companies (Irish governments generally have only invested in sinking state companies) and obstructed expansion or development plans. Further, Irish privatisations have not, to date, involved any major rip-off of the taxpayer and while a number of former senior State company managers have become seriously rich, this has been achieved discreetly.

Ownership does not determine whether enterprises are run efficiently. In the UK, most of the major restructuring of the nationalised industries took place under public ownership. Then they were privatised. Most of the industries which were nationalised in the majority of countries were not the "commanding heights of the economy", as the British Labour Party once loudly advocated, but rather the "heavy sunset" industries, such as steel, shipbuilding and coal, under pressure from workers, unions and local politicians of Left and Right. Continuous subsidisation, especially in recessions, was to become too heavy a burden for any government. Although some companies had serious problems in Ireland, the ruthless rationalisation and privatisation pursued in Thatcher's Britain was not followed here.

Irish Steel, badly run and facing imminent collapse, was radically restructured with the co-operation of the unions. The sugar monopoly, Irish Sugar, now called Greencore, was rationalised with the contentious closure of one of its three plants while under public ownership. It was then privatised. It is in a protected market under CAP and has expanded since privatisation. The largest insurance company, Irish Life, was also privatised and merged with Irish Permanent. Privatisation, through an employee buy-out, of B&I, a shipping company, was rejected by the Fianna Fáil government in preference to selling it to another shipping company, Irish Ferries, into which it was subsumed. A minority share in Telecom Éireann was sold to strategic partners in 1996 with the enthusiastic support of the unions, because the new partners brought technology and management expertise to the company. Cablelink, the cable subsidiary of Telecom and RTE, was sold in a trade sale to TLC for an unexpectedly high figure of £520 million in May 1999.

Several state-owned companies that had to be radically restructured did so in partnership with the unions, and employees received 5 per cent of the equity in return for the radical change and agreed downsizing. These were Aer Lingus, ESB, Bord na Mona and Telecom Éireann. All now face competition, and while some of them are dominant in the domestic market, they are small by international standards. At the time of writing, Telecom Éireann had recently being privatised and relaunched as Eircom, and ACCBank, ICC, Great Southern Hotels and Aer Rianta are likely to be privatised shortly.

❖ **Industrial Policy**

Ireland's active industrial policy has contributed substantially to its economic success. Industrial policy has been consistent since the early 1960s and offers certainty to foreign investors. It has placed great emphasis on achieving export-led growth. Ireland moved rapidly from high protectionism (taxes and quotas on imports) to an active, state-led industrial policy which sought out foreign direct investment (FDI).

Ireland's Industrial Development Authority (IDA) has had considerable success in attracting FDI, offering high grants, tax breaks, a skilled workforce and other benefits. Credit must be given to the IDA for choosing to pursue the right industries — electronics, pharmaceuticals, software and chemicals. The development agencies "picked winners" — not individual firms, but expanding industrial sectors. The main industries have lately included financial services and teleservices. The companies that have invested include Intel, Microsoft, IBM, Hewlett Packard, Kodak, etc. (see the list in the Appendix).

Therefore, investments have been in the fastest-growing industries, which have now contributed so much to the Irish success story. As has been seen, even with downturns in the main foreign markets, exports boomed. These industries demand highly skilled, flexible workers, which Ireland has been able to supply, and access to the huge Single Market.

Ireland offered a tax rate of only 10 per cent on manufactured goods; this was later extended to exported services, including financial services. It also gives very generous grants on investment and training. Yet these incentives did not increase in the period under review. Taxes on manufacturing had been zero until the EU forced the government to raise it to the nominal 10 per cent rate and average grants per jobs have fallen in real terms. (The 10 per cent rate will be replaced with a 12.5 per cent rate in 2003, which will apply to all companies in the country, including non-traded services.) So it was not a boost in incentives that helped. It is likely that the educated workforce (cited often by the multinational corporations), combined with the already high number of computer, chemical and pharmaceutical companies located in "clusters", helped to attract FDI. Industrial policy and the dependence on foreign companies will be discussed further in the next chapter.

❖ Institutional Change

The contributions of institutional change to economic growth and well-being have been neglected by economists until relatively recently. This was probably for the good reason that it is a difficult area to measure, or even to judge. Yet it is obvious that an oil-rich economy like Nigeria remains poor because of the institutionalisation of endemic corruption by the military dictators, which prevents efficient economic activity from taking place (though the election in 1999 may lead to change).

Similarly, but to a much smaller degree, Ireland has been criticised because there has been a weak spirit of enterprise in the country. In particular, in 1993, a report (NESC, 1993) on what had been the neglected area of the role of institutions in economic change, said that there was "a vicious circle" at work in the Irish economy. This was because there was a weak system of innovation, which had led to decline and emigration. There has been some progress in this area, and indeed a White Paper on Science and Innovation was published in 1996. Lars Mjoset, author of the NESC report in 1993 concluded that he saw the potential for a shift to a "virtuous circle" with the shift in exports from Britain; the shift by employers and trade unions from the British model of industrial relations to the Scandinavian one; the fall in dependence on agriculture; and the more modern demographic pattern (NESC, 1993b).

Other positive institutional factors include:

- Membership of the EU

- The strong educational system

- A substantial decline in the culture of dependency of business on the state

- Reforms of public enterprise

- Clearer and more effective competition law

- The spillover of knowledge and skill from the multinationals

- Increased recognition of "best international practice," not just in technical areas, but also in ethical standards.

There is also greater professionalism and greater industrial harmony in many areas.

There was a growth in entrepreneurship in the period under review. The numbers establishing their own businesses expanded and there was greater debate and awareness of the whole area, from the Culliton Report's emphasis on building small industry to the schools' "Young Entrepreneurs" competitions. There was a greater focus by the State on sources of finance for small business, including the role of the tax system, on encouraging innovation, the development of management skills and flexibility. There was also a growth of awareness at every level of progressive organisations (including not-for-profit organisations) of the need for an enterprise culture where people would be more accountable for their work, collectively.

The "mañana" or "'twill do" attitudes that had been pervasive in Ireland until the mid-1980s are not tolerated by Irish people at the end of the 1990s. It is not just individuals who became more confident and willing to help get things done; it became ingrained in organisational cultures. There was a decline in the "cute hoorism" or clever obstructionism that was prevalent particularly in the public service, from the central civil service and local authorities to some state bodies.

The Irish public sector is well motivated and professional. It is, however, clearly in need of reform. It is extremely over-centralised and is still largely based on the model designed by the British in the nineteenth century. The issues of pay determination and productivity in the public service are obstacles to continuing growth and they urgently require reform. Joe Lee (1989) is highly critical of the power and conservatism of the civil service, but since his book was written, it appears that the Department of Finance has assumed even greater powers, not just over other Departments, but over every quango, state company and local authority. While there has been change in a piecemeal fashion, no root and branch reform has taken place.

The Irish public sector had been more or less free from corruption and ineptitude, with four recent, controversial exceptions. The first was low standards in areas of the Department of Agriculture, which were revealed in the Beef Tribunal of 1991–93, and the second was the interference by the Taoiseach's Office with the IDA on beef export guarantees for the Goodman company. The third was the scandal at the Blood Bank, where hundreds of women were infected with Hepatitis C. The Beef Tribunal, which delivered a surprisingly weak report, especially considering the time it took and its cost, did, however, expose dubious practices at the very highest levels in the state — politicians, civil service, Revenue and State bodies — some of which have been remedied. Finally, the bribes allegedly accepted by George Redmond, Assistant Dublin City and County Manager, and former Foreign Minister, Ray Burke, and questions over monies allegedly received by former EU Commissioner Padraic Flynn in the late 1980s, demonstrated what many had long believed: that there was a certain level of corruption in land rezoning, planning permissions and ineffective tax administration. The Payments to Politicians Tribunal in 1998/99 revealed corruption and tax evasion at the highest levels, up to and including the former Fianna Fáil leader and Taoiseach, Charles Haughey.

There is still a certain *laissez-faire*, or rather "lazy fare", attitude in some areas such as tax inspection of the self-employed, policing and animal disease eradication. There are major reviews underway in both the civil service (*Strategic Management Initiative*, 1996) and local authorities (*Better Local Government — Programme for Change*, 1996). These are largely self-driven.

Another important institutional change in the economy was the reform of state intervention. Ireland still has a high level of state intervention, much of which is regressive and of dubious economic effectiveness, but it has been reduced. There was a culture of dependency by business on state aid, which was highlighted by the Telesis Report (1982). Business sometimes spent much time lobbying government for benefits instead of pursuing profits. At one time, a firm could expect the state or its agencies to find the site and build the factory, pay for much of the machinery in grants, train the workers and management, subsidise R&D, help find the domestic and foreign markets and charge zero tax on profits made on exports.

In 1999, a major ESRI report for the government recommended major cuts in state aids to industry, services, agriculture, tourism and parts of education.

> We see a reduction in support for the market sector, including industry, services, agriculture and tourism. With rapid growth, the justification for state intervention due to "market failure" is reduced in more developed regions. Existing subsidies should be cut back (ESRI, 1999: *xv*).

There was a reduction of grants in real terms per job to industry over the 12 years under review. However, the OECD (1997) shows state aid to private industry and services rising from £155 million in 1988 to £300 million in 1997. This may be accounted for by the increase in the volume of investment and additional projects. However, in 1999 a report actually recommended the reduction in state aid to industry, because job creation is no longer the pressing priority it had been for so long (ESRI, 1999).

Tax rates — corporation tax and income tax— were reduced over time, but the many tax allowances for business were also reduced, bringing the effective tax rate closer to the nominal one. The many state agencies which aid business and agriculture began to charge for their services.

There was also a reduction in subsidies to state-owned industry in the past decade, a large sector of the economy, though if the transport company CIE is excluded, the net flow has been from the companies to the Exchequer for at least two decades, contrary to popular prejudice. There was a substantial curtailment of costly tax breaks to the middle classes for housing, life and health insurance.

Finally, the large number of leading multinationals based in Ireland has given many Irish managers top-class management skills that are permeating to other areas. These companies often have good benefit packages for their workers, such as canteen facilities, medical care and training and these benefits have spilled over to the rest of the economy.

Overall, these changes indicate a profound transformation in institutions and attitudes to public spending. Some of the changes would have been regarded as "impossible" a few years earlier — like the curtailment of mortgage interest relief, once a regressive transfer that was of most benefit to those on high incomes with larger houses.

❖ The Educated Workforce

Another key ingredient in the prolonged Irish economic boom has been the young educated workforce. The ESRI (1997) holds that the changes in education policy in Ireland were of great importance in the recent prosperity. It describes the changes in education as "revolutionary", arguing that the high levels of education have also had major impacts on fertility, marriage, migration and labour force participation, especially by women. Thus education has impacted upon and changed many areas of Irish life.

The ESRI report also states that modern theories of economic growth place great importance on the role of the stock of human capital and the rate of its accumulation to the production process. It is clearly part of the growth process.

> The rate of human capital accumulation is defined both by the demographic trends within the economy and the level of investment in education and training. These are two of the long-term factors that we identify as significant contributors to the Irish growth process (ESRI, 1997: 46).

Today, between 40 and 50 per cent of those entering the workforce have experienced third-level education (compared to 20 per cent in the EU) and over 80 per cent have Leaving Certificates (i.e. completed upper second level). In contrast, of those aged over 65, only a third went beyond primary level, and less than 10 per cent had third-level education. This is a remarkable achievement.

This has been achieved in spite of gross neglect of education in the post-war period, when most other countries were investing in the area and in spite of a relatively low spend on education today. It was only in the 1960s that Irish governments began to reform and invest in education. It is held by many that the introduction of free education in 1967 was the most important change, and it certainly led to greatly increased participation rates. The recent expansion in third-level education has also been significant. The high educational achievements in Ireland, with a relatively low spend per pupil, have been achieved because of strong motivation and a good teaching system.

The contribution of education to economic output is one of the main reasons why many MNCs invest here. A survey of businesses, asking the reasons for the choice of country for investment, placed Ireland top in Europe for its educated workforce and second (after Germany) for the skills of the workers (OECD, 1997: 14). There are a high number of engineering graduates and the workforce is well educated in general, meeting the needs of modern industry and services.

In addition, while an average of one-in-ten Irish adults have emigrated and returned, many more educated people have done so, bringing back skills and experience. Of those aged over 40 with third-level education, a very high 39 per cent have emigrated and returned. Clearly they were not McAlpine's Fusiliers! While the participation rate of women with only primary education is very low, there was a 20 per cent increase in women in their 30s and 40s with third-level education returning to work after 1988, according to the ESRI.

The rapid increase in Irish productivity has been generated by improvements in capital and labour with the improvements in the former achieved through greater investment and technological change. The contribution of labour to productivity has been achieved not just by more people at work, greater participation, etc, but because quality is improved through education. Durkan et al. (1999) found that in the period of most rapid growth, 1986 to 1996, increased education of the workforce contributed to a measurable increase in productivity. They were also able to project that there will be growth in the education-adjusted workforce to the middle of the next decade, leading to continuing productivity growth, but at a lower rate than to 1996, and this will help the economy to grow rapidly.

Ireland is well placed to meet the demands of modern industry and services, with most people having at least a Leaving Certificate. Such people generally do find work, but for the first time most of them are likely to get work in Ireland in the future.

❖ New Forms of Work Organisation

At microeconomic level, in the firm, radical changes were taking place in the late 1980s. At national level, employers and trade unions were abandoning their traditional adversarial role, and while movement was slower at the level of the enterprise, change was still happening. Firms that failed to move from Taylorist production methods and to recognise the need for new processes that encouraged workers to include quality, would become uncompetitive. Modern industry demanded quality (Total Quality Management — TQM) and other concepts whose acronyms are now widely known (Just-in-Time (JIT), World Class Manufacturing (WCM), etc.) which a regimented workforce could not give.

Did Ireland have specific advantages? Part of the reason for the success is that many of the plants are new and, while US-owned in many instances, they employed the latest production methods, focusing on quality, and they had come to Ireland because of the educated workforce. Older workers, on the other hand, have been surprised at the new production methods. There is more flexibility and co-operation in many plants than most people realise.

Workers, who are increasingly better educated, do not accept mass production methods and prefer team-working, where there is scope for initiative and the need for supervision is gone. Many, to their surprise, find that they enjoy the change that being multi-skilled gives them, or the flexibility of annualised hours, while some like part-time working and others see the advantages of flexible payments systems such as gain-sharing. Human Resource Management (HRM) became "Change Management" as firms realised that product lines were getting shorter, products were diversifying and services needed continuous improvement; the key to satisfying the endlessly increasing demands of consumers and industrial customers lay in people. In the past, this was merely an empty slogan for many firms. In the 1990s, internationally, this has become the essential ingredient of competitive success. However, it must be recognised that there are still many old-style firms around. This important factor will be further analysed in Chapter Six.

❖ Cultural Confidence Building

There have been radical changes in Irish society, which have had profound effects, not just in social areas, but on the economy. These include a greater respect for a professional approach, openness, participation, accountability and more democratic institutions, equality for women and greater inclusiveness.

A number of key institutions changed radically, and this assisted participation and helped democratise and open up decision-making, which assists in economic development in a modern society. Success in Ireland was helped by the triumph of the modern or professional over traditional ways of doing things. The hegemony of the two great Irish institutions — Fianna Fáil and the Catholic Church — has been greatly reduced since the mid-1980s. Both had dominated Irish politics and society for a long time. This change has had a far-reaching effect, which has not yet ended. These changes have allowed the greater questioning of authority and have boosted the confidence of the modernisers, including the more forward-thinking members of both institutions.

One institution, Fianna Fáil, had been "the natural party of government" for many decades. Fianna Fáil, for the first time ever, could no longer form a government on its own in the late 1980s. To achieve power, it would have to share it. It had to open up its highly centralised (and remarkably effective) machine to outsiders. This, combined with other factors, helped in the development of a new political pluralism. The revelation that the once-dominating leader of Fianna Fáil and former Taoiseach, Charles Haughey, was a "kept man" of Irish business for years, including the time when he was Taoiseach, meant that even the most powerful can be successfully challenged.

The past decade also witnessed the growth of the Labour Party in both size and, more importantly, with a weaker Fianna Fáil, influence. Labour appeared to become the party that no government could do without. Two very different parliamentary parties also emerged in the 1980s, one of the right — the Progressive Democrats — and the other of the left — Democratic Left — both of which had participated in government by the mid-1990s. Up until then, Irish politics had been run by two parties, Fianna Fáil and Fine Gael, and the two had been very similar in policies, if not in attitudes, with Labour on the sidelines. Democratic Left and Labour merged in 1999, and it remains to be seen how the new entity will do.

Furthermore, the election of Mary Robinson in 1990, against a strong Fianna Fáil contender, against the odds, and her immensely popular, path-finding and modernising Presidency gave a great boost to many Irish people, breaking old certainties. She had been a crusading lawyer and the people knew they were getting a person of radical and challenging ideas when they elected her.

The other dominating institution that fell in the period under review is the Catholic Church. Once unquestioned, with a profoundly conservative view on social and economic matters, it fell victim to the abuse of its own power by a small minority of its leading members. Roy Foster (1989) described the highly politicised nature of Catholic authority in an almost uniformly Catholic state where "the ethos of nationalist Ireland would be unashamedly Catholic", and it was. The Catholic Church's leading political role in the state was undermined by revelations of many cases of physical and sexual abuse of children and also the scandals, initially denied, of priests and a bishop who had fathered children. It had appeared as if "poverty was God's will", according to the Catholic bishops, for many decades. Poverty had been ignored and sexual morality had been their apparent primary interest.

Yet the Catholic Church's control of schools had many positive aspects, not least of which was the great dedication of the clergy to education. However, for many years it had been based on strong discipline and authoritarianism. This undermined the confidence and self-esteem of children. This had negative effects on the economy, because many children came out of schools without confidence and self-respect. It is not just that they were unlikely to become entrepreneurs, but they were imbued with caution and were risk-adverse, wherever they chose to work.

Today, however, many leading Catholics and priests are now quite radical in seeking to address social issues. The monolithic institution is gone, forever. It is still very powerful, but is more open and participative.

A newer institution, the EU, has gained an influential position: membership of the Union has greatly assisted Ireland, its civil service, state agencies, local authorities, unions, employers and all institutions and all the people who work for them, to become more professional and confident in their own abilities.

Women's Work . . .

There has also been a recognition and acceptance of equality and of individual and collective rights. The change in the attitude to women has been one of the greatest transformations in modern Ireland, and the importance of this, to men and women, is yet to be fully recognised. However, equality, now recognised in law and socially, has a long way to go in practice.

Women in Ireland have long been regarded as second-class citizens. As recently as 1973, women had to resign from their jobs in the public service if they got married! Until the late 1970s, Irish women got lower pay rates than men for the same work. Women still earn less on average, largely because they do not get the promotional opportunities. Part of the reason for this is that it is they, rather than men, who often leave the labour force to care for children. Now women are rejoining the workforce in far greater numbers after taking time out, mainly to rear children.

Social Exclusion . . .

There is also widespread consensus in recognising that social exclusion is a serious issue and one that threatens stability. A wider distribution of income means that there is a greater propensity for consumption, which generates activity and contributes further to economic growth. Yet the real question is whether there is a will to tackle the problem with effective action. Most Irish people do believe that the achievement of substantial economic success that excludes a substantial minority is hollow. And while they will never go back to de Valera's image of an Ireland with "comely maidens dancing at the crossroads" and of "frugal living", there is a sense of fairness in society which awaits action. This crucial aspect of the boom is addressed in greater depth in Chapter Seven.

There is Something Else Stirring in Ireland . . .

Parallel to Ireland's economic success, there has been a great deal happening in the arts — popular, high, low, culture or entertainment, whatever name it is given — which have helped to boost Irish self-confidence. The disproportionate success of the Irish in literature has long been known. But instead of the literary giants feeling that they have to exile themselves away from the claustrophobia and censorship of 1950s Ireland, the Irish are now proud of them, like Seamus Heaney, Noble Laureate. And Ireland has provided some popular writers too, like Maeve Binchy, top of the bestseller lists in the UK and elsewhere, while Roddy Doyle continues to receive both popular and critical acclaim. Similarly, Irish rock musicians such as U2, the Corrs, the Cranberries, Boyzone and Sinead O'Connor have taken the world by storm since the late 1980s. Irish dancing, once thought of as boring, was transformed by *Riverdance*.

There are wonderful playwrights like Brian Friel and Martin McDonagh, and filmmakers such as Neil Jordan, Jim Sheridan and Paddy Breathnach, and even the visual arts are providing a living for some in Ireland, like Tony O'Malley, Brian Maguire and others. There are excellent festivals, summer schools and arts events throughout the land, from the internationally acclaimed Wexford Opera Festival to the Galway Arts Festival.

In sport too there were some great successes that boosted the national psyche, such as the World Cup performance in 1990. Self-confidence is important in all areas of life, and the Irish are moving to the new Millennium with confidence. As long as it does not turn into a swagger, progress will continue.

Economists are waking up to the fact that with rising living standards, arts, culture and entertainment are not just growing industries, but they can have multiplier effects into the "old" economy too. These areas are now major employers in Ireland and help boost Ireland's balance of payments.

People are increasingly better educated and more economically independent, with rising incomes and a wider choice of jobs. With the rapid growth in material wealth and a fall in the numbers of children, for the first time, people are inheriting substantial assets, which creates more financial independence. The fall of some powerful people who appeared to be beyond the reach of law has helped in the change in attitude. It means that the culture of the "meeting before the meeting", the "wink and nod", the "word in yer ear", seniority and the replication of the mediocre are usually no longer tolerated. It still goes on in many institutions and organisations, but to their peril.

Irish people, not just the young, have been given a great boost to their self-confidence by the fact that they can achieve a lot and do so well. It is a new, strange feeling. To be the top-performing economy in Europe for many years may be a bit hard to grasp, but in recent years, Irish people are beginning to see that they themselves, in their own work and lives, can equal the best.

There is growing recognition of the importance of social, historical and cultural influences on economic policy and performance. The changes in attitudes to women, to minorities, to those excluded from mainstream society, the positive developments in the arts, culture, music, film and literature and the opening up of once monolithic institutions to other influences, all add to the cultural confidence-building of the Irish people, which can translate into progress in economic activity.

CONCLUSION

Of the reasons listed for the Irish economic miracle, most of them were determined by domestic policy or by actions of the Irish people themselves. This may have lessons for other countries looking to replicate Ireland's success, though this must be qualified, since some of the factors are culturally specific to Ireland.

It is unlikely, for example, that any government could persuade its people to reduce the number of children they were having to the extent to which it happened in Ireland in the 1980s! The government had little influence in this, other than reluctantly making contraception legal, some years earlier. Other countries do not have the historical problems that Ireland had, such as the major demographic problem of high dependency ratios between 1960 and 1990. Yet there are lessons to be learnt from Ireland's record on consensus-building, macroeconomic management, attracting in foreign direct investment, and other areas.

As the majority of reasons listed for the progress of the Irish economy were under the influence of the Irish people, this underlines the role and importance of policy. Some people argue that policy is made up as politicians go along, and would probably say that the "benign conjuncture" was just that and no more. Perhaps policy formulation in the past was often made on an *ad hoc* basis, but it is much more rigorous today.

For example, it has been seen that the EU imposed long-term planning on virtually all sectors of the economy. For each sector, there was a well-researched "Operational Programme", setting out exactly how the EU funds would be spent. In addition, the national programmes, such as Partnership 2000, while often thrown together in the heat of negotiations, do reflect the main aspirations of all interest groups and, once agreed, become extremely important medium-term programmes, forming the basis for future policy execution. Importantly, they bring all the main players together and they all end up with common ownership of the problems, proposed solutions and strategies. Many subcommittees and technical groups are formed to execute each aspect of the agreements, where there is analysis and intense debate before consensus is reached.

The role of policy and of the state should not to be underestimated, even in the era of globalisation. States make the laws where FDI is invested, decide on public spending — current (e.g. pay) and capital (e.g. infrastructure) — and they determine tax policy. They regulate the labour market, industrial relations, social security, income distribution, equality, financial disclosure and corporate governance. The Irish State plays an important role as an equal partner in Europe and can have influence on EU policies too.

In Ireland, the state has moved from a relatively authoritarian to a more consensual model, with most interest groups involved not alone in decision-making, but in the methodical work of policy determination, which usually involves the swift abandonment of dogmatic positions. Most importantly, once the decisions are made, all have ownership of them, and this consensual approach means that their implementation is more effective. It is government which co-ordinates, facilitates, directs and pays for the policies to be implemented, with the consent of all interest groups.

There has been a strong emphasis in this chapter on several non-economic factors, such as institutional changes and the consensus. Such factors cannot be measured as easily as the economic ones, but they are extremely important. The social and institutional milieus in which enterprises operate are a vital, and some-times over-determining, aspect of their development.

The reasons for the emergence of the Irish Celtic Tiger — with its rapid growth rates, low inflation, booming exports of leading products and services, rapidly rising living standards and, at long last, rising employment — are complex and interrelated. The next chapter analyses industrial policy in a small very open economy in the context of the increasing globalisation of the world economy.

Chapter Five

GLOBALISATION AND INDUSTRIAL POLICY

World trade has being growing at a much faster rate than the growth of the world's economies, and foreign direct investment (FDI) by multinationals is also growing rapidly. In this chapter, the phenomenon of globalisation and the expansion of world trade and foreign investment will be explored to set the context for an examination of the dependency theory of Irish industry. It will be argued that while Ireland is dependent on foreign direct investment, it and other small open economies have little choice in the era of globalisation but to encourage it, while building strong indigenous companies and stronger linkages between domestic and foreign companies.

This chapter also examines Irish industrial policy, which has been fairly consistent since the late 1950s, with a heavy state interventionist but "hands-off" approach. The state agencies have been successful in attracting foreign investment, but have been heavily criticised for failing to develop indigenous industry. In 1998, for the first time, foreign companies employed more than Irish companies in manufacturing and international services. They are also more profitable, more productive and export far more than Irish-owned companies. They have become very dominant in the Irish economy.

However, it will be seen that the "visible hand" of industrial policy, which has become more directed, has been more successful in recent years, and that both foreign and indigenous companies appear to be working closer together to their mutual benefit, and indigenous companies are now performing better in many ways than they did in the past.

GLOBALISATION

Globalisation can be defined as "the process by which markets and production in different countries are becoming increasingly interdependent due to the dynamics of trade in goods and services and flows of capital and technology" (*European Economy*, 1997: 45). Another definition of globalisation is that it is the result of the removal of rules, regulations, quotas and barriers to trade, which has resulted in the freeing up of movement of goods, services and, particularly, capital, between countries. It has happened because governments have decided to open up, or have been forced to do so by mobile capital.

In the European context, the Single Market and the fall of the Berlin Wall have added momentum to the process of globalisation. Many developing countries, which would have been protectionist in the past, have opened up in recent years, and the Uruguay Round of GATT for agricultural products and another agreement on services have also facilitated the growth of trade. The emergence of the Internet and the rapid rise of e-commerce has also led to increased globalisation.

One vital aspect of globalisation is the rate of growth of FDI, which has been phenomenal. Ireland has been a particular beneficiary of this. Annual flows grew from an average of $50 billion a year in the mid-1980s to $200 billion by 1990. This was followed by a slowdown, but it rose again to $315 billion in 1995. In that year, the Union was the source of 42 per cent of global FDI flows and it received 36 per cent of inflows, mainly from the US, Japan and the Asian Tigers, which were seeking to invest in the Single Market.

Within the European Union, foreign investment between member states has grown to very high levels, from 20 per cent of outflows in 1983 to 60 per cent 11 years later. Irish multinationals are now investing substantially in Europe. Foreign investment in non-EU countries by the EU member states is small as a proportion of gross fixed investment in the Union (at 2 or 3 per cent), but it is growing. It goes mainly to other industrial countries, but this was declining in favour of the Asian Tigers and China, before the Asian crisis.

Growth in world trade has remained at a rate well above growth in world GDP. Between 1950 and 1973, the volume of world trade grew at an annual rate of 8 per cent, compared to GDP at 5 per cent in volume. It slowed down after the first oil crisis. However, since 1983, according to the EU, the pace of world trade accelerated to almost 6 per cent a year, again well above the growth in world GDP of 3.4 per cent. However, with the Asian crisis, it fell from a high of 10 per cent in 1997 to 5 per cent in 1998 and 1999, reflecting the slowing world economy, but it has begun to pick up again (OECD, 1997b: 47; OECD, 1998).

In 1996, the stock of foreign investment amounted to $3,200 billion. The flow of FDI grew faster than trade (which has been growing faster than GDP) between 1991 and 1996 at 12 per cent a year, against trade at 7 per cent. The share of MNCs' foreign affiliates in world manufacturing output rose from 12 per cent in 1977 to 18 per cent in 1992 (which is not as high as one might have expected).

Finally, globalisation has increased in another area, financial flows, which have also soared in recent years. The trade in foreign exchange had grown to $1,500 billion a day in 1997. Thus the world economy is becoming more integrated and interdependent.

States, MNCs and Power

Globalisation of the world economy is taking place at a rapid rate. In the globalised economy, it seems that the nation state can be largely ignored by foreign investors, MNCs and speculators. The integration of the world economy appears inevitable, with convergence of economic factors like interest rates. Unskilled jobs seem to be shifting from industrialised countries to newly industrialising ones, a trend that worries trade unions in the US, Germany and other countries.

While world trade and foreign investment by MNCs are growing rapidly, fears of globalisation and the power of MNCs are exaggerated. This trend is not new. At the beginning of the First World War, the level of trade for the major powers — the UK, Germany, France, Japan and the US — was much the same as it is today and the level of capital flows was very high. This was the time that Lenin wrote his influential book about foreign investment and capital flows, *Imperialism: the Highest Stage of Capitalism*, where he saw the main powers dividing up the world amongst themselves. He did not foresee that the terrible war that was beginning would soon give him his opportunity to run one of the great powers! In addition, labour migration was far greater then than it is today and there was also free trade. In this sense, the world economy even then was internationalised. What is different is that foreign firms once located plants abroad to supply the local market, but now they do so to export. It is precisely this change that provides a small open economy like Ireland with the opportunity to exploit its advantages in the globalising economy, provided it also looks after its own backyard — investing in education, developing linkages, R&D, etc.

Hirst and Thompson (1996) state that that the world economy

> . . . is dominated by uncontrollable global forces and has as its principal actors and major agents of change truly transnational corporations, which owe allegiance to no nation state and locate wherever the global market advantage dictates.

But they also argue that there is much that states can and should do about MNCs, foreign investment and capital flows.

Today's world economy is still far from integrated in terms of prices of goods and services, labour, access to capital, interest rates and tax rates. Most importantly, governments still have a lot of power, and while it is a little less than before, particularly for small open economies like Ireland, it is still considerable. Ireland may have less power over macroeconomic instruments than in the past, but it has substantial power over many other elements, especially microeconomic factors. Governments acting together can achieve much, as the 15 member states of the EU are still learning. The introduction of the euro in 1999, to a shaky start, should strengthen the Eurozone and the European Union.

Globalisation raises two key questions for the individual state. Firstly, how does a country exploit globalisation and the growth of international trade, investment and capital flows? And secondly, how does it regulate it? The answer to the first question is to look at Ireland's success. The answer to the second is that no country, especially a small country, can regulate it on its own, but regions or groups of countries, especially the European Union, can and should.

The competitive down-bidding for FDI, using costly incentives, by EU governments is a case where democratic countries are weakening their own power instead of working together to set clear rules. Governments, particularly in the EU, must act together on broad policy issues for their peoples' welfare, while competing ferociously, if necessary, for FDI after the ground rules have been agreed.

The boards of MNCs, while appearing to have enormous economic power (with 21 global MNCs having sales bigger than Ireland's GNP in 1998) still have to watch what is going on in each country in which they operate. They spend much time lobbying in Brussels, Washington and every capital city, leaving nothing to chance — or rather, to market forces! Most of them still have the bulk of their investments in their home country. Small countries like Ireland, where MNCs such as Smurfits and CRH have more investment abroad than at home, are the exceptions.

Ireland is one of the most open economies in the world, and while it opened up late, it did so with enthusiasm and has benefited greatly. Free trade has expanded immensely, and indigenous companies are now well adjusted to foreign trade, unlike in 1973 when the country joined the EEC.

The unregulated flow of capital has great potential for instability and even anarchy, and this is an issue which governments must address. The power of George Soros in whipping the pound sterling in the currency crisis of 1992–93 was something that the Union could and should have prevented. The level of capital flows has grown enormously. A staggering $1.7 trillion a day flies around the globe, much of it in speculation. The EU should consider joining with the other large economies in imposing a small tax on financial transactions of 0.02 per cent.

This "Tobin Tax", called after the Nobel economics prize winner, James Tobin, would be of no consequence to legitimate transactions, but would amount to a high tax on speculation. Tobin says that "0.02 per cent on a round trip to another currency costs 48 per cent in a year if transacted every working day in a year". It would see off the speculation-induced chaos, would encourage productive investment and would raise billions in taxes for governments.

The State versus the Market

In a cover article and supplement, the influential conservative magazine *The Economist* (29 September 1997) bemoaned the fact that, despite all the talk of globalisation, the state is getting stronger. It believed that there is a battle between "states and markets" and said that the popular view in the 1990s — that the market is winning — is wrong. It reached this conclusion by finding that governments' share of the economy has been moving only in one direction every decade this century, and that direction is "up". Even in the US and Japan, state spending has risen considerably.

And Conservative Britain was not a model, *The Economist* claimed, saying that before Margaret Thatcher's

> . . . Conservative axe, public spending accounted for 43 per cent of the economy. After nearly 20 years of ruthless cuts, radical dismantling of the welfare state and hard-faced suppression of the public sector unions, the state's share has shrivelled to just 42 per cent (*The Economist*, 29 September 1997, Supplement, p. 8).

It continued:

> . . . sickened in the end by this remorseless brutality, the
> British electorate earlier this year swept Labour back into
> power with a landslide victory.

Table 5.1 illustrates how the "power" of states has grown, giving
government spending in various years since 1960. *The Economist*
said that since 1870 it has risen "remorselessly" in virtually every
country, including the US, UK and even New Zealand.

Table 5.1: State Spending as Percentage of GDP

Country	1960	1996	1999
Australia	21	37	34
Austria	36	52	52
Belgium	30	54	50
Canada	29	45	42
France	35	55	53
Germany	32	49	47
Ireland	28	37	29.9
Italy	30	53	49
Japan	18	36	40
Netherlands	34	50	48
New Zealand	27	47	41
Norway	30	46	47
Spain	19	43	42
Sweden	31	65	61
Switzerland	17	38	n/a
United Kingdom	32	42	42
United States	27	33	34
Average	**28**	**46**	**45**

Sources: Adapted from *The Economist* (20 September 1997), European Economy,
1998, OECD, 1998.

What is interesting is that Ireland is the one country in the table where there was a very large drop in the share of total government spending (as a proportion of GDP), from 37 per cent in 1996 to 29.9 per cent in 1999 — the lowest in the 15 member states, where the average current government spending is 48 per cent. It is lower than even the US at 34 per cent or Japan at 40 per cent. Its highest level in Ireland was over 50 per cent between 1982 and 1986 (*European Economy*, 1998: Table 75). There has been a dramatic fall in a relatively short period. It is largely driven by the rapid rise in GDP, because government spending has actually increased in the 1990s.

The Economist should (but does not) classify Ireland as a "small government country" along with Singapore and Switzerland! What appears to be amazing is the dramatic and rapid fall in Irish government spending, especially in comparison with other countries and its own past. There is no exact figure or even range of figures for a country's spending as a proportion of GDP, but it is clear that even taking account of Ireland's inflated GDP, more public spending can be afforded without risk, especially if it is judicious.

The Economist says that it is the growth of transfers and subsidies that has driven up state spending. These include income support for the unemployed, disabled people, single parents and "above all, pensions". It advocates that the "confiscation" by "punitive" and "aggressively redistributive systems of taxation and spending" should be ended and that people be left with their money in their pockets so that they can spend it as they like on education, health, etc.

The Economist's argument that states are still gaining power, when market forces seem to have triumphed, does not focus on the main points, which are that governments, which are elected democratically, should have decisive influence on economic matters and that the size of public spending does not necessarily determine national well-being. Few will be aware that state spending in Ireland as a proportion of GDP has shrunk rapidly in a few years, when that of other states was static or growing. Most will not feel that there has been a right-wing coup. When it comes to globalisation, it is important, from a democratic perspective, to remember that, ultimately, governments set the rules.

It should be noted that the 1999 figures for most countries showed a fall in the last few years of the 1990s, as the new figures in Table 5.1 shows. This could be an important change in direction, with current government spending having peaked in the mid-1990s, though it could just be a temporary change.

Ireland Attracts

Globalisation is an opportunity for Ireland. Ireland is attractive for investors, but it is no longer a low-wage economy. The EU's trade with low-wage economies is still small, with imports at under 3 per cent of EU GDP and exports at about the same. The Commission argues that this is a benefit, because "cheap imports mean an increase in Community real incomes" and this "trade embodies the exchange of low-skilled work against high-skilled and better paid work" (*European Economy*, 1997: 53). It contends that a job created in a low-wage economy is not a job lost in the Union. It opens up markets, leading to new exports of skill-intensive products. It does admit, however, that globalisation does "exert downward pressures on the wages of low-skilled labour".

The world is not a uniform place, and economies have differing strengths and weaknesses. Dicken pointed out:

> Change does not occur everywhere in the same way and at the same rate; the processes of globalisation are not geographically uniform. The particular character of individual countries, of regions and even of localities interacts with the larger-scale general process of change to produce quite specific outcomes (quoted in Jacobson and Andreosso, 1996: 114).

Ireland seized the opportunity to win a large share of foreign investment in recent years, marketing itself as the type of country in which growing MNCs would wish to invest — and delivering on its promises.

The IDA believes that there are four key reasons for investment in Ireland:

- The high level of education and skills of the workforce

- The flexibility and adaptability of the workforce

- The low taxes on companies

- The "pulling power" of existing "blue chip" companies already located in Ireland.

The change in Irish industrial policy with the second wave of foreign investment, to ensure greater linkages with indigenous firms required responses from both foreign and Irish companies. There is a greater awareness today among multinationals of the importance of being good corporate citizens, as consumer boycotts have demonstrated, and it makes sense for them to source inputs locally. On the other hand, more Irish firms are capable of meeting the high demands for quality inputs by the multinationals. The IDA, Enterprise Ireland and the other agencies have successfully picked winning industries, indicating that Irish industrial policy is finally working fairly well.

In addition, Ireland also has increased accessibility to the Single Market, without tariffs or non-tariff barriers, an English-speaking population, political stability, good communications, reasonable infrastructure, low social charges on labour, and good financial, professional and services infrastructure.

US Leads the Investment

The US is the largest source of foreign direct investment in Ireland. There are over 200 American firms, with one-quarter of all manufacturing. American firms invested a substantial $10 billion in Ireland in 1994, which was $3,000 per Irish person, compared to only $2,000 in the UK. US MNCs are still strong because they have the technological edge, especially in computing and telephony, and they have led the way in introducing the new forms of work. However, much of their competitive strength, such as R&D and strategic decision-making, is located in their home country. The state agencies are aware of this problem and have attempted, with some limited success, to get MNCs to locate strategic functions here.

In the US, profits have risen steadily for 20 years, while wages held still, giving an increased share to capital relative to labour. Profits are still not as high relative to labour as in the 1950s, but because effective tax rates and interest charges (as a proportion of pre-interest profits for US corporations) have fallen, US companies have done well. US companies that have invested in Ireland are amongst the leading "blue chip" companies, as the IDA describes them, and they boast of average profits of over 20 per cent on sales a year in Ireland (boosted by transfer price fixing).

Irish Foreign Investment

Ireland's leading companies have expanded abroad successfully, largely by foreign acquisitions. The main targets have been the UK and US, where many Irish companies have subsidiaries. Smurfits, CRH and Kerry are leading companies in the US in their industries, with AIB and Bank of Ireland also major investors. There are 30 to 40 Irish companies with operations abroad. More recently, opportunities have started to open up in Eastern Europe. For example, several of the top MNCs investing in Poland are Irish.

There have been some very successful Irish companies. But to stay successful, they must invest abroad. The big success stories are not always the classical stock-market-driven companies, but important examples are CRH, which developed in Ireland as a monopoly in cement production, the dairy co-operatives and public enterprises.

Profits from Irish-owned companies abroad which have been repatriated back to Ireland amount to hundreds of millions a year. This is only a fraction of the exports of MNCs' profits *from* Ireland, though when transfer price-fixing by them is discounted, it is not so unimportant. It is likely to grow soon as more Irish companies, including a number of state enterprises and former state enterprises, are seeking further expansion abroad.

Indeed, if the accounts of the two largest industrial Irish companies are examined, their Irish operations are quite small as a proportion of their total sales. Smurfits' Irish sales are not disclosed, being aggregated with Britain at £564 million in 1996, or 22 per cent of total sales of £2.6 billion. In 1998, its segmented reporting standard declined and it only disclosed sales and profits in Europe as a whole, where 77 per cent of its total sales of £2.9 billion and 59 per cent of the profit were located. CRH's Irish sales came to £540 million in 1998 or just 10 per cent of the total, which was over £4.9 billion, but Ireland generated a very high 22 per cent of profits. In fact, CRH's Americas operations account for 53 per cent of sales (£2.8 billion), and it has been larger in both the UK and mainland Europe than it is in Ireland for some years, though the home country is disproportionately profitable. It is likely that the secretive Glen Dimplex has only a small proportion of its electrical goods manufacturing in Ireland, with most of them being in the UK, Germany and the Netherlands.

The failure to develop sufficient large indigenous companies to absorb our labour force has been the subject of many reports. It probably would have been almost impossible to absorb the labour force at the speed at which Irish people were reproducing, until 1980. It is only in recent years that indigenous firms have been able to face the chill winds of global competition. While many of the best have been sold off by their founders to foreign MNCs, there are still some big players, as has been seen, and those that have been sold off generally retain their plants or offices here. One problem, which has not been debated much, is the possible takeover of major Irish companies like AIB and CRH by foreign MNCs. This has already happened to some leading Irish companies, including the entire Irish whiskey industry. The privatisation of some of the largest indigenous companies leave them open to takeover.

One other question arises: what is an Irish company? Guinness was floated on the London Stock Exchange a long time ago, but it is still regarded as a symbol of Ireland, not least by tourists. Jacob's Biscuits, one of the oldest Irish manufacturing companies,

Irish Distillers, New Ireland Assurance and several other large Irish companies have been bought over by MNCs, with hardly a comment (the latter was bought back by Bank of Ireland in late 1997). Several new indigenous companies which grew rapidly were sold off, like Green Isle to the UK's Northern Foods, Wood-chester to GE Capital and GPA, also to GE. Some successful Irish software companies have also been sold off. The challenge for future industrial policy is to grow the indigenous sector, while still attracting foreign investment.

INDUSTRIAL POLICY IN IRELAND

The over-reliance on MNCs was first pointed out in the 1970s, but there was a decisive criticism in a radical report on Irish industrial policy, the Telesis Report (NESC, 1982). This report for the National Economic and Social Council was written by an American consultancy firm led by Ira Magaziner, who was to become an advisor to President Clinton. This report was incisive, and it strongly advocated a shift in state aid from foreign to indigenous industry; that the state should play a much more active role in developing indigenous industry; and it also advocated building structurally strong Irish companies rather than strong agencies to assist weak companies.

The government's industry agency, the Industrial Development Authority (IDA), was not impressed. This was not unexpected, as it was not just an executive agency helping industry, but had become the centre of policy-making, a point strongly criticised by Telesis. The Department of Industry had abdicated this policy-making role and Telesis recommended, largely in vain, that it re-assume it. The IDA and the government were against a more interventionist role for the state, and it is only recently that policies have changed. This is in stark contrast to the Asian Tiger economies (except Hong Kong) where state intervention was used to build strong independent exporting companies. O'Sullivan (1995) makes the case that the success of the Asian Tigers is not due to "getting prices right" or "reducing market imperfections", but to a strong central state with an active industrial policy.

Telesis recommended that policy should shift spending in grants from foreign to indigenous industry and that the state and its agencies attempt to grow the best Irish companies to become international players. A White Paper on Industrial Policy was published in 1984, which largely ignored Telesis. However, in 1985, the Company Development Programme and the National Linkage Programme were launched and both of these, with a more directed approach by the state, have proven successful.

Each subsequent change in industrial policy was not to come from the Department of Industry but from two commissions, which included the social partners. These were the Culliton Report in 1992, followed by the Moriarty Report (1993). The most radical suggestion of Culliton was to split up the IDA. It was following the essence of Telesis: to place more focus on Irish industry. It recommended that this be achieved by addressing the structures — that is, the agency. A state agency to focus solely on indigenous industry, Forbairt (now Enterprise Ireland), was formed out of a merger between the IDA and Eolas and later with An Bord Tráchtála; the IDA name was kept for MNCs; while the remaining component became Forfás, the policy-making body. Forfás leads policy formulation for the IDA and Enterprise Ireland, which are represented on its board, and it also has a co-ordinating role.

There have been two strong periods of growth in foreign investment in Ireland. The first wave was in the 1960s after the country opened up and the second has been in the 12 years under review. There was a qualitative difference in the two waves, with foreign investment coming largely for the cheap labour, grants and tax breaks in the early phase and for the skilled labour and access to the European market in the 1990s. In between, especially in the 1980s, there were a lot of jobs lost, though more were gained, as Table 5.2 below shows. The numbers of foreign firms grew from 670 in 1987 to 1,140 in 1998, a rapid growth in just over a decade. The quality of investment has been largely "blue chip". This did not happen by accident. As has already been stated, IDA policy targeted electronics, pharmaceuticals, software, financial services, teleservices and other industries. Policy had changed to one of "picking winners", by sector, if not by firm, in the foreign sector, and it was successful. The importance of manufacturing should not be underestimated, especially with the rapid growth in services jobs. GDP per person employed in manufacturing is over twice as high as in services and productivity is far higher too.

Table 5.2: Jobs Losses in Manufacturing, 1973–1994

	Irish	Foreign	Total
Total job gain, 1973–94	231,999	161,866	393,885
Total job loss, 1973–94	263,201	141,175	404,376

Source: O'Sullivan (1995) and Culliton.

There was a massive shakeout in industry between 1973 and 1994, as Table 5.2 shows, with the gross loss being far higher than the total numbers of 215,203 in manufacturing in 1973 — a massive 404,376 jobs were lost. The indigenous sector suffered very heavily, with a gross loss of 263,201 jobs. There was a renewal of employment and the shakeout of Irish firms meant that those remaining were survivors, capable of international competition. In 1994, Irish industry employed 31,202 less than in 1973, but there was an important change from net job losses to net job gains in the mid-1990s.

Table 5.3 shows the rapid growth of employment in foreign manufacturing firms — almost 60 per cent over the past twenty-five years — and the decline in Irish manufacturing industry, where numbers fell by 16 per cent in the period from 1973 to 1998. However, there has been a recovery in Irish industry, with the number of net new jobs growing by a substantial 12,190 between 1993 and its new peak in 1998. This is a very important reversal in the trend, because for a long time it was in the opposite direction — net job losses. Part of the reason for the economic success is that MNCs have no longer being making up the losses of Irish firms, but in recent years have been adding to their gains.

Table 5.3: Jobs in Irish and Foreign Manufacturing, 1973–1998

	Irish	Foreign	Total
Employment 1973	143,815	69,388	215,203
Employment 1998	121,073	109,222	230,295
Net Change, 1973–98	−22,742 (−16%)	+39,843 (+57%)	+15,092 (+7%)

Sources: IDA and Forfás Employment Surveys.

The growth of employment in foreign firms is impressive. In the five years to 1998 it had risen by a very high 20,595 or almost a quarter. Therefore, even with the Irish recovery and trend reversal, it seems certain that, soon after 2000, the foreign MNC manufacturing sector will be a bigger employer of Irish workers than will Irish manufacturing firms.

When internationally traded and financial services are added to these manufacturing jobs, the numbers employed in 1998 were 133,230 in Irish firms and 136,515 in foreign firms. Thus in 1998, for the first time, the number of jobs in foreign firms in manufacturing and internationally traded and financial services exceeded the number of jobs in Irish firms. The high level of foreign direct investment (FDI) has helped Ireland shift from a very high dependence on the UK market.

Cost of the Visible Hand

Irish industrial policy is the visible hand — intervention by the state on a large scale. This policy does not come cheap. In the past, however, it was the maximum tolerable to conservative economists, because it was very "hands-off" in approach. Money — lots of it — was given and little was demanded in return from companies in the past.

There are several large state agencies involved — IDA, Forfás, Enterprise Ireland, SFADCo and Údarás na Gaeltachta. Grants and administration amounted to several hundred million pounds a year in the late 1990s. These state agencies sometimes reveal symptoms of "regulatory capture". This is where a regulatory body or development agency can become "captured" by the industry and begins to articulate the industry view rather than the state or public interest view. Debate on industrial policy, helped by reports such as Culliton, is the best way to ensure that the relationship with industry is maintained on the best basis from the public's perspective.

Culliton costed total direct spending on job creation in the period 1981–1990 to be £1.6 billion in 1990 prices. There was only an increase of 7,000 net new jobs in the period. However, the 1980s were a very bad decade for Irish industry and the economy in general. What was surprising is that this major report, employing many consultants, did not attempt to examine the additional cost of tax expenditures. This was estimated at £5.9 billion gross in lost taxes, though the net cost would have been less than that. The actual calculation of the net cost is a problem, as there are many imponderables and it is a figure which can only be based on estimates (Sweeney, 1992). If the two were added, the cost of maintaining the visible hand of industrial policy would be seen to be expensive. Yet it would be incorrect to jump to the conclusion, as many did at the time, that this money was wasted. Without this public spending, the job losses would have been disastrous — possibly wiping out most industry in Ireland and leaving no base for the subsequent economic lift-off.

Forfás, conscious of the cost of job creation, points out that the cost to the state of a job has fallen from £22,587 in 1987 to £11,426 in 1998 (1998 prices) (IDA Annual Report, 1998).

Over-reliance on Foreign Direct Investment

The criticism that Ireland's success is based on multinational corporations (MNCs), which do not have allegiance to the country and which can close down and move out easily in the global economy, requires examination. There are many who believe that Ireland relies too much on MNC investment. And this is not just the nationalist perspective.

The nationalist economic policy of self-reliance was finally abandoned in 1958 by Fianna Fáil, and there was little opposition to the move. This was surprising, given the level of nationalist and self-sufficiency rhetoric in the past, even from the architect of this about-turn, Sean Lemass. The reason for the lack of opposition was simple. The 1950s were desperate times. The trade unions welcomed the new plants, as did the local populations. With few exceptions, the companies were reasonably good corporate citizens, albeit small spenders in the local economy for several decades. Today, most Irish people recognise that if Ireland is to go on the High Road as opposed to the Low Road strategy — the High Road being high technology, high productivity, high wages, flexibility, innovation and working in partnerships — it needs these companies.

The Left in Ireland also welcomed foreign investment, unlike the Left in many other countries, because of the increase in jobs, but was critical of the high dependence on it. Yet it is the small size of indigenous industry which is the cause of concern, not the large number of MNCs. O'Hearn (1998) is highly critical of "the dependent tigers like Ireland" which "ultimately will be unable to maintain its success as the expanding European periphery increases the competition for foreign investment". Many outsiders are also highly critical of this economic dependency.

However, the contribution of the foreign companies is very impressive and has improved substantially in the 1990s. As Ireland heads towards full employment, it can be more choosy in the companies it attracts. O'Malley (1995) found that there were more jobs created by backward linkages from foreign firms than by indigenous companies. He also estimated that for every 100 direct jobs in overseas companies, there were another 105 indirect jobs in existence in 1992. This has probably increased since, as the proportion of spending by foreign companies has grown, as will be seen below. The growth in skills in the foreign multinationals is higher than in indigenous firms and they are concentrated in a few sectors. While such a concentration can be criticised, it also leads to agglomeration economies, where the clustering of skills and knowledge are reinforcing. A crucial point is that foreign multinational manufacturing plants actually stay longer in Ireland than Irish-owned firms. They stay for 13 years on average compared to 10 years for indigenous firms, according to Strobl et al., (quoted in Barry et al. 1999: 70), though the shakeout of indigenous firms in the 1980s may have adversely affected the Irish firms.

However, autonomy and key decision-making and marketing etc. is still located overseas for most FDI companies. The growth in their spending in Ireland is constrained by their need to buy from their affiliates in order to avail of transfer price-fixing, according to Breathnach (1998). However, the IDA has moved from targeting low-paying, low-road industries to choosing which companies should be wooed.

On 26 May 1999, the Governor of the Central Bank of Ireland, Maurice O'Connell, warned of the high dependence on foreign companies; on the same day, Enterprise Ireland, the indigenous industrial promotional body, announced a new strategy for its client companies, which among several targets, would aim to double their sales within a decade.

Linkages with the Domestic Economy

The linkages between MNCs and the Irish economy have improved substantially in recent years. A Forfás study (1998) shows that total spending by MNCs on wages, raw materials and services in Ireland in 1996 amounted to £6.7 billion, which was £2.8 billion up on 1989, or a growth rate of almost 8 per cent a year. When food, drink and tobacco companies are excluded, it was still a substantial £4.8 billion, up 10 per cent a year since 1989. The excluded companies include Guinness, BSN (Jacobs), Pernod Ricard (Irish Distillers) and Unilever (HB, McDonnell's) — all of which have large plants in Ireland — and other MNCs that use a lot of indigenous inputs. A spokesman for Forfás has said that Irish firms had had difficulty in meeting quality standards required by the MNCs in the past, but this was no longer a problem for most of them in the late 1990s.

Business R&D spending rose to over 1 per cent of GDP in 1997 from 0.84 per cent in 1993, closing on the EU average of 1.2 per cent, and Irish companies doubled their R&D spend between 1991 and 1997. There has been good progress on the R&D front, but more needs to be done. The IDA and other state agencies do appear to be achieving greater linkages between the MNC sector and the domestic economy, which is important for the long-run health of the economy.

There has also been growth in exports by Irish manufacturing firms, which was 44 per cent of their output in 1996, down a little from the peak in 1995. A further indicator of the improving fortunes of Irish industry is that their profits, always very low in aggregate, have improved to 6.2 per cent of sales in 1995, from under 4 per cent in 1989. It was almost 9 per cent in general manufacturing, that is, with food, drink and tobacco excluded. There has been a diffusion of skills from the foreign to the domestic sector, and the clearest indication of this is the establishment of their own firms by some former senior executives of foreign firms.

The high level of conditions and reasonably good pay offered by MNCs have had an effect on Irish companies. With the boom, Irish owners of industry complained about the level of pay to Irish workers in MNC plants and the difficulty in retaining them. However, some foreign firms also complained of other MNCs poaching their best workers.

If many indigenous companies can now compete on international markets, then they have come of age. There has been a large growth in software development —a welcome skill — and export-intensive development in Ireland. Ireland exports 40 per cent of all packaged software and a massive 60 per cent of all business applications software sold in Europe, and while most of this comes from foreign MNCs, there is a spillover effect. Enterprise Ireland expects that early in the next decade, software will become the largest Irish-owned industry after food. Its development has been helped greatly by the presence of and links with the MNCs.

The turnaround in the fortunes of indigenous Irish industry is partly due to policy changes. The change was slow — far slower than Telesis recommended — but it did occur. The split-up of the

IDA into the MNC side (still the IDA) and the agency with the indigenous focus, Enterprise Ireland, helped considerably. The introduction of the Company Development Programme and the National Linkage Programme, and the insistence on business plans from companies looking for grants, all helped a lot. The agencies work more with the management of companies on long-term strategy, with an emphasis on research and development, training and management development. There is an increased share of agencies' budgets for these activities rather than for grants for machinery. The agencies no longer simply pay out grants and ignore the company until the next application. With the rapid fall in unemployment, the State agencies can be much more selective.

CONCLUSION

This chapter has examined globalisation, foreign direct investment and industrial policy. It was argued that, in spite of increased internationalisation, the democratic nation state can still be fairly powerful in setting the background against which business takes place. Combined with regions or groupings like the European Union, the nation state can determinate policy and set agendas. MNCs may occasionally bend the rules and laws of states, but in general, they adhere to them.

Foreign investment is less a problem for Ireland today than in the past, because even in the era of globalisation, Ireland's policy in attracting FDI has been very successful. Ireland appears to have the attractions that MNCs want, even if some of them are artificial. There has been a large increase in foreign direct investment in Europe, particularly by US firms, and Ireland's share had been disproportionately high. Better linkages have been developed under changed industrial policy, and this has helped root the MNCs here and to build stronger indigenous companies. MNCs have made a major contribution to the economy in jobs, investment, technology and entrepreneurship, and also in the transfer of these into the local economy.

With the second wave of foreign investment, the change in Irish industrial policy to ensure greater linkages with indigenous firms required responses from both foreign and Irish companies. There is a greater awareness today by multinationals of the importance of being good corporate citizens, as consumer boycotts have demonstrated, and it makes sense for them to source inputs locally. On the other side, more Irish firms are capable of meeting the high demands for quality inputs by the multinationals. The IDA, Enterprise Ireland and the other agencies have successfully picked winning industries — ones that are developing and expanding. These developments mean that Irish industrial policy is finally working well.

Irish companies have performed better and the downward slope in job losses was finally turned into job gains in the mid-1990s. In the past, foreign companies plugged the hole made by indigenous job losses and there was little progress in job numbers. In the last few years, both types of companies have created jobs.

Ireland, like all small economies, is dependent on foreign investment. However, all large companies, including Irish firms, are now investing abroad. Only the very biggest countries can escape dependence on MNCs. What defines a successful Irish company if most of its activities take place overseas or when its owner could sell it to an MNC overnight? This may be a negative argument, but it is a realistic one in a world where calls to patriotism and national self-sufficiency echo hollow.

The best response to the dependence on foreign investment is to ensure that investing MNCs remain in Ireland, set down roots, build linkages with the local economy and wish to expand here, as many of them are currently doing, and that they behave as good corporate citizens. It is also still important to develop and retain indigenous industry in Ireland and to build linkages with the MNC sector, in Ireland and abroad.

Chapter Six

COMPETITIVENESS AND NEW FORMS OF WORK

Two of the building blocks in the Irish success story are worthy of closer examination: competitiveness and new forms of work. Economic policy in Ireland is still focused mainly on macroeconomics, yet it is microeconomic factors — at the level of the firm — on which a small country can have a big impact. Policy aimed at improving the performance of the firm can be effective in building competitiveness. Competitiveness and new forms of work — in the factory, in the office and eventually even on the buses — are both examined because they are important, they are developing, they are relatively new concepts, and they can be misunderstood.

COMPETITIVENESS — THE BUZZ WORD OF THE 1990S

Every economist and businessperson is using the word "competitiveness". The word was even in the title of the national deal between the social partners in 1994, the Programme for Competitiveness and Work and there is a National Competitiveness Council which completes a major report each year. Yet in spite of its widespread use, there is confusion about what it means, though it is a vital concept in the modern economy.

Competitiveness is one of the major reasons for the Irish transformation. It is often confused with wage rises or with profitability. At the level of the firm it is easy to define. A firm is competitive if it can sell its products at the market price and be profitable. A dynamic approach — over time — changes the definition, because when a firm takes a longer-term perspective, it alters its strategies.

A country's competitiveness is harder to define. It is judged to be competitive by its external performance, which is often taken to mean its trade performance and/or growth. In Ireland's case, it has been seen that both of these are rising fast. The distribution of the gains of growth must be a factor too. Translating growth into jobs, raising living standards over time and facilitating the growth of firms are important components of an economy's competitiveness. However, factors like the appreciation of the exchange rate can have a large impact on these indicators. Japan has seen its exports lose out since the mid-1980s and the Asian Tigers' exports boomed in recent decades, until the crisis in 1997. Thus, export or cost competitiveness is but part of the complex whole.

Paul Krugman (1995) warned that it is "trouble with a capital 'C' that stands for 'Competitiveness'", when it means one country waging war against another over trade. He sees competitiveness as destructive when trade is viewed as a war where there is a winner and a loser. This mercantilist idea is long dead for most economists, who see trade as a form of economic activity where all gain because each country exploits its particular advantages. This is what is being discussed here, with Ireland building up its comparative advantages in the post-natural-resource-based industrial revolution. The new industrial revolution is ultimately reliant on the efficient use of the whole intellectual capacity of the people in the economy.

Productivity is a Key

If a country can raise its productivity higher than the levels of its main trading partners, which are at similar levels of development, while also having high employment and economic stability, they can contribute much to competitiveness. For example, in comparing productivity growth in the Triad — the EU, US and Japan — the European Commission found that the EU's productivity has grown at 2 per cent a year over 20 years, or three times the rate of growth of the US. Japan's productivity growth was very high for 30 years until 1990, when it fell because of recession. The EU's productivity growth is faster than that of the US, whose actual productivity *level* is the highest in the world. The EU has seen a steady catch-up of its community-wide productivity with the US from 45 per cent of its overall level in 1960 to 82 per cent of the US level in 1995. The EU's productivity level is well above the level in Japan, which is held down by the low productivity in many areas outside those areas of manufacturing where it is so strong. Table 6.1 shows how much the EU's productivity growth has been ahead of that of the US since 1960 in segmented periods, and it shows how the Japanese levels have moved, actually falling in the first half of the 1990s.

Table 6.1: Trend in Triad's Productivity Growth (total factor productivity in %)

	1961–73	1974–85	1986–95	1986–90	1991–95
EU	2.8	1.0	1.2	1.5	1.0
US	1.6	0.4	0.8	0.6	0.9
Japan	6.3	1.1	0.9	2.3	–0.5

Source: European Economy (1997)
Note: Total factor productivity is average labour and capital productivity weighted by factor income shares.

Employment in the US is higher than in Europe, which gives it much of the edge on overall living standards, but the EU worker is now producing about the same amount of wealth as a worker in the US. If the EU had lower unemployment, then its overall living standards (measured as GDP per capita) could be close to those of the US. EU employment performance is, in the word of the Commission, "dismal". However, it has risen a little in the late 1990s. It has also been seen that Ireland's employment growth in recent years has been superb and its productivity growth has also been high.

A key way of improving competitiveness is to use modern machinery efficiently. The EU has consistently out-performed the US in productivity over many decades, but it has achieved this by substituting capital for labour. The Commission estimates that half of Europe's labour productivity growth since the first oil crisis in 1973 has been due to the substitution of capital. In the US, productivity growth has only been at one-third the level of the EU, but very little of it has been because of capital substitution. However, since the mid-1980s, total productivity growth (of both labour and capital) has been strong in the US as a result of more investment.

Some US economists have argued that their country's productivity growth is underestimated. This is because of the growth of the service industry, where it is difficult to measure productivity, and also because of the importance of "complex goods" like electronics, where increasing quality and falling prices dominate. Compared to measuring the unit cost of a ton of steel, it is harder to measure improvements in services, or a better but cheaper computer. In the US, figures for services' productivity have seen no improvement at a time when employment growth in services has been high. If growth in these two areas has been understated in the US, then the same must apply to Ireland, where the real growth in jobs has been in services, and also in its relatively large electronics sector. It would, of course, also apply to other countries too. Therefore, if a better measurement of these sectors is devised and productivity is revised upwards in the US, a similar revision must take place in other countries, including Ireland.

With 17 million unemployed in the EU in 1999, there is a very serious problem. While the use of capital ensures a high level of productivity growth, the Commission attributes high wage costs as the cause of the substitution of capital for labour in the EU, after the first oil shock. Of course, workers in the US have had stagnant real earnings since 1983; only in the last year or so has there been a rise. A huge gap has opened up in wages in the US, especially between skilled and unskilled workers. The EU is against following the US path: "it is neither feasible nor desirable as it would mean a dramatic change in the European social model". It would, it says, lead to a reduction in welfare benefits and would ultimately lead to greater income inequality. It would:

> . . . introduce into the Community the working poor syndrome — a form of exclusion just as harmful for the social fabric as unemployment (*European Economy*, 1997: 60).

The Commission opts instead for the higher employment growth strategy which was adopted at Essen. It recommends cutting taxes on low incomes, a policy that should have been adopted in Ireland years ago (to be paid for by control of spending and higher environmental taxes, urges the Commission). It also recommends more flexible working time, more voluntary part-time work, and greater pay variation for workers with different skills, in different regions and different sectors. While employment in Europe began to grow again in 1997, it remains to be seen if the new euro currency and the sacking of the Commission by the Parliament will lead to more effective policies, under European President Prodi.

Does Competitiveness Mean Low Pay?

For many years, most economists believed that you could tell if a country was competitive if its wage levels were low or rising more slowly than competitor countries. Up until the early 1990s, major economic reports from international agencies like the OECD defined competitiveness solely in terms of relative wage movements, generally citing only manufacturing. They actually used tables called "Germany's Competitiveness" or "Ireland's Competitiveness", showing the level of wages or earnings or the rise in earnings compared to other countries. Measuring wage levels or rises is *not* a measure of competitiveness. It is just a measure of the wage! Wages are a component of competitiveness, but only one small component.

In the mid-1980s, economists began to acknowledge that there were many other factors involved in competitiveness. Even trade unionists who had abhorred the term — because of the crude attempt by government to intellectually browbeat them into wage cuts with a major report narrowly focused on wage levels — came to recognise its importance to their members' well-being.

The view was that low pay or small pay increases would result in more jobs. This was the official line of government, and in 1981, the Irish government's Minister for Finance, John Bruton, commissioned three leading economists to prepare a report on competitiveness, the *Report of the Committee on Costs and Competitiveness*.

The Three Wise Men recommended that wages should only rise by a certain amount — 11 per cent for 1982. This seems very high today, but inflation was then at 20 per cent. Thus they were advocating a big cut in real wages. While their report said that all incomes should be subject to the same kind of discipline, it was clear that they were talking about wages. They reduced their recommendation to a rise of only 6.5 per cent later, because one of their assumptions on the exchange rate turned out to be incorrect.

This was a political report — an intellectual justification to attempt to keep wages down. The report was destined to play a key part in the adversarial industrial relations system of the time. Yet this kind of thinking was dominant, not just in Ireland, but internationally.

However, a strong counter-argument was put forward by a group of socialist economists in 1983 *in Jobs and Wages — the True Story of Competitiveness* (Socialist Economists, 1983), arguing that competitiveness must be more broadly defined, incorporating more than costs, especially labour costs. It highlighted the complexity of the issue, particularly for economists, where it is difficult, if not impossible, to measure factors such as quality, innovation, the role of the state, political stability, human resources, education and marketing. Economists distrust factors that cannot be measured.

They pointed out that competitiveness included many factors far beyond the level of the firm, which could contribute or detract from this competitiveness. These included national attributes such as the quality of the banking system, investment in human resources, outward orientation or participation in international trade and levels of investment.

They highlighted the 1982 European Management Forum (EMF) report because it gave this broad definition; in that year Ireland's best score was, ironically, in the area of "industrial efficiency", which includes costs and productivity! This EMF report is still compiled and now attracts more attention. It has useful concepts but some of the factors are very subjective like the "size of government in the economy", which is seen as negative, or "openness of the economy" which is seen as positive (though small economies are more open than large ones). It also makes the crucial mistake of running country league tables. It is extremely difficult to measure country performance accurately, as the discussion of Irish GDP in the previous chapter has shown.

The Socialist Economists (1983) argued that:

> wage costs are a small proportion of total costs, and while they do influence costs, they are not the most important factor. . . . Sales and profits generally depend much more on design, service, marketing, investment and management.

They pointed out that price is only one part of competitiveness and that "Ireland needs a growing efficient industrial sector based on modern technology . . . at decent wage levels" and that "it should not compete with low wage economies like the Asian Tigers, but instead should produce 'sophisticated high value products'".

The report recommended that "instead of resisting industrial and structural change, we should encourage it, and develop our non-wage advantages like quality, design, service, marketing ability, skills and capacity for change". This was aimed at the trade unions, which have generally resisted change, as well as managers and opinion formers. It was very different from the orthodox view of competitiveness back in 1983.

Jobs and Wages also warned against wage "militancy" as self-defeating, and was an early advocate of "a greater say in the management of the economy" through national agreements, and at enterprise level. The report recommended that workers should "accept the hitherto uncharacteristic role of encouraging innovation, new technology, diversification, improved service or even wiser investment". This was revolutionary at the time, greatly anticipating partnership and human resource management.

They also urged workers to move from supporting loss-making state industries to investment in "profitable growth industries", and to "challenge the assumptions in the present (adversarial) management–worker relationships in industry". They advocated that:

> shop stewards should no longer ignore the quality of what is being produced, where it is being sold, how it is being marketed, the margin of profit, the delivery date or after-sales service — if they are to protect jobs and secure wage improvements (p. 42).

Much of this is now happening in Ireland, though there is still a long way to go to real partnership at local level. These economists concluded that "while such change requires a radical departure from our tradition of defensive trade unionism, it is the *only* approach which offers any prospect of success for workers in an increasingly competitive economy". It was to be more than a decade before implementation of these ideas began. But the seeds of a sound perspective on competitiveness, which could be acceptable to workers, were sown.

Indeed, the major industrial reports, Culliton (1992), *Shaping our Future* (Forfás, 1996), and the National Competitiveness Council (1999) had a clearer understanding of the complex concept of competitiveness. The development agencies — IDA, Enterprise Ireland, SFADCo, Údarás na Gaeltachta — working in the real world, knew that they would not attract or build up industries if they focused only on wages or costs. Today the debate about competitiveness in Ireland is much more realistic, though some government departments still occasionally attempt to focus primarily on wages.

Competition and the Entrepreneurial Firm

Michael Porter's influential *The Competitive Advantage of Nations* (1990) examined the attributes that contribute to a nation's competitiveness and pointed out that it is really firms that are competitive. He also focused on what he termed the world's eight most competitive economies and gave a list of things that governments could do to improve their nation's competitiveness. He argued, as has been presented elsewhere in this book, that even with globalisation, nations do matter. He held that national or regional circumstances have played a crucial role in making firms successful. A central thesis was on the clustering of firms in industrial districts like clothing or ceramic tiles in the Third Italy[1], or German engineering firms. In Ireland, there are clusters of chemical and electronic firms in Cork, furniture, poultry and mushrooms in Monaghan, etc. This enables them both to compete and to co-operate in areas where co-operation is useful, like international marketing. Porter did not investigate the degree of co-operation between firms in Italy.

NESC (1996) urged a programme of collaboration between Irish small and medium-sized firms through wider and deeper networking, to overcome problems such as transaction costs, problems with bargaining, innovation, etc. Such co-operation between small Irish firms was also urged as long ago as the early 1960s by the Committee on Industrial Organisation: "instead of the traditional encouragement of competition among firms, co-operation on a massive scale is recommended" in areas like purchasing, production rationalisation, training, and export development (quoted in O'Sullivan, 1995: 389). This would have been similar to the co-operation embarked upon by the Asian Tigers. However, instead of following this recommendation, it was decided that industrial policy would encourage investment in fixed capital through grants and tax breaks.

Michael Best (1990) also advocated "co-operative competition", where firms compete hard in most areas, but co-operate in areas where this will be of benefit to them. He has a wide international

---

[1] Third Italy is the name given to the North Central area of Italy — as distinct from the industrialised North and the agricultural South — where groups of small firms have outperformed the large firms in the North since the Second World War.

perspective and analyses Japan and the success of the Third Italy, where many small firms work co-operatively in international marketing, while competing in production. There may be more co-operation amongst firms in Ireland than managers are even aware of. Pat Byrne, MD of CityJet, a small Irish airline, has openly called for all Irish airlines to co-operate on some areas, such as fleet management. The NESC recommendations may assist in the development of this form of economic activity.

In what Michael Best calls "the new competition", the entrepreneurial firm is distinguished from the hierarchical firm, with its emphasis on continuous improvement and product-led, rather than price-led, strategies. Best focuses on the firm, unlike most economists, and has a clear understanding of what makes firms competitive. He pays a lot of attention to small and medium-sized firms, co-operative competition and the role of institutions.

Best says the "new competition is about business enterprises that pursue strategies of continuous improvement in product and process within a regulatory framework that encourages industrial restructuring". He holds that many efforts in industrial restructuring fail because they are imposed within the context of a Taylorist work organisation, which is alien to the integration of thinking and doing. He says that there is a need to break out of the old legacy, which is rooted in big business, with a new definition of the role of workers and managers, who are often the remnants of the resolution of a country's class struggle.

Best believes that small firms can be technologically advanced, generate high-income jobs and produce internationally competitive goods and services. He recognises the role and importance of history but believes that Japan and the Third Italy show that the "transformation of economic institutions is possible". This is what occurred in Ireland in the past decade — the legacy of history was overturned.

NEW FORMS OF WORK

Many in Ireland have long blamed others or external circumstances for Ireland's lack of development. The country failed to industrialise in the nineteenth century, and again after Independence, not because of the colonial legacy, but because of the economies of scale required to compete with British and later American industry. Today, in the modern economy, many firms do not need to be large to be competitive. Increased globalisation and rapid technological change provide opportunities for countries like Ireland where the basic infrastructure, workforce, political system, institutions and all the other factors contributing to competitiveness are reasonably developed.

At the turn of the century, mass production, with repetitive tasks, producing only one product on long lines, was organised scientifically according to Taylorist principles, after Frederick Taylor, the founder of "scientific management" in the early years of the century. Henry Ford's production lines epitomised this, where immigrants who could not speak any English could find work and be productive, doing the required task over and over, producing any car, "as long as it was black".

Peter Drucker, the management guru, wrote as long ago as 1946 in his *Concept of the Corporation* that the firm is a social system, not just an economic organisation. He also came up with a few other ideas, which were to take time to root in the real world. These include such ideas as the "knowledge worker" — that is, the head is more important than the hand — flexible production and worker empowerment. He now argues that workers own businesses through their pension and insurance funds and he preaches that management should tell workers that they are, in fact, the new bosses.

In a much-cited but very valuable quote from the founder of the huge Japanese company named after him, Konosuke Matsushita said, in 1988:

> We will win and you will lose. You cannot do anything because your failure is an internal disease. Your companies

are based on Taylor's principles. Worse, your heads are
Taylorised too. You firmly believe that sound management
means executives on the one side and workers on the other;
on the one side men who think and on the other side men
who can only work. For you, management is the art of
smoothly transferring the executives' ideas to the workers'
hands.

We have passed the Taylor stage. We are aware that business has become terribly complex. . . . Only the intellects of
all employees can permit a company to face these challenges (quoted in Best, 1990).

Since Matsushita's harsh criticism of Western business methods,
many companies in the West have moved from the old mass production, hierarchical organisation and the "do as I tell you" systems to new forms of working. This is not because of his searing
criticism, but because technology allows, and competition forces,
great changes in production and in the way services are delivered.
There is evidence that Ireland is high on the list of countries
where these changes are taking place, which has added to the
overall performance of the economy.

There are a number of very positive factors which give Ireland
an advantage in introducing new forms of work: the high level of
modern industry in Ireland, much of it owned by industry-
leading MNCs; Irish plants are relatively new; shorter product
cycles of goods give Ireland's relatively small, flexible factories
opportunities; many companies have been willing to experiment;
and the workforce has been agreeable. The high level of education
and training and relative youth of Irish workers has meant that,
for the most part, they have welcomed the changes and have
shown themselves to be flexible. The IDA cites this flexibility as a
key attraction to foreign investors.

The trade unions recognised the way Britain was going under
Margaret Thatcher in the mid-1980s and consciously decided to
embrace the new working methods. While some trade unionists
were, and still are, backward, most saw that their own members
would happily embrace changed working conditions where they

would have control over their own work environment and where they could use their initiative to a greater degree than in the past, if the changes were negotiated fairly. A minority of trade unionists still oppose partnership, national agreements and the new forms of work, especially partnership at enterprise level, regarding it as a sell-out to employers.

In the new competition, it is necessary that the firm's organisational practices impact not only on workers' quality of life and well-being, but also on their productivity. Irish firms must be competitive if they are to survive, yet "competitive" does not mean being the lowest-cost producer, if the product is of poor quality. A truly competitive firm must harness the collective intelligence of its workforce, motivate them and win them over to identify more with the firm. This can only happen when the workers are treated with respect. Innovation is a continuous process and seldom occurs in major leaps. It is boosted by design and marketing, but it also occurs at the production level and in the way in which goods are produced or services are delivered. All workers must be involved if innovation and efficiency are to be part of a continuously improving process.

The new developments associated with the so-called World Class Manufacturing (WCM) have the potential to alienate workers through the increased pressures associated with procedures such as Just-in-Time (JIT) inventory and quality control aspects such as Total Quality Management (TQM). These soulless acronyms, however, present real opportunities for workers, if properly managed, and this is being increasingly recognised.

Concurrent engineering — where new products are developed through co-operative teams of designers, engineers, workers, distributors and consumers — represents a new, holistic approach to product development. The emphasis on production through multi-skilled teams of individuals, rather than unskilled workers on assembly lines, has the potential to humanise the production process and to recognise individual contributions. Bord na Mona, a state company, was one of the first to introduce such work practices in Ireland.

The introduction of World Class Manufacturing into Ireland by Irish subsidiaries of multinationals has had a knock-on effect on local companies supplying these firms, which have in turn been encouraged to adopt JIT and other procedures, incorporating built-in quality and product design flexibility.

For several years it has been fashionable for employers to state that their employees are their best assets. Often this was empty rhetoric, accompanied by massive downsizing. The financial markets loved downsizing. It appeared to them that when a firm announced a downsizing, it was doing something radical, which would, in the language of business "add value to shareholders' capital". These analysts, who knew all about numbers on screens but little about the way business actually worked, seldom asked: why did a company need to downsize? The obvious answer, which usually evaded the analysts, was that management had not been doing its job effectively up until then to ensure continuous improvement in its processes!

In an interesting study of well-run businesses, Frederick Reicheld (1997) found that two-thirds of companies that engage in large-scale downsizing under-perform on the stock market in the long-run. He cites profitable Rank Xerox's announcement of 10,000 job cuts, which briefly boosted its share value by 7 per cent on the day of the announcement (did its promise of 1,500 new jobs in Dundalk cause a fall in its stock price?). He questioned the effect on the remaining employees. The average US company loses half its customers in five years, half its employees in four, and half its investors in one, showing how far things have gone in the US. Reicheld's book is on loyalty, which he believes is an overlooked area of management.

In another study, a strong link was found between companies that invest in their employees and their long-run stock market performance. It was based on 100 German companies, and focused on "intrapreneurship". This means giving employees the freedom to make decisions and to use their initiative. Linda Bilmes summarised the study, of which she was a co-author, in the *Financial Times* (10 February 1997) and noted that the leading companies, like BMW and VW, had focused on human resources for many years and were developing their approaches further, but Audi, Ford and Opel were slow to change. She found that "employee-focused companies not only deliver the best shareholder value; they also created the most jobs". The companies with the lowest employee focus, based on four criteria, had the lowest total shareholder return (TSR), which is share price increase and dividends, over a given period of years.

Bilmes pointed out that the huge Californian institutional investor, Calpers, which invests over $100 billion a year, has a policy of preferring to invest in companies with a good employee focus. Other companies have found that consumers can react very rapidly to perceived poor corporate behaviour — two late 1990s examples being Shell (the treatment of the Ogoni people in Nigeria and the Brent Spar oil platform) and Nike (alleged use of child labour). Consumer boycotts will probably become more common than strikes in the future.

Thus it is clear that, in spite of downsizing and the apparent growth of atypical working, a new era is emerging where companies find it in their interest to actually do what they say in regard to valuing their employees, from production, marketing and shareholding perspectives. This is the stakeholder approach.

In the past, trade union responses to industrial change were dictated by relatively simple analyses. The answer was, all too often, to say "no" on principle. Today, trade unions are examining, accepting or rejecting each development on its own merits. Where new technologies benefit workers and society as a whole, unions are generally prepared to co-operate in their introduction. As Roche and Gunnigle (1997) concluded:

> it seems to be increasingly accepted that the adversarial model of industrial relations no longer provides a viable basis for relations between employees, unions and employers in Ireland.

The Irish trade union movement is ahead of other European countries in accepting the need to develop partnership at enterprise level. Part of the reason for this is that Irish trade unions have recognised the imperatives of competition, in all its complexity, faster than unions in other countries because of the high level of multinational penetration into the economy and because they have become accustomed to change. As has been seen in Chapter Four, employers have embraced partnership in theory, and progress has been made in a proportion of companies, but many have yet to fully embrace it. Most collective agreements state that there is partnership in the enterprise, but they do not "walk the talk".

Industrial relations specialist Bill Roche (1995) identified four types of industrial relations model practices in Ireland. First is the non-union human resource management model, where there is no union and the firm is usually a subsidiary of an MNC with high pay, good conditions, especially for core workers and flexibility, with atypical work contracts.

The second model is a partnership between unions and management which attempts to build a genuine co-operation to develop the business, products, systems, design, etc. This model usually operates in MNCs' plants (Analog Devices, Apple Computer) as well as most commercial state companies (Bord na Mona, Aer Lingus, Aer Rianta), and several large indigenous companies.

The third model is the deregulation model, where the company tries to keep unions out. It is usually associated with the low-cost, low-road strategy which attempts to circumvent legislation on conditions, etc.

The fourth model is the adversarial model with management and unions engaged in traditional pay, demarcation and productivity disputes. Here, management implements parts of world class manufacturing in order to control workers and get flexibility in the short term, and workers generally oppose everything management proposes.

This fourth model is still widespread in Ireland, but there is no empirical evidence of the division among these four categories. However, it is clear that the partnership model is the one that is growing rapidly, often developing concurrently with other models. The EU is keen on the partnership approach because it sees it as the best way forward for industry and employees and it is in line with the European social model. The European Commission (1997b) published a Green Paper on it, advocating that competitiveness can be improved through better organisation of work based on high skill, high trust and high quality.

The potential of flexibility in manufacturing can only be properly harnessed nationally if it is matched by similar flexibility in other institutions, including local, regional and national authorities. The civil service, local authorities, Garda and health boards, all huge employers and not subject to competitive pressures, are nonetheless tentatively examining the way they do their business.

Such is the pace of change today that, unless these institutions are transformed rapidly, they will act as a block on Ireland's economic progress. Despite their hierarchical organisational structures dating from the nineteenth century, they actually have the potential to be radically reformed in a short time. They are highly unionised and the unions, using the partnership model, have experience of the changes elsewhere in the economy and know how to import them into the new structures. The old structures are so antiquated in many instances that they should be easy to abandon. The big losers will be middle management and the winners will be the public, as consumers of services, and most employees. Privatisation of many public services is now more feasible than before with changes in technology, but the Irish public has not shown a great appetite for it, nor are the employees likely to accept it, particularly for its own sake.

The pace of competition is now faster, driven by changing industrial structures as firms use both old and new ways of increasing power through mergers, acquisitions and strategic alliances, or by concentrating on core competencies. There is also the consequence of strategic trade policy, which was successful in South East Asia, and there are new localised networks of small firms (like in industrial districts) achieving success beyond local markets through co-operative competition.

There is increased competition driven also by technology and
EU rules on competition and state aid. Part of the drive on competition is to ensure that there is no more state aid, not just to state
industries, but also to private ones. Articles 85 and 86 in the gov-
erning treaty of the European Union, the Treaty of Rome, are
driving the pace of change in Europe. Yet these changes are not a
free market triumph over those who want social matters to be
taken on board. They are European, and have a certain ambiguity
that allows social issues to be seriously considered. The European
move to deregulate is different from that of the US, as has been
seen from the Commission's earlier quote on employment.

Another driver of change, from the employers' perspective, is
that the changing nature of work and its organisation demands
that workers should work in teams, unsupervised; they must focus on quality, Just-in-Time production and all the other acronyms such as WCM. The only way forward for Irish trade unions
and employers is to work in a *genuine* partnership at enterprise
level, where there is a comprehensive sharing of information,
where there is trust, where there is dialogue and where workers
can take ownership of company problems and vice versa.

Aer Rianta, the airport company, probably has the most comprehensive strategy for developing partnership in Ireland. It has a
"Compact for Constructive Participation" and all in the company
are involved and participate in change. The Compact is well
written and detailed, is working very well and should make the
process of change in that company smooth. Other state companies, which in differing degrees are engaged in greater dialogue
and partnership, include Bord na Mona, Aer Lingus, ESB and the
now privatised Eircom (previously Telecom Éireann).

However, MNCs, both unionised and non-unionised, are well
along the road to partnership. A large number of the more recently arrived MNCs in Ireland do not recognise trade unions.
They can do this successfully because they are leading-edge companies, making very high profits and can afford to pay top rates
and offer good conditions. They often believe in open dialogue

with their employees, partly to keep out unions, but also to adopt new effective forms of working in their plants.

An OECD report on partnership in Ireland by Charles Sabel (1996) found that the new forms of work, especially partnership between employers and workers, appear to be fairly widespread. He found that both the multinational and domestic sectors have begun to adopt the new methods extensively enough to contribute to the recent performance of the Irish economy. He examined the changes in a number of MNC plants and also looked at some domestic industries, and tentatively concluded that Ireland appeared to be ahead of Europe on workplace change. There is much evidence of change at enterprise level throughout the country.

CONCLUSION

In this chapter, two micro-economic factors that have contributed substantially to Ireland's economic success were examined in detail. The concept of competitiveness has only been developed in recent years and while the world of work has always been evolving, there has recently been unprecedented change, with new forms of work organisation entering the factory, which will spread to all areas in time.

Competitiveness as a new way of looking at economic factors is not clearly understood, having been seen in terms of labour costs by some and profits by others. However, there has been a major change in Ireland and the more recent major reports on industrial policy have taken a broad view of the concept. It was seen that productivity is an important factor in competitiveness, but when there are underemployed resources — such as high unemployment — then overall living standards are reduced.

There have been major changes in industrial relations in Ireland with both employers and trade unions moving partnership at the national level down to the level of the firm. This move was particularly evident in Partnership 2000, the fourth national agreement. The concept of partnership is widely accepted in 1999, but there are widely differing opinions on what it means and how it

should be effectively applied. Employee involvement in work decisions is an idea whose time has come. Like a lot of good ideas, it is
not universally applied and many companies operate in the old
authoritarian ways.

The new forms of work, in an era of shorter product cycles,
greater product differentiation and innovation are welcomed by
workers who are better educated and who want to control their
own work environment. Irish trade unions have probably moved
ahead of their European colleagues in adopting the participative
approach. MNCs have led in the introduction of the new forms of
work in Ireland because many of them are new, innovative firms
and they have even newer plants in Ireland than at home. The entrepreneurial firm, often small or medium-sized, may have a special role in the new competition because it can be especially flexible,
adaptable and innovative. These changes will make work both
more attractive and more productive.

Chapter Seven

UNFINISHED BUSINESS

There are six factors that appear to detract from the Irish economic miracle: high long-term unemployment, widespread poverty, lack of tax reform, a housing crisis, exaggerated growth figures and over-reliance on multinationals. The last two factors were dealt with in Chapters Three and Five. This chapter will examine the first four: Part 1 will deal with poverty, Part 2 with unemployment, Part 3 with tax reform and Part 4 with the housing crisis.

Poverty is *the* major economic and social problem, which the Irish success has not eliminated, and which policy has not effectively addressed. The lack of tax reform is important, not least because it impacts on poverty. The historic problem of unemployment has been dramatically reduced over the decade of the 1990s, but the boom has created a major housing crisis. Emerging labour shortages mean that Ireland could safely import skilled Germans, French, Italians, Greeks, Belgians and Spaniards, where unemployment is over 10 per cent, but they would have to live in tent cities!

A serious assault on poverty would make Ireland one of the most attractive countries in the world, with a fine economic and social system. The disparity between rich and poor may not be as wide in Ireland as in some other countries, but the boom has widened it. It impacts on other social issues, such as drug dependency, alienation and crime. This chapter will also assess whether those with power in Irish society are willing to deal with the twin evils of poverty and the residual problem of prolonged unemployment, and also tax reform and the housing crisis.

PART 1: SHARING THE WEALTH — POVERTY

The extent of poverty in Ireland is surprisingly high, with over
one million people classified as being poor by authoritative research. This is a very high level of poverty. With a population of
3,721,000 in 1999, over one-third of the people were living in poverty in 1997 (Callan et al., 1999). These figures use an income poverty line of 60 per cent of average income. If an income poverty
line of 50 per cent is used, there were one-fifth of the population
living in poverty.

The Combat Poverty Agency would like Ireland to move into
line with the more progressive EU countries by aiming to bring
those living below the 50 per cent income poverty to well below
10 per cent by 2007. The level of those living in persistent poverty
showed a significant fall from 9–15 per cent in 1994 to 7–10 per
cent in 1997, using basic income deprivation indicators such as
adequate heating and a warm winter coat. One-third of children
continue to live in poverty, though this figure was reduced between 1994 and 1997 with the rise in employment, and is likely to
have fallen since. In June 1999, the government revised its targets
for reducing poverty set in the Anti-Poverty Strategy, setting a
new target of reducing consistent poverty to below 5 per cent by
2004.

The distribution of the fruits of the economic boom is a major
indicator of the economic and social management of the economy
and of citizens' well-being. It is clear from the preceding chapters
that Ireland does not lack the resources to tackle the problem of
poverty.

In the period under review, the social consensus ensured that,
while public spending increased slowly, social welfare payments
grew at a rate above inflation and were targeted at those most in
need. Yet the level of poverty remained exceptionally high and is
still crying out for radical action.

Poverty here is not defined as "absolute" poverty, which is just
sufficient food and basic shelter. It is "relative" poverty, where
people's resources are so limited that they have a standard of living that is unacceptable by the general standard of living in the

society in which they live. This standard of living is not just measured by financial and material resources, but also participation in activities that are considered normal in society. This means that those who are excluded from participation in the mainstream of society are also in poverty. Thus in the 1980s, the concept of "social exclusion" became important. Poverty is not just located in urban ghettos, as some of the worst poverty is in isolated rural areas.

Those most at risk from poverty have been identified by research as:

- The unemployed, especially the long-term unemployed and their families

- Children, especially in big families

- Small farmers

- Lone mothers, and

- People with disabilities.

The Combat Poverty Agency is the government body whose task it is to address poverty. It is recognised as a professional and competent organisation that has done excellent work in highlighting the problem of poverty and in drawing together a broad consensus on how it should be tackled. There are other bodies whose work in the area is invaluable, including the Conference of Religious in Ireland (CORI) and the Saint Vincent de Paul Society, both of which now focus on the causes of poverty, with the former developing a very radical solution in the form of a basic income for all.

A Little Progress in the Boom

There has been some progress in reducing poverty in the boom period from 1987. The greatest impact on poverty has been the rapid growth in job creation, though this did not really begin until 1994 and the level of unemployment remained high, with most of the new jobs going to those other than the unemployed. However, there was a rapid reduction in unemployment in the late 1990s and this helped reduce poverty.

Much of the period has been analysed in a study (Callan et al., 1996) which showed that poverty was reduced somewhat between 1987 and 1994, and again between 1994 and 1999 (Callan et al., 1999), but that much more needs to be done. The study set a number of poverty thresholds, with the most accepted being 60 per cent of the average household income.

A major initiative in the area of poverty was the National Anti-Poverty Strategy (NAPS) introduced by the Government in 1995. This seeks to ensure that the reduction of poverty is firmly on the agenda of every government department and agency. The NAPS requires all policy to be poverty-proofed (e.g. proposals for reductions in tax) — which could prove radical, if effectively implemented.

The Rainbow Coalition of 1994–97 concentrated welfare improvements on children, doubling child benefit. Most poverty is found in families with children. For the many who are dependent on welfare in Ireland, this move was beneficial.

In spite of the central wage agreements, income disparity widened since 1987. The hourly earnings of the lowest-earning 10 per cent (decile) of the population stagnated in real terms, or even fell a little, while those of the top decile grew by over 4 per cent each year. The ratio of earnings of the top decile to the bottom decile (for men) increased from 3.5 to 5 between 1987 and 1994. The change was less marked for women. With stagnation at the bottom of the pile, the share of the labour force earning less than two-thirds of median earnings was almost a quarter of the total — one of the highest rates in the 29 members of the OECD (OECD, 1997: 91–2).

Another way of examining the trend is to compare the "free-for-all" up to 1987 with the central agreements since then. Research has shown that for workers on average earnings, the national agreements saw real increases in their living standards, especially when compared to actual declines in take-home pay in the period from 1980 to 1987 (SIPTU, 1996a).

However, the boom changed little for a substantial minority in Ireland. Breen et al. (1990: 97) describe how the once minimalist Irish state became a large interventionist one after the late 1950s, developing a welfare system as big as those in countries with larger incomes. This meant relatively high taxes and spending, but "it did not significantly reduce income inequity and certainly failed to abate the importance of class in determining life chances".

Overall, it is reasonable to estimate that poverty was reduced somewhat in the last decade or so, that many enjoyed improvements in living standards, but that there is still a very serious problem of poverty as Ireland enters the twenty-first century.

Five Ways of Tackling Poverty

The five main policy instruments for influencing the share-out of income and wealth are: (a) the welfare system; (b) the number of jobs created; (c) the distribution of the "national cake" between profits and wages; (d) the tax system; and (e) in the longer term, education.

(a) The Welfare System

No Irish political party favours cutting welfare. Chapter Two described how the old-age pension was cut in 1924 by Ernest Blythe, in the absence of an opposition. Most parties in government today give reasonable increases in welfare — generally above the rate of inflation, and on a par with wage increases. With the national partnership approach, the trade unions took the lead role in protecting welfare, and they have been joined at the negotiating table by the unemployed and the voluntary sector. There was a Commission on Social Welfare in 1987 and its recommendations were broadly accepted by most in society. It recommended that various anomalies be eliminated and that certain rates be increased. This was done incrementally over the years.

There has not been a radical debate over the future of the welfare system in Ireland, as there has been in the US and UK. Only recently has there been a more strategic approach taken to welfare, by the Rainbow government, when it became more focused and the NAPS was introduced.

The crucial problem in Ireland was, and still is, the large numbers who are dependent on welfare. The reductions in the number of unemployed since 1994 means that welfare costs were reduced, freeing resources for a more strategic approach. While the level of welfare increased above the rate of inflation, it did not keep pace with the rate of increase in wages and particularly with the increase in take-home pay. Thus there was more focus on the employed than those on welfare by government in the late 1990s, in spite of the fall in the numbers on welfare. On this count, the gap between rich and poor widened at a time of unprecedented Exchequer surpluses.

(b) Increase in Jobs

The increase in jobs, already highlighted, has had a large impact in reducing poverty and so this has contributed to a reduction in the gap. Employment is the big enemy of poverty. However, in Ireland most new jobs were taken up either by those leaving education or by returned emigrants until the late 1990s, when unemployment finally began to fall. Many of the longer-term unemployed have had little access to jobs, and with low levels of education, their opportunities are limited. Thus, serious government action in addressing the problems of the long-term unemployed is urgently needed. Unemployment will be dealt with in more detail in Part 2.

(c) Sharing the Cake

The share-out of the national cake — or national income — is achieved through negotiations all over the country and it is largely determined over a long time-frame. The main share is the traditional one — between capital and labour. This is determined by collective bargaining, and the share generally changes slowly over time. There is also the share taken in taxes by government, some of which goes in transfers to people on welfare, on pensions, etc., and much of it in public sector wages and salaries, which are determined by the collective bargaining system.

While reliable income distribution data is not available, the distribution of earned income in the period from 1987 widened substantially. This was because the share of national income going to profits increased substantially and because the rates of tax on high incomes and on profits were reduced, giving more disposable income to profit earners and high-income earners.

Figure 7.1: Wage/Profit Share of Irish Economy, 1987 and 1999

Share of National Income, 1987

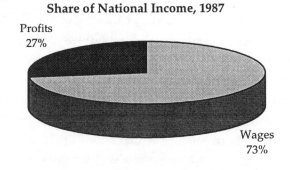

Profits
27%

Wages
73%

Share of National Income, 1999

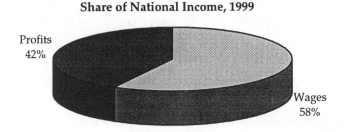

Profits
42%

Wages
58%

Source: European Economy, No. 66, 1998.

The wage share of the Irish economy fell dramatically from its peak of 84 per cent of national income in 1974, to 73 per cent in 1987, and to 58 per cent in 1999 (*European Economy*, 1998, Table 32). This shows a shift in income distribution from labour to capital in Ireland, as labour's share moved to the lowest share in the 15 member states. The share of labour's income in Ireland had remained a little above the European average of 73 per cent in the 1980s, at 75 per cent on average. Indigenous business was barely making profits in the late 1980s and many of them failed. There has also been a shift in distribution from labour to capital in most countries in the period. In 1999, the EU average is a share of 68 per cent for labour and 32 per cent for capital. The capital to labour ratios in the US, the UK and Japan were slightly less at 30:70, 28:72 and 27:73 per cent respectively.

National income and OECD data confirm this shift from labour in the period of the national agreements between employers, unions and government, which began in 1987. It has been argued that profits were low in earlier years in Ireland and the large increases in the share going to profits help investment, etc. It is also clear that the wage moderation under the national agreements assisted the increased share to capital.

On the other hand, in spite of an increase in self-employment, there has been a large increase in the numbers in employment — that is, on the labour side — which should be reflected in a larger share for labour. It has also been seen that there had been modest wage increases, assisted by tax reductions, giving real increases in take-home pay in the period under review. On the other hand, profits have been rising rapidly, from 8 per cent return on capital in 1987, to 11 per cent in the early 1990s and to 17 per cent in the late 1990s — nearly the highest in the OECD (OECD, 1998, "Rates of Return on Capital in the Business Sector"). This rise in profitability has helped the shift from labour to capital.

When allowances are made for the effect of transfer pricing (which artificially boosts profits), the Irish shareout appears to be low for labour (for further discussion of this, see Lane, 1998). By 1999, the Irish figure was well out of line with the rest of Europe, and capital's share was well above the US and Japan. It is clear from the emerging shortages in labour and from this data that the market will begin to operate more efficiently, with the price of labour rising to dampen down demand. In short, there will be wage rises and, in aggregate, such rises can be afforded. The data may be too broad for a definitive picture of inequity, but the shift is clearly a move away from redistribution, away from the reduction in poverty. If the trend in the shift from labour were to continue, it would indicate a serious widening of income disparity. This, however, is unlikely.

From Revenue Commissioners' data, it appears that the self-employed are under-represented in the league of high-income earners, where the high earning professionals, publicans and large farmers should swell their numbers. There has also been a lower proportion of the total national income going to the state in taxes in recent years. As welfare payments were maintained and more targeted, and there was an increasing cake, a lower proportion of taxes is not necessarily regressive. However, from the perspective of reducing poverty, the shift in the share of the cake from labour to capital would appear to be regressive, particularly if those on lower incomes are not protected.

(d) Tax Reform

The whole issue of tax will be examined in some depth separately in Part 3, as it has important effects on many areas of the economy, as well as poverty. Tax can be used as a redistributive instrument or as an incentive, in addition to raising revenue. Irish policy-makers have had a strong belief in the powers of taxation in giving incentives to industry. For many years, every week seemed to see a new tax scheme proposed to help an area or an industry, which the proposers knew would at least be heard. However, there is greater recognition that the tax system is an inefficient, unfair and costly way of boosting employment (of course, it no longer needs to be boosted in many areas).

Ireland is a tax haven for the global corporate sector. The industrial development agencies and some others argue forcibly that this is how it should be. Therefore, as the state must raise taxes for its daily activities, it does so mainly on labour and consumer spending, which have to be relatively high to compensate for low taxes on profits, property and wealth. The issue of tax as an instrument for redistributing income or wealth has not been widely debated.

Tax reform, for those on the Right, primarily means reduced taxes. In the context of poverty reduction, reform for most people means having a tax system where those with high incomes and wealth pay proportionately more tax — in short, it should be redistributive. There is also a broad consensus that there should be some well-considered incentive schemes for some sectors, which will, therefore, cut across the progressiveness of the system.

One radical solution to the problem of poverty has been put forward: a "basic income for all". It has been proposed in various forms by the Left and Green parties in the past, and is currently strongly advocated by the Conference of Religious in Ireland. A full basic income, as proposed by CORI, would mean that every adult would have a basic income of £70 a week in 1997. This amount would not be taxed and would apply to everyone in the state, with smaller amounts for children and more for the elderly. The tax rate for all income in excess of the basic amount (£3,650) would, however, be close to 50 per cent, a very high effective rate. This contrasts with current average effective tax rates (the proportion of total earnings paid in tax) for a single person of around 23 per cent and 15 per cent for a married person.

A basic income for all might be attractive in a greenfield situation. To introduce it today would be politically and economically difficult. To sustain and increase it could prove even more difficult in times of economic recession and/or changing trends in demography and dependency. It would cost a lot and, as the average effective rate of tax (not the top rate, but the average rate paid) would rise substantially, it would not be popular with most taxpayers. Moreover, the difficulties it seeks to remedy can perhaps be tackled in other, less problematic ways.

The Rainbow Government of 1994–97 went quite some way towards a basic income for children with substantial increases in Child Benefit. A full basic income is a very radical solution to poverty. It has been subject to serious study by various government committees and several independent researchers and was examined by a Working Group on Basic Income established under Partnership 2000. A Green Paper on Basic Income is expected in

1999. It may be worthy of further study to ascertain if it could be introduced in the future, or at least to see how it can be applied to children.

(e) Education

The power of education in increasing life opportunities is internationally recognised. It takes some time to work its way through the system, however, and the fruits of progressive educational reforms, begun in the 1960s, are now evident in the Irish success. Those leaving school early have the lowest potential earning power, and indeed have little public money spent on their education. There is a strong correlation between educational achievement and high income over a lifetime. Children of professionals have a far greater chance of following their parents' profession than those of lower socio-economic groups.

The following figures show how much is spent on pupils at different levels — and, of course, third-level education requires more spending than primary level. But the figures show who gains from public spending. Combat Poverty have shown that, in 1995, spending per pupil at primary level was £1,425, at secondary £2,225, and at third level £3,750. The *Early School Leavers and Youth Unemployment* report of the National Economic and Social Forum (NESF, 1997) showed that, on average, a total of £11,400 is spent by the education system on each child who leaves after primary school, and £15,850 is spent on each child who leaves after two years of second-level. This contrasts with the £37,525 spent by the State on a student who completes a four-year programme at third level. The educational changes over the decades have contributed to better opportunities for all in Ireland. Those who are disadvantaged have special needs that must be addressed. Overall, there is progress in the area of educational opportunity.

Conclusion on Poverty

The level of poverty is remarkably high in Ireland, affecting over one-third of the population by the 60 per cent average income benchmark, or one-fifth of the 50 per cent poverty line. The economic boom has not reduced it. Everyone's boat rose, but the bigger boats rose faster and higher. In a time of plenty, it is the smaller boats that should have risen fastest. This did not happen.

There was no assault on poverty in the 1990s, though some effective measures were introduced and the fall in unemployment helped. Policy-makers have a clear understanding of its extent, its depth and what should be done to radically reduce it. There is widespread consensus that poverty is a problem. There is a clear understanding of how to deal with it effectively and how to reduce it swiftly and dramatically.

The job creation success of the 1990s has greatly helped, but the division of the national cake is more problematic, and the other areas of redistribution — through tax reform, welfare increases which track real earnings and education — have not been seriously addressed by those with power. There has never been a better time to tackle poverty effectively, particularly with tax and welfare reform, financed by the rising incomes and wealth generated by the economic boom and fairer investment in education.

PART 2: UNEMPLOYMENT

Main Features of Irish Unemployment

Unemployment has been the historic problem in Ireland since Independence and before. It was not particularly high until the late 1970s when it soared to double digits and remained there until 1998. It would have gone far higher had not so many Irish people emigrated, as has been seen in Chapter Two. The most remarkable economic fact in the period under review has been the very high job creation. This was not initially accompanied by falling unemployment for a number of years, but then from 1994, it began to fall rapidly.

The rate of unemployment in Ireland at 17 per cent in the mid-1980s was the second highest in the European Union, after Spain. In 1997, it fell below the EU average of 10.7 per cent for the first time since 1963; in late 1998 it fell to 6.4 per cent and is likely to fall further. Labour shortages became a real problem in 1999.

However, there is still a serious problem of long-ter~ ployment and of young people without jobs. Unemployment is a waste of resources — of output, in welfare costs and lost taxes — and it adds to poverty. It is the unskilled who are at greatest risk of unemployment — this group has suffered the worst job losses since 1981 while, at the other end of the skill spectrum, it was professional service workers who gained most jobs. Most of the unemployed have lower educational qualifications. The rate of unemployment for those with primary or lower secondary education was over four times higher than for those with third-level education in 1995.

Long-term unemployment in Ireland had been almost twice the rate of the level in the OECD, with 58 per cent of the unemployed having been without a job for more than a year, compared to 30 per cent on average in the OECD in 1995. For Irish males, the situation then was particularly bad, at 64 per cent of the unemployed compared to 49 per cent for females. It was and still is most severe for middle-aged men (45 to 54 years of age). Most lost their jobs because of downsizing in traditional industries such as clothing, textiles, food and drink. These men, with less education, get pushed to the back of the dole queues and have little chance of getting jobs in the new industries.

There were 52,000 long-term unemployed at the end of 1998. This may be less of an employment problem and more of a social one, particularly affecting certain urban areas, but it is one which should be addressed by action. The level of long-term unemployment peaked at 128,000 in 1994, or 9 per cent of the labour force. At 3 per cent in late 1998, it had been dramatically reduced. But at 52,000 people, many with families, it is still to high, especially in such an unprecedented boom.

The Costs Are Unequally Shared

In Ireland, over 70 per cent of people in work never experience unemployment. Those with low educational achievement are most at risk of long-term unemployment. Ireland is in keeping with the European-wide pattern of high unemployment. The scale of unemployment imposes huge economic and social costs, which are apparent in a number of ways:

- Loss in output for the unemployed and for businesses;

- Additional welfare benefits and foregone tax revenues;

- Effects on the health and psychological well-being of the un-employed;

- Impact on society at large (e.g. crime, alienation);

- Increased burden on social services (e.g. housing, education, health);

- High risk of poverty.

The burden of unemployment and its costs are not equally dis-tributed, as a rather small segment of the population — the long-term unemployed — carry the greatest share. This extremely vul-nerable group is in danger of near-permanent detachment from the labour force and society in general. This pattern is replicated at household, class and community levels, with a growing con-centration of unemployment in work-poor families, among semi-and unskilled workers and in local authority housing estates.

There were no net new jobs created between 1978 and 1987. In stark contrast, in the following decade, between 1987 and 1996, the total numbers at work increased by 216,000, and in the period from 1987 to 2000, over half a million additional jobs have been created. Even more impressive is that job creation accelerated rapidly after 1994, as has been seen. The growth in Irish employ-ment has been astonishing and, if there is no major upset, it is forecast to continue for at least ten years, though there will be a slowdown in the rate of growth. Unemployment should fall to a level close to full employment.

The interaction between taxes and welfare is important for those on low incomes who find themselves hit by taxes, particu-larly in Ireland where taxes bite into low incomes. The OECD rec-ommended that Ireland "reduce the high marginal tax rate on low-paid workers". This was begun in the mid-1990s, albeit slowly, and the introduction of tax credits in 1999 was a progressive step. The OECD also recommended welfare benefit changes, though the OECD admits that benefits to jobless persons "are not high in Ireland" (OECD, 1997: 81). If the additional revenue flowing into the Exchequer was put into increased personal allowances or, even better, into tax credits, then all would gain, but the low paid would gain most, helping to reduce poverty and unemployment and assisting vulnerable industries and services.

According to a major study of flexibility of employment and working time, Ireland is the second least regulated country after the UK (Koedijk and Kremers, 1996) and another study shows it as the third least regulated country out of 16 European countries (see Table 7.1). Irish firms face some of the lowest regulations and least regulated labour legislation covering working time, temporary employment, dismissals, notice, severance pay, etc. In spite of this apparently low level of employment protection in Ireland, employers' organisations IBEC and ISME regularly complain of the strictness of legislation and cite it as a major obstacle to employment. On the other side of industry, unions seek steady improvements in employment legislation and are able to use it to defend their members' interests.

Surprisingly, spending on active labour market schemes in Ireland is high by international standards. It is double the average OECD level or equivalent to two-thirds of the benefits to unemployed persons. With the high level of unemployment, it seems that this money is not spent effectively. There is a need to rationalise the many schemes (there are over 30 at present); integrate the government agencies dealing with the unemployed; focus on targeted programmes; invest in increasing the skills and competencies of people; and encourage the diffusion of technology from foreign to domestic firms.

The Government set the goal of "full employment" in 1996, with the publication of *Growing and Sharing our Employment* (Department of Enterprise and Employment, 1996), making a decisive break with past policy, which had sought to avoid the issue of full employment. It had a twin approach: to increase the number of sustainable jobs; and to improve access to jobs for all, especially the disadvantaged. Substantial progress has since been made.

Table 7.1: Rankings on Employment Protection Legislation

Country	Regular Procedural Inconvenience	Notice and Severance Pay for No-fault Dismissals	Difficulty of Dismissal	Overall Ranking for Strictness of Protection against Dismissals
Austria	10	10	11	13
Belgium	4	13	3	5
Britain	4	5	1	2
Denmark	1	11	5	4
Finland	14	9	4	9
France	9	7	6	6
Germany	13	2	12	9
Greece	8	12	10	12
Holland	16	1	8	7
Ireland	6	3	6	3
Italy	3	16	15	14
Norway	6	6	14	8
Portugal	12	15	16	16
Spain	15	14	13	15
Sweden	11	8	9	11
Switzerland	2	4	2	1

Note: The country rankings are based on the situation in the late 1980s. Rankings increase with strictness of employment protection, i.e. 1 is the least strict.

Source: OECD, Jobs Study, 1994

Measuring Irish Unemployment

There are two ways of measuring unemployment — the Labour Force Survey, which is known as the International Labour Office (ILO) approach, and the Live Register, which measures the numbers signing on at Labour Exchanges.

The Live Register includes part-time workers, seasonal and casual workers. Half of those on the Live Register would not be classified as unemployed by international definitions. A quarter were not economically active, with most of them not looking for jobs; some were students or retired; some in part-time work; and 11 per cent were working full-time! This explains the reason why the Live Register is not accepted as the accurate measurement by economists, who opt for the International Labour Organisation (ILO) definition.

The ILO definition gives a much lower figure. While the Live Register is an overstatement of the problem, the ILO definition understates it, because it neglects discouraged workers — those who would work if they had the opportunity and all those on schemes (41,000 in 1999), and some older workers who are classified as retired.

Table 7.2 shows that Ireland's overall level of unemployment was high compared to most, though not all, countries. It also shows that it is moving in the right direction and indeed, since this table was computed, the rate has fallen to just over 6 per cent for early 1999. Ireland's position improved greatly from having been one of the worst in the Union. There is still the problem of long-term unemployment.

Table 7.2: World Unemployment Rates, 1996, 1997 and 1998 (ILO Definition)

Country	1996	1997	1998
United States	5.4	4.9	5.0
Japan	3.4	3.4	4.5
Germany	8.9	11	10.75
France	12.4	12.4	11.5
Italy	12.0	12.2	12.2
United Kingdom	8.2	7.0	6.5
Canada	9.7	9.2	9.1
Total of above countries	6.8	6.6	6.6

Country	1996	1997	1998
Australia	8.6	8.7	8.2
Austria	4.3	4.4	4.4
Belgium	9.7	9.2	8.3
Czech Republic	3.5	3.8	4.6
Denmark	6.8	5.5	4.2
Finland	15.3	13.1	11.7
Greece	9.6	9.6	9.4
Hungary	10.6	10.5	10.4
Iceland	4.3	3.8	3.5
Ireland	11.9	10.3	7.8
Korea	2.0	2.7	2.8
Luxembourg	3.0	2.6	2.4
Mexico	5.5	4.5	4.2
Netherlands	6.3	5.2	4.0
New Zealand	6.1	6.7	6.0
Norway	4.9	4.1	4.2
Poland	12.4	11.7	11.1
Portugal	7.3	6.8	5.7
Spain	22.2	20.1	18.9
Sweden	9.6	9.9	8.3
Switzerland	3.9	4.2	5.0
Turkey	6.5	6.6	6.5
Total of smaller countries	8.7	8.5	8.2
Total OECD	7.6	7.3	7.0
Total European Union	10.9	10.7	10.0

Source: OECD (1997b and 1998); *European Economy* No. 66; and QNHS, Nov. 1998.

Tackling Long-term Unemployment

There has been a good reduction in long-term unemployment, from over 10 per cent in 1988 to 3.1 per cent (52,000 people) in late 1998. Yet this is a high proportion of the total numbers of unemployed at half, compared to one-third in most countries. Progress in the reduction has been fast with the rate being halved in just over two years. But there is a hard core of unemployment which requires the proactive management of the labour market in four main ways:

1. Targeting particular categories of the long-term unemployed for priority attention, while ensuring that people are not ghettoised in second-class programmes, from which their chances of entering the formal labour market are minimal;

2. Re-focusing the resources and structures of the employment and welfare systems to support the transition from unemployment to work, while avoiding cuts in welfare or mandatory participation in programmes;

3. Intervening directly in the operation of the labour market, not by old-fashioned and now discredited public sector recruitment, but by other more creative ways which minimise the long-term cost to the state;

4. Adopting preventative as well as curative measures, mainly via the education system, so as to stop the problem of unemployment being reproduced at source.

Conclusion on Long-term Unemployment

Employment (and unemployment) is a key economic factor. Unemployment, while directly affecting only a small proportion of the population, has a devastating effect on those without jobs and their families. It also has a large indirect affect on all people through taxes and lost output, and it is a cause of crime. It is the largest cause of poverty, hitting those who are weakest — the socially disadvantaged, particularly those with poor education — hardest. It hits the children of those affected hardest of all.

Great strides have been made on reducing unemployment and Ireland may be heading for full employment. The serious problem is long-term unemployment. Many of the long-term unemployed are not benefiting from the jobs boom because they are unskilled, are older workers, have the "wrong" addresses, or have been unemployed for so long that employers do not favour hiring them. The jobs are going to the new labour market entrants and to those who return from abroad and, lately, even to immigrants. This means that the market alone will not provide the solution to persistent long-term unemployment.

In addition to the 52,000 who were long-term unemployed in early 1999, there were 40,000 on government-sponsored schemes. These schemes need radical reform so that they can give the long-term unemployed the skills and real training which will enable them to get back to work, particularly when there are job opportunities for those with skills.

The problem of long-term unemployment is now intergenerational — the children of those who have not worked have little hope of work. The boom is only alienating them more because they are getting relatively poorer as others get richer. The boom is passing them by. They are the truly marginalised.

The first step in the solution is to ensure that the children of the long-term unemployed are given particular opportunities to break out of the cycle of despair. Next, and in tandem, the long-term unemployed themselves must be targeted. There is recognition that market solutions will not address the entrenched problem of long-term unemployment and that state-led approaches are the only ones which will work, provided they are well constructed.

PART 3: TAX REFORM

Ireland is a tax haven for companies and capital and consequently has high taxes on labour and spending. In the context of reducing poverty, tax reform in this chapter means using tax as a mechanism of redistribution, while recognising its role in industrial development. There were some reforms made in the last 10 or 15 years, which redistributed income more progressively, but nothing radical. There was a reduction in tax allowances and breaks to companies (including Section 84) and tightening up of other avoidance schemes and a reduction in relief to income tax payers.

However, there has been a huge reduction in the top tax rates on companies (from 50 per cent in 1988 to 28 per cent in 1999, to be further reduced to just 12.5 per cent by 2003; this will also be extended from manufacturing and trade services to all companies, irrespective of status). The top rate of income taxes have been also been reduced (from a top rate of 65 per cent in 1984/85 to 46 per cent in 1999). Property taxes were abolished and inheritance taxes were reduced in recent years. There were also a number of investment schemes introduced that benefited the wealthier sections of the population: the Business Expansion Scheme was introduced in 1984; Section 35 (Film Relief) in 1987; Urban Renewal in 1986; the Temple Bar scheme in 1991; Urban Renewal (Resorts) in 1995 and Urban Renewal (Islands) in 1996. These generous investment incentives in a time of property boom, when they are least needed, shows how biased the Irish tax system is. There is no reason for continuing such incentives in an overheating property market, except to distribute money upwards.

The low taxes on some areas, such as the 10 per cent tax on manufacturing and exported services, limited VAT coverage, no wealth taxes and taxes only on commercial property, means high taxes elsewhere. Therefore, tax has to be high on employees and on spending, and this is one reason why there is tax on low incomes in Ireland, hitting the poor, and not helping unemployment. The overall tax level in the economy has been reduced in the period under review because increased economic activity boosted Exchequer revenue.

Taxes and Companies

A key component of government industrial policy in the past was that multinationals and Irish companies paid no taxes at all on profits on exports; this was changed only at the insistence of the European Commission. It was replaced by the low 10 per cent tax on manufacturing and export services, which remains until 2003.

A powerful lobby of industrialists and the Government's own industrial agencies persuaded the Rainbow Government in mid-1997 to extend this in a modified form.

This competitive down-bidding between democratic states to attract foreign direct investment through lower and lower tax rates is ultimately self-defeating. The Commission, by allowing the extension of the low 12.5 per cent rate to all companies in Ireland, set a major block on the road to a common taxation policy, which is necessary for the effective working of the Single Market. Similar tax rates across Europe are required for a level playing-field on taxes on companies and savings, and on speculation.

Powerful forces in the EU opposed the low Irish corporate tax regime, including various German Finance Ministers, and Mario Monti, the former EU Tax Commissioner, who wanted to reverse the trend towards an increased tax burden on labour and also to stop serious losses of national tax revenue, by such down-bidding. He wanted to end this tax competition and to institute its opposite — tax co-operation — within the EU member states.

In a front-page article in the *Financial Times* in 1996, the then German Finance Minister warned that Bonn was campaigning against tax havens in the EU. He mentioned the UK, Ireland, Netherlands and Belgium as countries that weakened the competitive position of the German financial services sector (*Financial Times*, 23 December 1996).

In an editorial called "Living with Tax Rivalry", the same paper (14 January 1997) singled out Ireland's Financial Services Centre for criticism. It said that the OECD was assessing tax competition in member states. It said that tax competition erodes the tax base and that artificial regimes to lure mobile capital "can drive effective tax rates to zero or even make them negative, in which case they make them a subsidy". In October 1997, the British Revenue announced that it was clamping down on transfer price-fixing by multinationals, leading to squeals of protest from the big accountancy firms. Big fines were to be imposed on firms that move profits offshore to low tax regimes like Ireland.

Irish officialdom, lobbying for the low tax regime, caused strong resentment in other countries, which may have unintended effects, particularly loss of goodwill. Commenting on this, one EU official said, "the days when Ireland could expect to provide an attractive tax regime and still get EU funding are coming to an end" (*Financial Times*, 14 October 1997). The criticism of Ireland's position was very strong in 1998 and the country clearly burnt up a lot of goodwill with its European partners. With a tightening labour market and high taxes on labour and spending, it is surprising that the drive to achieve the low corporate tax regime was sustained.

The argument that the elimination of tax havens within Europe would mean that MNCs would move offshore to Bermuda or the Cayman Islands, ignores the perspective that Europe, as a Union of 15 countries, should and must co-ordinate tax policies and insist that companies which trade in Europe should pay taxes in Europe. With far less need for incentives, there is a strong case for a prudent government to increase the 12.5 per cent rate progressively to 20 per cent with a minimum effective rate after 2003.

Taxes on Wealth and Property

There are no taxes on wealth in Ireland, unlike many OECD countries. There was a Wealth Tax for a few years in the 1970s. The opposition to it from every quarter was the strongest opposition ever to any legislation in modern Ireland, even though it only affected a few hundred extremely wealthy people (see below). There were also taxes on all property until 1977 when Fianna Fáil abolished rates on houses. There was a minimal tax on expensive houses for those with high incomes, but it was reduced and then abolished in 1996.

Most countries have taxes on property and many have taxes on wealth. The abolition of rates also undermined the system of local democracy in Ireland. Virtually every authoritative report on the Irish economy dealing with tax advocated some form of property tax. If properly structured, it can be equitable and redistributive, and it has the added advantage of being difficult to evade. It also encourages investment in industry rather than property. The 1999 OECD report advocated reforms to take the heat out of housing, including the phasing out of mortgage interest relief, the reintroduction of property taxes, a restructured capital gains tax and, to strike fear into the hearts of the property-owning bourgeoisie, a tax on imputed rents on owner-occupied housing!

Wealth tax was supposed to work in tandem with the new inheritance tax (CAT) which replaced rates. CAT is almost completely ineffective because most of its thresholds are high and its rates are low. It is not a progressive tax and the few who might be liable use schemes to avoid it.

Finally, progressive taxes on inheritances encourage efficient use of capital because those who are fortunate enough to inherit businesses may have to borrow to pay the tax, encouraging them to run the business more efficiently. Alternatively, they can sell the business to those who would run it more efficiently.

Income Tax

It has been seen that the top rates of income tax have been progressively reduced over the past 20 years. This has been accompanied by some reforms and a little, but not much, has been done to help the lower paid. Low earnings are taxed in Ireland and single workers on average earnings have paid at the top rate for many years. In spite of many expert recommendations that the low-paid be exempt from tax, little was been done until recently.

One of the reasons why the Rainbow Government lost office in 1997, in spite of the booming economy, was its failure to address this problem. The extent of this error was revealed in September of that year when it was found that the Department of Finance had underestimated tax revenue for the year by £500 million. Any fear of overheating the economy was ill-founded, as inflation remained low. And this was even after paying out £280 million in equality payments over the previous 18 months. There also had been two tax amnesties, which further skewed income distribution, rewarding evaders, who were often big earners.

With rising incomes, unless there is redistribution through the tax system, more of the new wealth goes to those at the top of the pyramid, as happened in the US and UK. Much is made by some of "high" pay-related social insurance (PRSI) in Ireland, but the combined employer and employee rate is actually below that in the UK and is only half of the continental average rate. As a proportion of GDP, it was under 4 per cent in Ireland in 1999, compared to 15 per cent on average in 14 of the EU member states.

Table 7.3 shows social security costs in selected EU countries as a percentage of GDP. Denmark's and Ireland's are the lowest of the 15 member states, and only Ireland, the UK and Denmark are in single digits. In the decade, there was a small rise in most countries, but a fall in Ireland (with rising GDP and reductions in PRSI). Some economists and others have focused on social security contributions as the biggest obstacle to employment in Ireland. Yet these costs are particularly low in Ireland, both as a proportion of GDP compared to the EU states, as Table 7.3 shows, or as a percentage of labour costs.

Table 7.3: Social Security Costs in Selected EU States (% of GDP)

Country	1987	1999
Austria	15	16.9
Belgium	17.8	16.8
Denmark	3.0	3.2
Finland	16.6	13.2
France	20.9	19.1
Germany	17.6	19.4
Ireland	5.2	3.8
Italy	13.8	12.6
Netherlands	20.5	18.2
Spain	12.8	13.9
United Kingdom	6.6	7.8
EU 14	15.0	15.1

Source: European Economy (1998)

There is a school of thought that sees these contributions as part of general taxes. The reduction in labour costs to employers, including social security costs, is seen as a boost to them and to employment. However, social security charges pay for most work-related welfare benefits, and their reduction would mean shifting the burden to general taxation. These are an integral part of the social insurance scheme and, as such, are not taxes.

A Brief History of Tax

Ireland had its greatest street protests since Independence in 1979 and 1980 over the inequity of the tax system. Taxes had been rising after the 1973 oil crisis. The catalyst was the government backing down on a small levy it tried to impose on farmers, but the real reason was that taxes were increasing as a result of increased spending, in response to the 1973 oil crisis, compounded by the necessity to raise income taxes to pay for the abolition of property taxes and car taxes and for further increases in spending after the 1977 election.

The great tax marches, involving around 750,000 people in late 1979 and 1980, were protests at the unfair burden on Pay As You Earn (PAYE) workers, largely employees, while the self-employed and farmers were paying little. PAYE workers, making up around 70 per cent of those at work, were paying 89 per cent of income tax. Farmers had been exempt from income tax until the late 1970s and it was to be many years before they would be liable on the same terms as other citizens. The self-employed, while paying some tax, had ample opportunity to avoid (which is legal) and to evade (which is illegal) paying the full tax amount owed. Public attitudes to evasion began to change substantially after the protests, but were to have little impact on official attitudes or actions for many years. Until the mid-1980s, Irish tax inspectors seldom left their desks, there were no audits, and to this day, nobody has been jailed for tax evasion.

The disparity between revenue and spending was to necessitate continued high taxes, even throughout most of the 1990s. The big burden of the national debt at a time of high interest rates meant that taxes had to remain high and, for some years, almost all income tax went to pay interest on the debt. The debt rose from 75 per cent of GNP in 1977 to over 100 per cent five years later.

The government's response was to set up a Commission on Taxation, chaired by Miriam Hederman O'Brien. It produced surprisingly comprehensive and radical reports. These were shelved, though not forgotten. They are the benchmarks for all later reports on tax here, and indeed abroad.

While there was little reform during most of the 1980s, there was some progress in the late 1980s and in the 1990s, but it was piecemeal, slow and cautious. Total taxes are very low in Ireland as a proportion of GDP, at 33.3 per cent in 1999 compared to 46 per cent on average for the EU. Irish taxes are the lowest in the EU, the US and Japan by this measure. They fell substantially in the period under review from 41 per cent in 1987, as GDP rose.

The mountain of debt grew with the recession in the 1980s, reaching 125 per cent of total GNP by 1987. Some economists were in a panic; it was the big economic issue in the 1980s. Drastic action was proposed by some. Yet the problem was painlessly resolved and the rate of reduction was such in the 1990s that it surprised many dismal scientists, falling to 44 per cent in 1999, the lowest in the EU (excluding Luxembourg). In the late 1990s, the overflowing coffers of the Irish State present the best opportunity to reform the tax system by taking the low-paid out of the tax system, reducing poverty and unemployment. Instead, only piecemeal, conservative changes have been made. There has been no vision, few ideas and little action.

The introduction of tax credits to help the lower paid was one small reform, but tax still bites at low incomes and amazingly, many of those on average industrial earnings still pay at the top rate of tax! At a time of massive Exchequer surpluses, falling debt, low overall levels of taxes, low levels of government spending, it is clear that governments have their priorities mixed up. Or do they?

The Opposition to Tax Reform

How strong is the opposition to dealing with poverty and long-term unemployment? Some may be callous and not care about the problems of others, while others feel they pay their taxes and that is enough. Most who would hinder moves to reduce poverty or long-term unemployment would not do so deliberately, but would generally advocate some other policy that clashes with poverty-fighting policies.

The slow pace of tax reform is because the power of the interest groups frightens government, which is by nature short-termist in thinking. The Department of Finance, which is vitally influential on this issue, does not like the "big bang" approach to reform. Its officials tend to be well informed, technically brilliant and persuasive, especially over Ministers for Finance. Most Finance Ministers cannot compete with the officials in their knowledge of the complexities of the tax system and, in this author's view, none of them has had a clear vision of tax reform. The Department always errs on the side of caution.

The self-interest lobbies are well entrenched and have most of the establishment well in their grip. In effect, they *are* the establishment! Those with money and power in Ireland held onto it and increased it in the period under review.

A further problem is that the administration of taxation is weak. In spite of the evidence of serious problems of commitment in the Revenue Commissioners, no government has had the courage to change the senior personnel. It is particularly poor in uncovering evasion by the self-employed and companies. This is not just minor evasion, but includes millions of pounds in offshore accounts, secret payments, etc., as the amnesties, the wealth of the millionaire drug barons and the various frauds and tribunals, such as the Beef Tribunal and the Dunnes Stores Payments Tribunal, have revealed.

A radical change in attitudes on the part of the senior officials in the Revenue Commissioners would greatly help build a more equitable society and deepen the success of the economy. Embarrassed by the exposure of their incompetence by the various Tribunals in 1999, the Commissioners, in an extraordinarily feeble fig-leaf ceremony, announced in May 1999, with great publicity, that they were hiring an extra 26 professional staff (out of around 3,000 staff in taxes). The success of the Criminal Assets Bureau in taxing criminals is in stark contrast to the poor record of the Revenue. It is not more staff that is required at the taxes division of the Revenue, but the implementation of an effective investigative and administrative system which ensures ethical treatment of all, where the rich and powerful, from the Taoiseach and beef barons, down to PAYE workers, are treated equally.

Breen et al. (1990) found in their major study of the role of the state and class structure in Ireland that:

> This reluctance to tax the profits from enterprise, along with the sacrosanct status of wealth in the form of capital, confers enormous advantages on proprietorial households relative to others with the same income and facilitates the inheritance of wealth and its concentration among a small number of families (Breen et al., 1990: 82).

They concluded that the benefits of Ireland's economic development since the country opened up to foreign investment in the early 1960s were very unevenly distributed.

There are probably few in Irish society who do not wish for more equity and social justice. Everyone has their views on how taxes are raised and spent, and those untouched by poverty often assume the state is dealing with it, especially at such a time of rising incomes, lower taxes and relatively large cuts in government spending. There is a new awareness that more taxes (and private money if it gives value) should be spent on infrastructure — roads, public transport, water and sewage, and environmental protection. This consciousness has yet to spread to a concerted attack on poverty. But there are some positive signs. Few wealthy or powerful Irish business people have come out against poverty. Many do give to charity, which is different. One notable exception was the financial director of one of Ireland's largest multinational companies, Gary McGann of Smurfits, who warned against the growth of a two-tier society in the Celtic boom (*Irish Times*, 15 May 1999).

It is not easy to reduce poverty radically and though long-term unemployment can now be dealt with easily, many people are untouched by these problems and are indifferent to them. This means that, on the one hand, the tax system as a method of redistribution in Ireland is far less effective than it could be, and on the other, a serious concerted attack on poverty would require a courageous and motivated government. There is a lot of knowledge out there, but there is a need for less analysis and more passion.

PART 4: HOUSE PRICES BEYOND REACH

House prices, driven by real economic factors, demographic change and a consequent shortage, have soared well beyond the reach of ordinary workers. This section will analyse the reasons behind the housing crisis, review the government's response and will attempt to forecast future demand. The average new house price in 1999 in Ireland at £115,000 (£144,000 in Dublin) is well beyond the reach of workers, even those with twice or three times average industrial earnings.

FIGURE 7.2: DUBLIN SECOND-HAND HOUSE PRICES, 1990–1999

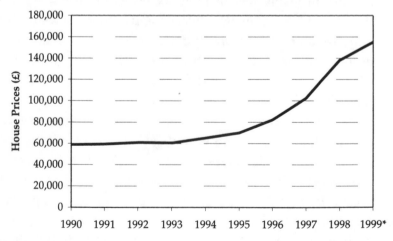

* 1999 is an estimate

The housing crisis may not get worse, but it is unlikely to lessen in the short to medium term and demand will remain high for a decade. It has been fanned by inappropriate government polices. It is one of the biggest obstacles to the continuation of the current economic progress.

The drivers of the housing crisis are as follows:

- The spectacular and sustained increase in jobs
- Rising real incomes
- Population increase, especially of those over 20 years of age
- Immigration
- More household formation, and at earlier ages
- Smaller and therefore more households
- Low interest rates
- Easy credit
- Panic buying
- Low inflation (but high house price inflation)
- The abolition of the small tax on property
- The halving of capital gains tax
- The lack of serviced land in some areas
- Delays in planning
- The large reduction in social housing by the state in the 1980s.

If one was to highlight a single key driving factor, it is the success of the Irish economy since 1987, with rapid growth, substantial job increases, low interest rates and low inflation and rising incomes, which in turn has led to rapid population growth, immigration and smaller household size. All of this has led to increased demand for housing.

On the supply side, the government has not helped with crazy, contradictory and costly policies. It is subsidising wealthy people to fan the fire with tax relief for inner city investment, investment in resorts and cuts in capital gains tax. The abolition of the small property tax on the top range of houses took the lid off higher priced houses and affected the whole chain. The OECD (1999) has recommended radical and equitable solutions to the current crisis, which include a property tax and even a tax on imputed rents of owner-occupiers.

While inflation is low at 2 per cent, second-hand house prices have risen by as much as 42 per cent in Dublin in one year (1998), and by 37 per cent for the rest of the country (Central Bank, Spring 1999), which must encourage investors into property, in spite of the government removing interest relief for them after a major report on housing (Bacon, 1998). There has been rent-seeking (profiteering) by land owners and builders; poor public transport and infrastructure also exacerbated the problem; and there is an alleged lack of serviced land. The cuts in capital spending of the 1980s; the very low density and ribbon development, unchecked by coherent policy; and particularly the massive cut in social housing investment, have all added to the problem.

In 1994, average house prices were 4.3 times average incomes. By 1998 the ratio was up to 6.4 nationally and 8.2 in Dublin. Thus a couple with earnings of £20,000 each would fall short by £54,000 of the average new house price in Dublin in 1998 (Drudy, 1999). Therefore, house prices were far beyond the reach of most people.

On the other side, builders, landowners and those who already owned one (and particularly those with more than one) property benefited enormously by the house price boom. Those who inherited even a modest house were doing well too.

Housing — The 80:10:10 Society

It is important to recognise that housing is a social issue. High house prices mean that many people will not be able to afford their own home. Ireland has the highest home ownership in Europe, greatly assisted by government policy in the provision of what were once very generous tax incentives, especially to the wealthiest.

Eighty per cent of Irish people are owner occupiers (up from 60 per cent in 1960), with ten per cent in social housing and the remaining ten per cent in the private rented sector (almost half the 1960 level). This is the 80:10:10 society. It is worth noting that half of the owner occupiers own their own house outright, with another quarter having relatively small mortgages. This leaves 20 per cent of all households with large mortgages. And at the end of the 1990s, many of them are very large loans.

But it is those without homes who are in the toughest position in 1999, because they have the least possibility of being able to afford a house or to get a local authority home. The state's spending on housing maintenance payments will probably have to increase; this is current spending, not an investment in the future nor a step towards helping people to self-sufficiency in housing. There were 42,000 private renters on housing welfare, at a cost of £113 million. This spending has increased from only £9 million in 1989 (Fahey, 1999a).

The local authority housing sector has seen 73 per cent of its stock of 330,000 houses sold off in the century and only 90,000 are left in 1999. This stock of social housing has been further reduced by a massive reduction in social house building from 1987. In 1999, only one in ten houses of the 45,000 built will be social housing, even though there were 43,000 families on the previous year's waiting list, representing over 100,000 people. This is in contrast to only 18,000 on the waiting list at the beginning of the boom in 1987.

It has been seen that the jobs boom really began in 1994, and it is in this year that house prices began to take off. Between 1994 and 1998, inflation rose by 9 per cent, while new house prices soared by a staggering 71 per cent. This was three and a half times the house building index, showing that builders and landowners were doing very well from home buyers. Reports that it is the lack of serviced land which is pushing up prices may be off the mark. According to the four Dublin local authorities, there is enough serviced land in Dublin to meet demand for over four years and unserviced land adds approximately a further four years, depending on the demand (Dublin Local Authorities, 1999). From the evidence, it appears that landowners have driven up prices by holding onto land. It is clear that builders have also enjoyed huge profits on house sales.

Fahey (1999a) points out that the distributional aspects of housing are across income categories, with about one-third of wage earners unable to purchase housing, and across age cohorts and life cycle. Existing householders benefit from falling interest rates and rising house values and, at the other end, new entrants who are young people with families are hit at the vulnerable time of family formation.

While the number of social and local authority houses increased substantially from 1994, it was only at half the levels in the 1970s and early 1980s, in spite of a rapidly increasing population. The cuts in this sector were severe. For example, the number of such houses built in 1989 was cut to one-tenth the level of 1984. In addition, there had been massive privatisation of the public housing stock. Thus while the stock of public housing has been substantially reduced, the addition to that stock had also been curtailed, while demand was rising. This meant that those with low incomes were being forced to find accommodation with relatives or pay high rents in the too-often sub-standard private rented sector in Ireland. The waiting list for local authority housing grew, but it will rise more rapidly now.

There has been a major positive change in local authority housing away from vast housing estates to smaller more integrated and socially mixed schemes. Tenants are now being asked for their opinions on facilities and design, which is a big change. Furthermore, the type of social housing is more imaginative than simply local authority rental or purchase. The problem is that there are just not enough houses, of any category, and that prices may have been pushed up by builders and landowners.

The Government Response

Housing policy is very influenced by government policy in most economies and this is particularly true in Ireland. Governments have, in the past, encouraged a high degree of home ownership, rather than rental accommodation, through large tax incentives. This has been exacerbated by their neglect of the rented sector and of social or public housing. This was because ownership was popular and it helped the building industry. There is a poorly developed rental sector in Ireland and with little security, people prefer to own rather than rent.

The government policy response to the current crisis has been very weak. It did act on the Bacon report, but this was not enough. It disallowed interest for investors and it expanded the social and local authority house building programme. However, the numbers of local authority houses being built in 1999 was still much lower than in the 1970s and early 1980s, when housing demand was less than half the level. The government established a Commission on Security of Tenure and may do more in a Planning Bill to be published in mid-1999. However, it was still unwilling to intervene on land hoarding/speculation and on builders' margins. The government has also ignored the distributional aspects of the housing crisis, which are so important. The evidence on soaring house prices points to extraordinary gains by builders and particularly by landowners. It is clear that the government is not acting in the public interest by failing to act against these profiteers.

There is no sign of long-term strategic physical planning. There are planning delays and investment in water, drainage, waste treatment and sewage and transport, while increasing, is insufficient. Tax incentives, wasteful in a booming economy, go to the wrong people. The state subsidy to those on low incomes was increasingly going to private landlords through the huge growth in spending on supplementary rent allowance.

Future Demand for Housing

The economic drivers have been analysed in preceding chapters, and it is worth teasing out the demographic pressure on future demands for housing. The labour force grew by 11,000 a year in the 1980s, but then by a massive 30,000 a year between 1991 and

1996, helped by net immigration. Increased participation in work by women and the decline in the birth rate gave families greater purchasing power. The population grew by 8 per cent between 1993 and 1999 and the rate of growth of employment was very high. Real earning were also rising. The upskilling of many jobs meant that incomes were rising too in another way and the growth in self-employment and the lower effective rate of tax on such incomes in Ireland further pushed up aggregate incomes. The population is forecast to grow to over 4 million by 2010, a growth rate of between a half and one per cent a year, and there will be further net immigration.

Age and marital status are important factors in the demand for housing. The numbers of those over 20 years of age, the biggest household formers, will grow by 300,000 between 1996 and 2006. If Ireland is to follow the UK, as it used to do, then by 2011 the numbers of households will increase from 1,180,000 in 1998 to 1,590,000 or by over one-third. This implies a growth of over 30,000 households a year. In addition to replacing older homes at around 8,000 a year and demand for holiday homes from the better-off, this figure rises to 40,000 a year. Immigration boosts this to a final figure of between 42,000 and 45,000 a year (much of this analysis is based on ESRI, 1999). The annual average house completion for the three years to 1998 was just over 38,000, though it was over 42,349 in 1998.

Thus there is no major long-term gap between supply and demand that cannot be met with a once-off boost to deal with the current high demand. Demand will still remain strong for many years and it requires a careful policy approach. It is likely that current high house price levels will remain, but if government policy tackles those landowners and builders who have been profiteering on this crucial social need, and more social housing is built, then prices could be reined in.

A radical programme of compulsory purchasing of land in and around cities and towns, with fair payment to landowners is needed. Re-zoning by local authorities should not enrich landowners. The situation is too serious not to be addressed. If it is necessary, a referendum should be undertaken against the archaic special position of private property in the Constitution, in the interests of the public good. Government could also curb demand with some form of property taxes (if only to address the "polluter pays" principle for use of water, sewage and land), and it should end the regressive and costly housing subsidies and begin to build and assist in the financing of social housing.

In conclusion, the housing crisis is different to previous ones because it is not just affecting the poor, but also many on middle to higher incomes. Demand is real and will continue for many years. Potential supply is not too far off demand, but prices are very high. The government response has been weak.

CONCLUSION

The economic success of the Irish economy in the twelve years from 1987 has been superb. This is particularly true when compared to the previous decade, to Irish economic history, or to the performance of most other countries. Even the boom in the 1960s pales into the shadows compared to this success, which is well-rounded and deep.

Poverty does not parade itself in *Hello* magazine or in the gossip columns of the Sunday papers. Poverty is hidden. It is in remote and often in beautiful rural Ireland, as well as in endless, barren housing estates in Dublin, Cork and Limerick. Its victims are inarticulate and impotent. Yet there is a clear understanding of the problem by the excellent voluntary agencies which now focus on the causes and not just the symptoms of poverty. The radical reduction of poverty and unemployment must become the priority to complete the Irish success story.

The economic boom has helped reduce poverty and unemployment, but the disparity between the top and bottom of Irish society has increased. Policy did attempt to address the problem and every government has increased welfare a little above inflation. The state's Combat Poverty Agency has quantified the problem and has set out coherent policy proposals. Poverty and long-term unemployment are not easy problems to solve, but the resources, material and intellectual ability are there to do so.

The great job creation success of Ireland — surpassing even the best international success — has not been of benefit to most of the long-term unemployed, who number 52,000 people, many with families. And it is these families where serious poverty and disadvantage lie. Their children are the ones who are growing up without even indirectly experiencing employment in their homes.

There are over 30 active labour market schemes and many government departments and agencies dealing with the problem of unemployment, and public spending on them is high. Progress has been made and the unemployment rate, which was predicted to fall to seven per cent by 2005, had done so already by 1999. If the problem of long-term unemployment is easing, it is not because of conscious action by government or its agencies, but because of the economic boom. A hardcore of unemployed will remain, with intergenerational problems, unless a more concerted effort is made to deal with the issue.

It is beyond the scope of market solutions. The long-term unemployed require special attention and specific directed schemes. Training and upskilling are essential to give the unemployed the skills to get jobs. There has never been a better time for a successful assault on the persistent problem of long-term unemployment. The failure to use the tax system to deal with poverty is particularly shameful when there are large budget surpluses, falling national debt, less dependants.

The housing crisis is affecting the poorest most, as usually happens, but price rises have been so high that they have gone beyond the reach of many citizens. Demand is likely to remain strong for a decade or so, but there appears to be a strong redistribution of wealth to those with housing, to builders and particularly to those with land, away from those without property. This has both social and economic consequences — immigrants will not work in Ireland's tight labour market if too much of their income goes on housing. And others will be forced to leave.

A society cannot be proud of itself with such a wonderful economic success as Ireland's if it excludes such a large minority of its citizens. The failure to address poverty and high long-term unemployment is no credit to the Irish people. In James Plunkett's *Strumpet City*, the south Dublin bourgeoisie were cast as indifferent and indeed callous to the hunger and poverty of many of their fellow citizens during the 1913 Lockout. If the Irish middle classes were to feel that they would be cast like their forebears, then they might be shamed into action. Will history judge us as uncaring people who reaped the benefits of massive economic growth while many in our midst were in poverty and excluded from much of the best in their own society? The recent economic success, and especially the jobs boom, makes this unfinished business easier to complete successfully.

Chapter Eight

WILL THE BOOM CONTINUE?

The Irish economy's rate of growth will slow down to a level that is more sustainable in the longer term. It is unlikely to collapse, unless there is some unseen calamity. The boom has given Ireland the leg-up that it needed to catch up with the rest of Europe, and with good management, the country's economic welfare should be sustained into the future.

De Valera's dream of "frugal living" for the Irish people has been decisively rejected by them in the 1990s economic boom. Never were there so many Mercedes Benz, BMW, and Lexus cars choking the streets of its cities. Never were there so many ostentatious houses built on their half-acres, exotic foreign holidays and packed restaurants in every town, demonstrating how far the Irish have come from the "potato and buttermilk" diet of their forefathers.

What can go wrong? Many things can go wrong, and the main possibilities will be examined to see what is likely to change or fail. This chapter is speculative, but it is worth anticipating the areas of potential disaster and the reasons for them.

There are eight main threats to the boom:

1. The government could undermine the boom with poor policies.

2. Bottlenecks such as the housing crisis, lack of essential infrastructural investment and skilled workers could undermine economic progress.

3. A break-up of national partnership — extensive industrial unrest would discourage investment.

4. Over-dependency on a few products and a fall in demand could hit the economy hard.

5. Tax changes in the US or in the EU might cause disinvestment by MNCs.

6. A collapse in stock market prices in the US or elsewhere.

7. Lack of EU funds and the need for real CAP reform could lead to a recession.

8. A general downturn in the world economy could hit Ireland hard.

Each of these will examined to see which pose the greatest threats to the Irish economic boom.

1. The government could undermine the boom with poor policies.

Policy has been extremely influential in generating the Irish economic success of the 1990s. It has been seen that most of the key drivers in delivering the success are the result of domestic action by the government, institutions or the Irish people. Several of the main reasons for the success have been long in the making, such as the public investment in education or the change in the structure of the workforce from agriculture to services. While policy was a major determinant in these progressive changes, they took such a long time to develop that they would be hard to stop, even if a radical change in policy was tried. For example, the investment in education will bring benefits for a long time. Such investment in "human capital" is important for the economy.

Already the government's response to two major bottlenecks is very poor and does not augur well for sustained growth. These are the housing crisis and lack of necessary infrastructural investment. The third challenge — labour shortages — has yet to become a crisis.

Consumer inflation is unlikely to become a problem, though the rapid rise in asset prices is one already. Wage rises can lead to inflation, but with labour shortages, high productivity and high profits, it is likely that most companies can sustain a wage rise somewhat after Partnership 2000 terminates from the beginning of 2000.

There are areas of institutional change that require further reform if Ireland's economic progress is not to be halted. These include company law, tax reform, corruption at high levels and the implementation of existing laws.

International companies thinking of investing or just doing business in a small economy need to be assured that Ireland is a well-managed and well-regulated economy. They should not have to go to any great trouble to be assured of this. It should be automatic. This is not so today. There have been financial scandals at all levels, from theft of small savings to large sums being given by several businessmen to a former Taoiseach. Self-regulation has been seen to be ineffectual in Ireland in the 1990s. It cannot work in a small country where members of professions know one another and find it difficult to sanction each other. Effective systems of regulation and compliance are required so that foreigners doing business in Ireland come to expect, as a matter of course, standards at the highest international level.

Much of Irish business today is adverse to openness and transparency; not only does this undermine the confidence of foreign investors, but in an era of social partnership, workers should have access to company information as a right, not as a privilege. The hostility by the Stock Exchange and the Institute of Directors to even mild reform of disclosure of executive pay in 1999 demonstrates that the elitist attitude is still around in some influential quarters. On the other hand, the decision to set up a company law enforcement office, long overdue, is a good step.

Financial disclosure has improved in Ireland, but it is still behind most modern countries. Several areas of company law need reform, and the Irish Companies Office still does not contain basic corporate information required in a modern economy.

A reduction in growth could put the government under pressure to reduce spending, and this could lead to recession, wage demands to pay for reduced or privatised public services, etc. It is possible that a slow-down in growth would lead to pressure for fiscal rectitude, but with the gradual and continuing institution-alisation of the partnership approach, it is possible that negotiated cuts could be made where they hurt least.

But it is too much spending, not cuts, which economists tradi-tionally fear. Spending is as easy for a government to do as it is for Ivana Trump on Fifth Avenue. High spending could lead to another fiscal crisis. Again, it is hoped that the lessons of 1977 are etched deep on the minds of Irish people and would come to bear on any such reckless spending. The Exchequer is in very good health, with large surpluses on the current account and the na-tional debt is falling rapidly and should be the lowest in the union by the end of 1999.

The real problem is that the Irish government has a tendency to respond cyclically — to increase spending and/or reduce taxes in a time of boom and to do the opposite in times of recession — ac-centuating the business cycle. It is argued that it should be build-ing surpluses and setting them aside, cutting taxes or repaying the national debt, all of which it has been doing to some degree. However, the real need is for capital investment at a far faster rate than it has been undertaking.

An ageing population is a threat to some European countries, with a pensions "time-bomb" waiting to go off, but this is not a problem in Ireland as the percentage of the population which is ageing will not be significant for many years.

In conclusion, when the list of drivers in the boom is examined, it will be seen that several of them are independent of government and are part cultural, institutional or demographic. Therefore, they are unlikely to change overnight. The country's fiscal situa-tion is very strong and it would take a reckless government to undermine it. This augurs well for the short to medium term. However, its response to some problems such as housing and in-frastructural bottlenecks has been slow.

2. **Bottlenecks such as the housing crisis, lack of essential infra- structural investment and skilled workers could undermine economic progress.**

Bottlenecks do pose a threat to the economic boom, but most of them could be overcome with a little planning. The labour short- ages, if not tackled successfully, will be exacerbated by the hous- ing crisis. Meanwhile, progress in many other areas in Irish life should not be countered with despair on the issue of progress on urban transport! Aside from the lack of initiative on these bottle- necks, the economic management of the economy has been excel- lent, but it has been argued that it has been a relatively easy task with such levels of growth.

The housing crisis — discussed in Chapter 7— is already se- vere and it has been clear for some years that it was looming. It most affects those who will help to sustain the economy's prog- ress — young, mobile, skilled and professional workers. The fail- ure to invest anywhere near enough in infrastructure is adversely affecting the economy with delays, bottlenecks and frustration, which must lead to disinvestment. This has been at a time when the government's coffers are overflowing and, simultaneously, total (including capital) spending is at a record low level of under 30 per cent of GDP, below even that of the US. Clearly more capi- tal spending by the government in many areas is urgently re- quired, and the programme can be accelerated with appropriate and additional private investment through Public Private Partner- ships (PPPs). These are private investments in traditionally public projects such as roads, bridges, water and schools, in partnership with the public sector.

The main bottleneck problem is likely to be labour shortages. There is a shortage of certain skilled workers in Ireland. In Ken- mare (Dublin Economics Workshop) in 1997, Brendan Walsh of UCD forecast that the boom would lead to overheating of the la- bour market and there might be full employment (which he put at a relatively high 5 per cent) within a few years. It is now likely to fall to 5 per cent by 2000. Ireland has long had a common labour market with Britain and any shortage soon attracts workers from the UK, which has occurred. In 1997, Connell and Stewart had forecast net inward migration and that the population would grow to over 4 million by 2016. With the Single Market for labour, Ireland, with its booming economy, is now also attracting people from European countries other than Britain and elsewhere.

It is clear that when the Structural Funds reduce after 1999, the Irish government will be able to maintain the level of capital investment required for a modern, booming economy from its own funds. The Structural Funds gave Ireland a great start in investment in all kinds of capital projects such as better roads, ports, airports and telecommunications. After 2000, it would be self-defeating to wind down investment if economic growth, even at lower levels, is to be maintained. Not to invest in necessary capital projects is merely to postpone them. Such postponements or poor capital spending is already costing the country dearly.

The discipline imposed by the EU's planning requirements on major investments must be maintained and Ireland must not revert to the poorly planned approaches of the past. It has been seen that the European funds came at just the right time for Ireland, when there were major capital investment cuts. Investment in each sector had to be justified to Europe in detailed Operational Programmes. The establishment of bodies like the National Roads Authority meant that there is national co-ordination and planning of investment in major roads. The Environmental Protection Agency reports on drinking water, waste disposal, sewage treatment and integrated pollution control licensing, providing the basis for co-ordination and planning of environmental services to ensure best international practice. They also underline the need for more investment and environmental control.

The most glaring failure by government to deal with a major consequence of the boom is the traffic congestion in the capital city. There is such congestion in Dublin, other urban areas and main national routes that the economy is suffering from substantial loss of output. The number of cars has doubled in just a few years, and little has been done to curb those driving to work every day. The policy of "zero tolerance" on traffic offences in Dublin in the absence of a decent public transport system is not working. The city has a Dublin Transportation Office, but it has no teeth. There is no one government minister in charge of urban transport and it shows! The government's subsidy to the very poor city bus service, at a miserable 5 per cent of revenue, is the lowest for any European capital city. It is now clear that the bus services must be reformed, then generously subsidised, and that there should be one powerful Transport Authority for Dublin. The existing service is unreliable and expensive, without even a ticket transfer system. Without serious traffic management and a reduction in the numbers of private cars in the cities, the bus services cannot really be brought up to twenty-first century standard (speeds are lower than in the nineteenth century).

No single agency is in charge of Dublin's transport system. The Department of Public Enterprise does not have responsibility for co-ordinating the solution. The first thing that is required is one government Minister to be charged with urban transport for a term to get the city moving. This Minister could be given the brief of unblocking the infrastructural deficit nationally, but an accelerated programme for urban transport within a specified time should be their priority. The solution requires a multifaceted approach, including taxing congestion; taxing all free parking in urban centres, especially in private offices as benefit-in-kind (BIK); greatly increasing the subsidy to the bus companies, but only if they provide a reliable and efficient service; enforcing traffic laws; the acceleration of all urban transport systems; and the rapid completion of an *integrated* and expanded urban rail system, overseen by a dynamic Government Minister for Urban Transport or with the wider brief of Minister for Infrastructural Investment.

There is a planned Light Rail system, called Luas, but the company building it, CIE, has not even considered linking with the existing DART system! As if to bury Luas, the Minister for Public Enterprise, Mary O'Rourke, delayed it substantially by deciding to put it underground against her own expert advice, in spite of the unknown additional costs. If the private sector can build the underground section fast and for a reasonable price, it should be done as soon as possible under a Public Private Partnership (PPP).

The demographic dividend means that the numbers at primary and secondary schools will decline, but demand for third-level places will grow, as participation is at a lower rate than in other countries. Therefore the state will have to continue to invest in it. More effective training in industry and for the unemployed is required and, as the Structural Funds dry up, the State must take up this funding, as it is of vital importance in economic development. There will also be continued demand for housing and this market, which is overheating requires greater policy intervention by the State. Housing demand will be high for at least ten more years. It appears that the bottlenecks are already hitting the economy. While the main losers are residents, some multinationals are already put off by the traffic, high housing costs and labour shortages.

3. A break-up of national partnership — extensive industrial unrest would discourage investment.

There is now general consensus among rank and file trade unionists that the rises in basic pay under the Partnership 2000 agreement were too low compared to increases in profits. There is pressure on the trade union leadership because: (a) profits are booming — the annual growth in profits averages three times the growth in workers' earnings; (b) corporate tax rates have been reduced regularly (from 50 per cent in 1988 to 28 per cent in 1999) and will be further reduced progressively to 12.5 per cent by 2003 for all sectors of the economy; and (c) the share of national income going to profits has grown substantially in recent years.

To date, most trade unions have adhered to the terms of the agreements, though some stronger groups have made substantial gains above the term of Partnership 2000. These gains and the low nominal wage increases which workers see in their pay packets, and the fact that they see employers getting a double bonanza in both historically high profits and a gift (which was not even sought) from the government in the form of large reductions of corporation tax, may lead to industrial unrest. Workers would also see themselves as having to meet the shortfall in corporation tax of around £500 million a year with the large corporate tax rate reductions, though the exchequer surpluses have postponed this.

The agreement was fairly inflexible on pay, though there was an element of flexibility on profit-sharing and/or gain-sharing, which barely materialised. Most trade unionists and many employers do not clearly understand what these mean and most employers did not discuss these items.

Yet it has been seen that take-home pay under the agreement was far better than under the previous "free-for-alls", and if many workers recognise this, then another agreement could be forged.

It is still likely that a collapse of a national agreement would not lead to anarchy or even to extensive industrial unrest, because other institutional systems will come into play to replace it. If it does break down, a deal will still be hammered out in the public sector and workers in the leading sectors — the best paid workers — will gain most, as always happens under the so-called "free-for-all". With very high profit levels in Ireland, at 17 per cent on aggregate, the large shift in national income to profits and the labour shortages must mean that there will be substantial increases in wages in the early years of the twenty-first century. This will also help to reduce the demand for labour.

4. Over-dependency on a few products and fall in demand could hit the economy hard.

Ireland's manufacturing is concentrated in a few industries: office equipment, chemicals, pharmaceuticals and health care products. "Office equipment" is computers and related products, such as printers, ink cartridges, silicon chips, leads, software, etc. Ireland is clearly an industrial economy. But is it now over-dependent on, say, computers?

If there is a downturn in the demand for computers, will Ireland be hit? The most likely answer is no. It has already been seen that the exports are not just in personal computers, but in very many computer-related products, and they are from many different companies, and many markets, which spreads the risk.

There is already flexibility, as a few examples will show. The closure of a very large mainframe manufacturing factory by Digital in the mid-1980s appeared to demonstrate Ireland's vulnerability, but within a few years, the same company, Digital, was employing as many again in software development in Ireland. Another example is Apple Computers, Cork's biggest employer, with 1,600 direct employees in early 1999. Cork had been innovative during the lean years for Apple. However, in spite of a dramatic upturn in its fortunes with the iMac, which was made in Ireland, the bosses in California decided to move most of the jobs offshore. Intel's Irish operation is huge by Irish standards, employing 4,000. Intel is booming, but even if it was hit by a downturn, most jobs would still survive for a while until recovery. If it was to close, most workers could be absorbed elsewhere, especially if the boom continues.

But more importantly, sales of computers and related products are unlikely to fall significantly in the foreseeable future. The information age is spreading at a phenomenal rate. Computer penetration is still small; this second industrial revolution is only in its infancy. Competition is driving the cost of computers down; Ireland is responding by using its highly skilled workforce as a competitive advantage.

Computers themselves only amount to 2 per cent of US capital stock, but when all the equipment used for transmitting and processing information is added, this rises to 12 per cent. This is about the same as the railroads at their peak in the late nineteenth century, when they gave a big boost to America's economy (*The Economist*, 13 September 1997: 78).

As has been seen in Chapter Two, Northern Ireland was very prosperous in the nineteenth century with just a few industries, largely because of agglomeration economies. Similarly, the relatively high dependency on a few industries (although there are many products within these industries) of the Republics is not a major problem. It looks as if Ireland will be a major player in the second industrial revolution as many of the world's leading computer companies have branches here.

5. Tax changes in the US or EU might cause disinvestment by MNCs.

It has been seen that there is a cosy consensus of policy-makers and other opinion-formers in Ireland on the merits of the 12.5 per cent tax on manufacturing and export services. This consensus ignored the negative attitudes in other countries to it. The EU is not happy with it. Germany and Ireland's other partner states in Europe are not happy with it. The US government has long been unhappy with it.

They tolerated it because Ireland is small. The two other reasons for their indulgence were that it was due to expire in 2010 and Ireland was relatively poor. Both of the subsidiary reasons have gone. It has been seen that the government intends, not alone to extend it indefinitely, but to attempt to overcome other country's objections by charging *all* company taxes at only 12.5 per cent.

The European Commission agreed to this change, with much reluctance. Ireland lost a lot of goodwill from other member states. Ireland is no longer poor. Other countries are strongly of the opinion that it should no longer be allowed to do unneighbourly things, such as being a tax haven for the world's richest companies in the heart of the Single Market. The concept of a tax haven, which bids down company taxes within Europe, is also against the principle of the Single Market. The issue of harmonisation of taxes is still a live one, albeit within bands rather than at specific rates.

If Ireland is still dependent on a low tax regime as one of its key artificial attractions to foreign investment, then it will have failed to diversify and develop. It has been demonstrated in the preceding chapters that Ireland is well on the road to sustainable development that is not dependent on single factors like a low tax on profits. Therefore, if this tax were to be raised to levels acceptable to trading partners, particularly our partners in the European Union, it is unlikely to lead to recession.

Therefore the government should indicate soon that it will increase the rate of corporation tax to 18 or 20 per cent. At the very least, the 12.5 per cent rate must become a minimum tax, not the maximum. This would send positive signals to our European partners and with labour shortages emerging, Ireland no longer needs to offer this artificial, wasteful and inequitable incentive. Some plants, at the end of their productive life, may pull out, but they were going to do so anyway. The low tax rate has served Ireland well and will do so for some more years. By then, other, less artificial, attractions to foreign investment should be well developed.

6. The fall in EU funds and the need for CAP reform lead to a recession.

The importance of the European funds in assisting the Irish economy were examined in Chapter Three and it was seen that these funds (including the Common Agricultural Policy) played an important role, amounting to 2 per cent of GNP. Ireland secured a further £2.9 billion in European Structural Funds in 1999 for the period from 2000 to 2006. While this is less than half of the previous tranche, it is a lot more than many expected. It is clear that after then, Ireland's living standards will have reached such a high level that the country will no longer qualify for much in transfers.

The reform of the Common Agricultural Policy appeared to be inevitable, for four reasons, up to 1999. Firstly, the enlargement of the Union after 2005, with the mainly agricultural Eastern European countries joining, means that before this happens, the Common Agricultural Policy would have to be reformed; otherwise it would be too costly for the Union to bear. Secondly, the EU will come under intense pressure to cut agricultural subsidies at the next round of world trade talks under the World Trade Organisation. The US has reformed its agricultural subsidies and its support system is no longer linked to production. It will not tolerate any further tardiness by the EU on CAP reform.

The third pressure to reform CAP should have been dealt with in the negotiations in 1999 on the EU Budget ceiling for the following six years. They should have focused on the largest item of spending, the CAP, which comprises almost half of the Budget, and the next largest item, the Structural Funds. However, no real CAP reform was agreed in 1999. The final reason why the CAP will have to be reformed is that when reform was suggested in 1992 by Agricultural Commissioner Ray McSharry, it was opposed strongly — watered down, but reformed nonetheless — and today's consensus is that it was both necessary and worthwhile.

Ireland does gain overall from the CAP. Irish agriculture is potentially capable of being competitive and of facing a freer market for agricultural produce. If the government, under pressure from the powerful farmers' lobbies, were to "re-nationalise" the huge subsidy system (the Irish taxpayers used to pay the subsidies to the farmers before EEC membership), it would cost the taxpayer dearly and Irish farmers would continue to be insulated from the marketplace. Such a drastic and costly policy would be compounded by the phasing out of the Structural Funds at the same time.

It is not beyond the realms of reason to suppose that Irish governments would re-nationalise agriculture, at least to some extent. Since Ireland joined the EEC in 1973, successive governments have had a very simple policy — maximise the size of the CAP budget. Consumer interests were ignored, and only a few politicians opposed these policies in the past. They have not favoured a freer market for agriculture, and in this sense, Irish governments have been very anti-market! But Irish farmers are resilient and have shown themselves to be capable of responding quickly to change.

The reduction in the Structural and Cohesion Funds and the reform of the CAP, which were expected in 1999, must still be tackled before enlargement. Therefore it should be planned for by prudent policy-makers. These two changes will not pose major problems for Ireland as a whole.

7. A collapse in stock market prices in the US or elsewhere.

It has been seen that multinational investment has played an important role in the boom and US companies are predominant in Ireland. These companies mirror the Dow Jones or S&P indices, which are exceptionally high in mid-1999. The companies' investment plans reflect both the real world of business and the value the stock market places on them. In the US there has been a bull market for several years. The S&P 500 index rose by a substantial 174 per cent between the end of 1994 and 1988. In the same four years, corporate profits rose by less than 40 per cent. Thus the driver of the stock rise has been expectations, not company performance. The price/earnings (P/E) ratio doubled from 14 to 28, and 80 per cent of this is due to expectations.

Fortune (1 February 1999) which likes to be optimistic on shares, said "the stock market party may soon be over". It examined nine large companies (including Coke, Microsoft, IBM and Dell — all of which have operations in Ireland) and calculated that if they were to achieve a third less than their share growth since 1994 over the next five years, then they would need to generate 20 per cent return on capital a year. This would be very difficult to do. For example, Coke would need to grow profits by 24.2 per cent a year to generate a 20 per cent annual return to 2003. It would have to treble sales and in fact supply all of the world's soft drinks (it sells half now). It pointed out that several large blue chip companies had already issued profits warnings in early 1999, including Coke, Caterpillar, 3M, Mattel and Compaq.

The average rise in profits historically in the US has been 7 per cent a year and the P/E around 14. Even if there was a rise in profits to 8 or 9 per cent, this would bring the P/E to 18, well below recent performance.

A stock crash would both hit the companies and cut through the personal net wealth of the senior executives who pay themselves very large share options, and this would hit their confidence and judgement. In the old days they were paid mainly salaries and concentrated more on the business than on the value which the stock market placed on it. There has been a bull market since 1982, and only in 1990 and 1994 did the indices fall. Some people appear to believe that stocks and shares only go up.

The gap between the real value of many US companies and that which the stock market has placed on them is very large. Many believe that there will be what is euphemistically called a "stock market correction" soon. This could take any form and if there is a crash, it would have a major effect on Ireland. If it is severe, it could lead to a world recession and a reduction in investment in Ireland. This would probably hit house prices first, and jobs next. However, there is little or nothing that anyone can do about this, other than be aware that it may occur.

8. A general downturn in the world economy could hit Ireland hard.

Some people believe that "the boom won't last for long", or "it will fizzle out", or "it's a flash in the pan". It is true that there could be a downturn in the world economy. It could either be a sudden major crisis which adversely affects trade— such as another oil crisis or war (like the Gulf War) —it could take the form of a slow recession in the main European markets, or it could be the result of a trade war.

Such scenarios are possible. It is extremely difficult to predict the future. A big crisis could suddenly emerge. It is more likely, however, that a slow downturn in the world economy would lead to a recession.

A major world crisis would mean a sharp downturn, which would hit a small trade-dependent economy like Ireland very hard. This would rapidly reduce most economic activity and lead to a sharp recession, with all the usual economic problems — rising unemployment, a financial crisis for the state, etc. A general downturn or slowdown internationally would also hit the economy. It was argued in Chapter Four that many of Ireland's exports have been relatively insulated from small recessions in our main markets. If there were deeper and more prolonged recessions, then the Irish economy would be more adversely affected. Even with a small downturn in the world economy, many economic agencies still forecast good rates of growth for Ireland. It should be noted that many economists are like stock market analysts and brokers — they tend to run in packs, in the same direction, and at the same time.

However, the Irish economic boom has lasted for 12 years to 1999. It has been prolonged and is now deeply rooted within the economy. There are no major obstacles on the horizon. Most forecasters are predicting that it will last at least several more years.

The ESRI's Medium Term Review (1997), the most respected and detailed of all forecasts, said "the Irish economy looks set to grow at more than 5 per cent a year over the next decade, raising the standard of living to at least the EU average". It had forecast that unemployment would fall to less than 7 per cent in 2005. This target was surpassed in 1998. It said that this would be achieved, not by emigration as in the past, but by "continuing buoyant growth in employment well into the next decade".

The ESRI set out the policies required to achieve this forecast, and holds that most of them are within our control:

- Public finance and social partnership

- Policies aimed at minimising congestion

- Institutional reform

- Continuing role of education and training

- Policy on the environment

- Preparing for EMU membership (which has been successfully achieved).

The ESRI had forecast that growth (GNP) would be around 5.5 per cent in the second half of the 1990s (around 8 per cent was achieved) and it would be around 5 per cent until 2005, and then about 4 per cent to 2010. The forecast on disposable income growth was a little lower than this but still well above that of most countries, giving most people rises in real incomes. Inflation would remain low and employment continue to grow, giving "an exceptional performance by the standards of the past and by the standards of the rest of the EU" (ESRI, 1997: vii).

The ESRI had also forecast an excellent fiscal performance, with the debt to GNP ratio being reduced to only 33 per cent by 2010, no government borrowing soon and budget surpluses by about 2005 — providing there were no shocks or surprises. The outcome is already far better than this forecast. If, however, there are serious problems, then the forecast could be reduced by around 2 per cent a year, it said. Therefore the growth in GNP would be in the range of 3.5 to 6 per cent a year, with some years fluctuating. The ESRI sees Ireland as having come of age, of having had a renaissance.

The European Commission described Ireland's performance with superlatives such as a "remarkable performance," "exceptional" and "remarkably successful". In its 1997 Annual Economic Report (February), it forecast that there would be continued growth but it would be slower "over the medium term." Its projections were 8 per cent GDP growth in 1996, 6 per cent in 1997 and over 5 per cent in 1998, compared to between 2 and 3 per cent for the EU. In October, it revised the growth statistics upwards. The IMF had offered its most optimistic report on the world economy in decades. It saw the prospects for Europe as particularly good. It did not anticipate the Asian crisis.

The OECD, slow to praise, described Ireland as having had "an outstanding economic performance" helped by "sound economic management". It forecast that "the Irish economy seems likely to maintain its rapid pace of growth. The increase in GNP may total over 12 per cent in 1997 and 1998" (OECD, 1997). It concluded that GNP growth of the level of 5.5 per cent to 6 per cent a year "should be sustainable in the period to 2002" (OECD, 1997: 32). In its 1999 country report, OECD said that "Ireland can potentially continue to grow at superior rates", and as we have seen, called the Irish performance "stunning" and "astonishing" (OECD, 1999: 4).

In conclusion, it is difficult, if not impossible, to forecast what the future holds, but most agencies see a rosy future for Ireland for the next five to ten years, based on real economic fundamentals.

CONCLUSION

This chapter has set out some of the potential problems that could occur in the Irish economy. Many people wonder if the current boom can be sustained. It has been worth anticipating some of the problems and the possible results if they do emerge. Some reports from the main economic agencies that make forecasts have been assessed and it can be seen that they are optimistic, not just for the next year or even two years, but for many more years. There could be a major crisis, but a slowdown is more likely to occur and the policy challenge is to maintain a strong level of sustainable growth. Even a slowdown from the high rates of growth of recent years is likely to still be high by international standards. Many of the potential problems can be dealt with by the Irish themselves. Ireland's future looks good, for the first time in a very long time. In spite of globalisation, its future is largely in its own hands.

Chapter Nine

CONCLUSION

Ireland has moved dramatically from being one of the poorest countries in the industrialised world to close to the European Union average and will soon be one of its richer countries. It has had the fastest rate of growth in the world in the last years of the twentieth century and employment, stagnant for most of the century, grew rapidly in the 1990s — with a staggering increase of 45 per cent between 1987, when the boom began, and 2000.

A returned emigrant or a first time visitor cannot but be impressed by the sheer buzz, the excitement, the vibrancy all over Ireland. Even the once dreary small rural towns and villages are now brightly painted and lively. The country is full of young people, the skyline of the capital city is criss-crossed with cranes, the streets are choked with traffic, and people are walking with an air of confidence which they never had before. They are more economically independent and educated than ever, they are working harder and more effectively and they now expect the best from their compatriots.

Major reports of the main economic forecasting agencies were assessed in the previous chapter and were found to be optimistic on Ireland's economic prospects, some for the next year or even two years, but others for many more years.

Investment in people has been substantial and industry and services are modern and approaching world class standards, and infrastructure is being slowly modernised. Many employers and trade unions have a new outlook and the old adversarial ways have been replaced by greater participation and co-operation.

Thus the country is well equipped to move forward at a rapid pace.

This book has examined the performance of the Irish economy over the years from 1987 and has found that there has been a sustained economic boom. Each year since 1987, economic growth (GNP) has averaged 5.2 per cent a year and it has been even higher in the last few years, averaging 8 per cent in real GNP growth in the six years to 1999. The size of the economy has doubled between 1987 and 1998. GDP growth is higher than GNP growth in Ireland, and in some years its growth has exceeded 10 per cent. In the six years to 1999, it averaged almost 9 per cent each year. Growth rates of between 2 and 3 per cent are generally accepted by economists as being as good as it gets. Ireland's rates of growth are far above the rates of other countries. And it is expected that the rates of growth, while slowing, will still be high over the next five years or more.

The rate of growth of employment has been astonishing. A total of 513,000 extra jobs have been created in the period — a growth rate of 47 per cent. This is higher than even the lauded US jobs machine, particularly in the later years from 1994. Total employment had been more or less stagnant for seven decades and was actually lower than at Independence until the mid-1990s.

A key contribution to this growth has been the labour inputs, including the rapid productivity growth, the increase in the labour force, increased participation of women, of the former unemployed and of immigrants and, importantly, in the quality of the workforce, which is better educated and more skilled.

There are many Irish people returning from abroad and there is the relatively new phenomenon of voluntary emigration of well-educated people, who typically return with experience. Inflation is low, the trade surplus is high, the country is running a budget surplus, the national debt is falling rapidly as a proportion of GDP, profits are booming and workers' real after-tax earnings are growing by a reasonable amount each year. There is a new approach to work and industrial relations, and there is a more consensual and participative economy and society than before.

After examining the economic history of Ireland, the figures were analysed to see if the boom was real, prolonged and well balanced in all areas of the economy. Analysis confirmed that the boom was very real, sustained and balanced. It was also found that there are still serious problems in the Irish economy that have not been dealt with, even though there are the resources to do so, particularly in recent years. The road to the radical reduction of poverty and long-term unemployment is mapped out in many studies. Tax reform and urban public transport have not been addressed. Then there are problems which have emerged because of the economic success — a severe housing shortage and a pressing need for investment in infrastructure — roads, bypasses, bridges, school buildings, water and waste treatment and European-style (people-centred) public transport for its cities.

In the initial years of economic growth, the figures did not translate into jobs or increased living standards, and it was the foreign press and commentators who noticed the boom before the Irish did. There was a caution initially, but the physical manifestations of it became difficult to ignore, in the massive increases in the numbers of cars, in house prices, in the new factories and offices and eventually in jobs. It is believed that the Irish economic boom will continue for several more years, if there is no major external crisis.

The "feel-good factor" of increasing incomes and wealth does stand the test of analysis. It is not just happening in Dublin, or in the electronics industry, or just for some people. All economic indicators have greatly improved in the decade under review. All areas of the economy have benefited and continue to benefit.

This economic "miracle" is, of course, not a miracle. It did not just happen. It was created. If there was luck involved, it was that many economic, social and political forces came together in a benign conjuncture in which the economic boom took off. After a long history of poverty, two centuries of massive emigration, with over five million having emigrated since the Famine and deprivation for many, Ireland finally entered a virtuous circle, where each factor in the success reinforced other factors to generate rapid, positive economic improvements.

In the nineteenth century, was it British rule that held back Ireland's industrial development? Ireland, like other parts of the then United Kingdom, did not suffer active discrimination, but because its industries, such as they were, could not compete with superior British factory products, it did not develop, except in the north-east.

The Industrial Revolution began in Britain, where it benefited from close, large markets and from coal and iron. It was also the leader in mechanisation and it had an early concentration of industries and scale. Northern Ireland got a kick-start in the first wave of the Industrial Revolution.

Ireland's economic history shows that it was in the shadow of the world's leading economic power. It was very difficult to compete with the power of British industry. Other regions in the UK suffered relative decline too as the developing clusters of industry sucked in labour and capital, producing cheap goods with the latest mechanisation and economies of scale.

There was a massive decline in population after the Famine, due to emigration and reduced fertility. There was large-scale de-industrialisation and agriculture shifted from tillage to pasture in response to demand for beef in Britain. Those who stayed in Ireland saw their incomes rise, even without innovation or industry. The per capita increase in income was largely a result of the declining population. These changes led to a deep conservatism, which was to remain dominant until the 1960s, when increased economic wealth finally allowed people to express differing views.

The first government after Independence pursued free trade policies until the late 1920s and adhered to the ruling economic orthodoxy of *laissez-faire*. However, it did establish a few state companies in the late 1920s and this was built upon by Fianna Fáil, for pragmatic rather than ideological reasons. Despite this, these companies were to become some of the largest in Ireland, becoming centres of excellence for management, production, marketing (e.g. Kerrygold) and some research and development, and a number of them expanded overseas.

In this century, Ireland experienced free trade, protectionism (and an economic war), and then free trade again. In each case, Ireland was following world trends, though the type of protectionism prevalent in the 1930s did not help develop the country, but rather held it back. Its laws did not allow foreigners to own more than 50 per cent of a company; it was also illogical, as there were many exemptions, many for political rather than economic reasons.

The major lesson of the 1930s was not the economic war with Britain, which Ireland both won and lost, but that the government did not encourage indigenous firms to export. Therefore, most of them were unable to compete when the country eventually opened up. Ireland had nurtured weak industries in its protectionist nursery.

Ireland opened up, late, to foreign direct investment in the late 1950s. Had it opened up a decade earlier, then the lean, mean and miserable 1950s could have been avoided. But there were intense debates going on for many years behind the scenes, with disagreements between de Valera and Lemass.

The radical change in industrial policy — called the "visible hand" by conservatives — to encourage foreign investment in the early 1960s was very successful, encouraging excellent rates of economic growth. The type of industrial policy put in place in the 1960s was largely unchanged until the mid-1980s. The visible hand was more the "open hand" than the "pointing hand". It was a hand open with grants and tax expenditures, but it was non-directive. Irish industrial policy was based on state intervention on a large scale, in terms of cost in grants, tax expenditures and the size of the state agencies engaged in the work. The first wave of foreign investors in the 1960s boosted growth rates substantially. Indigenous industry was weak and after Ireland joined the EEC in 1973, it did not grow.

In the mid-1980s, policy did switch to a somewhat more directed approach and, not surprisingly, the results were better by all criteria — jobs, linkages, etc. However, there had been a shake-out of industry in the 1980s with a gross loss of hundreds of thousands of manufacturing jobs. Those firms remaining were the survivors, capable of international competition and were able to demonstrate export capacity and growth in the 1990s. This was an important contributor to the boom. Prior to this, additional jobs created by MNCs were just covering the job losses of Irish firms. In the early 1990s, the level of net job losses in indigenous industry slowed, stopped and reversed. The additional jobs from both foreign and indigenous sectors meant a large increase in the numbers of jobs and, as Irish firms have greater linkages into the economy than foreign firms, there has been a greater economic effect in the domestic economy. By 1999, almost half of all manufacturing jobs were in foreign-owned companies? After 2000, they will employ more than Irish manufacturers do. Most jobs being created are in services, including international services.

Ireland declined from one of the richer countries in the world at the beginning of the twentieth century, but it begins the twenty-first century again up close to the top of the league of wealthy countries. This book has shown how Ireland finally step-changed in the late 1980s and became efficient and competitive.

Landes attempts to find out why some countries are wealthy and why others are poor (1998). He places a lot of emphasis on innovation and also on the environment which engenders it. He focuses on such historical detail as the invention of spectacles, which doubled the working life of craftsmen. He looks at natural endowments, which of course matter less today, on imperial power, on war, the role of culture in responding to markets, as well as the role of the state. This book shows that there are lessons for other countries, but there were a multitude of factors which came together at one time and there were also cultural influences. There is no simple formula to emulate. However, countries do not necessarily remain poor, and the correct policies can deliver change. There are, however, major outstanding problems that have yet to be dealt with if the success is to be more complete.

Ireland has serious problems which its leaders have yet to face up to directly. There is extensive poverty, and while the poor are somewhat better off at the end of the successful period to 1999, the boom has accentuated the differences between the top and bottom of society. There is a consensus that much needs to be done about poverty and long-term unemployment. While both problems are complex, there appears to be a high level of indifference or even a hardening in some quarters not to share the new wealth with those who have not benefited from the success. Failure to deal with these problems detracts from Ireland's otherwise excellent economic success.

Ireland has had a long, sad economic history, with too much grinding poverty and mass emigration for two centuries. The rapid gain in overall wealth, which takes Ireland near the top of the league of wealthiest countries, must also give pause. As wealth and income distribution are fairly unequally distributed within the country, some people have being doing spectacularly well in a very short period.

Do the Irish people wish to pursue an endless consumption of material goods for their own sake? Is the emergence of Ireland as a leading consumer society, where success is measured largely by material goods, the best way forward? It can be argued that one of the benefits of being a latecomer is that the country avoided going through the heavy industrial phase and as a modern economy, its environment is largely intact and it now uses far less material inputs. In the new century, consumption will consist less of material goods and more of services, which is more sustainable. Nonetheless, endless consumption and accumulation is the hallmark and the driving force of the modern capitalist economy and society. The politician or leader who believes they know when it is time to call halt, when to decide that we have enough, is facing a difficult if not impossible task.

Without a measure of economic growth, economies stagnate. The US and European economies are growing at a far lower rate now than in the post-war Golden Era. The challenge is to make this growth self-sustaining. As Ireland is now reaching average

European standards of living, it can afford to slow down. All economies will have to grow at levels that are truly sustainable.

In spite of domestic inequality and vast global problems of starvation and poverty, as we move into the twenty-first century, society's values are firmly focused on economic growth, on production, on consumption and on endless demand for new products and services, however trifling.

A brief review of what can go wrong showed that many of the potential problems can be resolved with foresight and planning. Most external factors are beyond influence in the short to medium term. Investment in infrastructure should continue at a high level, even after the Structural Funds dry up. There is a housing crisis where even middle income people cannot buy their own homes. It has been seen that supply can match demand, but the government must get off its hands and act against the minority who are profiteering — builders and particularly landowners. It also needs to accelerate the provision of integrated social housing. Action in dealing with urban traffic congestion should also be a priority, as it is hindering economic activity as well as frustrating so many people.

The tax system is overdue for reform and this would have a major impact on the problem of poverty and also on levelling the playing field by helping make the economy more competitive. The failure to reform the tax system, even when Tribunals, family feuds and criminal investigations in the 1990s revealed negligence by the tax authorities, demonstrates a stasis in tackling urgent problems.

The disclosures of the Flood and Moriarty Tribunals in 1999 of payments to politicians, of tens of millions of untaxed money hidden away in offshore accounts, etc., showed that the "nod and wink" is still alive in important quarters. Indeed the Tribunals have revealed that some politicians have even enacted laws solely to reduce wealthy individual's taxes! People of substantial means have waged some very tough campaigns against even mildly redistributive taxes, and many in the middle classes, with little to gain personally, have weighed in against the mildest reform.

There was concerted action against the wealth tax in the 1970s; a campaign for the abolition of a negligible property tax in the 1990s; and the hundreds of millions of pounds taken in amnesties was only the tip of the iceberg.

A small economy that is dependent on foreign investment should not tolerate dubious practices in business, government and financial circles for long. In the 1990s, there has been widespread exposure of very questionable activities by a small minority of powerful people, assisted with acumen by some professionals. This has been exposed by the theft of money from many small savers by "pillars of the establishment" in their marbled offices, hiding behind professional associations, by widespread tax evasion, dubious property transactions, money hidden in offshore accounts, and the role of certain professionals in laundering drug money. This demands the ending of so-called "self-regulation" of the professions, particularly those in financial services. Irish company law also needs strengthening and enforcement. The ethical practice of business has to become synonymous with high standards, if Ireland is to continue to be a favoured place to do business.

There was a great increase in new jobs in the period under review, 1987–1999. This job creation is better than any other economy and was hugely superior to previous achievements. There has been a large fall in unemployment, though long-term unemployment is still high. Strong, coherent policy intervention is required. The required policies are reasonably well developed, and if they require more money to be successful, this investment in human capital would be well spent. These policies would also help address the modern problems of drugs, poverty, crime and alienation.

Many books on the Irish economy have been doom-laden, with titles like *Ireland in Crisis* by Raymond Crotty, *The Irish Disease* by Cathal Guiomard, *Black Hole, Green Card* by Fintan O'Toole and *Poverty Amid Plenty* by Peadar Kirby. Others have been critical, including those by Joe Lee, Eoin O'Malley, Kieran Kennedy et al., Tim Callan et al., Richard Breen et al. and Peter Shirlow et al. (the latter included this author). These writers argued forcefully that Ireland had many economic and social problems requiring radical action and that policy was not addressing them. Each had their policy prescriptions. Their criticisms were correct at the time. However, things have improved radically in Ireland in a short time. Yet much remains to be done.

A number of reasons for the economic success in Ireland were outlined in this book, with many more within those headings, and it is argued that no single factor was over-determining. All the influences came together to reinforce one another. It would be simplistic to say that the boom was unleashed by the flow of EU Structural and Cohesion Funds. They helped, as did the inflow of investment from MNCs, but the boom was not the result of any one influence.

The exogenous reasons were the external environment which is vital for a small trade-dependent economy, EU funds, the money invested by MNCs and the revolution in communications, which undermined the argument that our woes were due to our status as "the island, off the island, off Europe". Foreign investment was also vital for jobs, technology and management transfers. Fiscal reform, the stable economic environment and changes in education, attitudes, self-confidence and family size were part of a quiet revolution in economy and society. This had been progressing for some time and reached a critical phase in the 1990s and all the factors combined to give the lift-off required to create the Irish boom.

Other domestic elements include the consensus at national level, where the social partners agreed on many aspects of the economy and society over the medium term, in addition to the growth level of earnings. The consensus approach is slowly moving to enterprise level where new forms of working, and a shift to more devolved decision-making and participation, are assisting in making industry and services more flexible and competitive. There is also a shift to a more open and participative society. There is a clearer understanding by most of the often misunderstood word "competitiveness". The state monopolies and other state companies have faced competition through commercialisation, rather than privatisation. There had not been much privatisation until 1999 and where it occurs, it is generally dealt with through consensus with unions and employees. There is also a good understanding of the need for change because of the impact of technology and EU rules on competition and state aids.

The contribution of confidence-building is important. This has long been recognised by business people, but it is vital for the economy. It involves more than businesses taking risks, but includes positive attitudes by people at all levels throughout enterprise. A collective shift upwards in confidence can be a boost to an economy, manifested in extra consumer and producer spending on investment and consumables, which in turn encourages others to invest in the country.

The role of policy has been emphasised. In this age of globalisation, it is easy to neglect the importance of the state and its institutions. The decisions to invest in education and to encourage multinational investment were policy decisions. As a result of government decisions, Ireland joined the EEC in 1973, accepted the Structural and Cohesion Funds and invested them wisely. It was the people themselves who put a premium on education, on consensus-building, and on the move from adversarial industrial relations; and government policies reflected these changes. By having less children after 1980 the people themselves generated the demographic dividend and the election of Mary Robinson in 1990 symbolised how attitudes had changed.

The figures on growth, employment, inflation, interest rates, the balance of payments, productivity, etc., have all shown that Ireland has, at last, picked itself up and run and run and run. It has run as fast as a Tiger.

Many economists, including the prestigious Economic and Social Research Institute, forecast that the boom will continue for at least several more years, though at a slower rate. The boom is not a "flash in the pan". It has not been done with mirrors. It shows the hallmarks of a trend that has set down deep roots in investment and work, in the education system, in attitudes, in infrastructural investment, in foreign investment, in the approach to problems and in the way people work and even interact as consumers. The Irish people appear to have built a launch pad for continued success, which is well constructed, has good foundations and is strong.

Ireland has beautiful, unspoilt countryside, a very low population density and has everything going for it. In their history, the Irish people have never had such opportunity. They are now particularly well equipped, with a new confidence, a sound economy and a new sense of identity as members of the European Union. They have generally competent management and an educated and flexible workforce which is conscious of international trends and developments. Ireland made excellent progress since 1987. It enters the new Millennium confident, prosperous and capable.

APPENDIX

APPENDIX: FOREIGN COMPANIES INVESTING IN IRELAND RECENTLY

Company Name	Location	Origin	Number of Jobs	Product
3Com	Dublin	US	775	Computer network products
ABB Industrial Sys. Ltd.	Louth	Switzerland	40	Software centre
Abbot Laboratories	Sligo	US	50	Manufacture of diagnostic kits and sterilisation facility
Accuris Telecom Software Solutions	Dublin	JV	315	Software development centre
Allied Signal Ireland Ltd.	Waterford	US	150	Automotive turbocharger components
Alps Europe Ireland Ltd.	Co. Kerry	Japan	250	Automotive parts manufacturing
Ascend Communications	Dublin	US	580	Customer Support
Bard	Galway	US	500	Medical instruments
Bausch & Lomb Ireland	Waterford	US	100	Contact lens manufacturing
Berg Electronics Corp.	Cork	US	310	Connectors for telecommunications and computer industries
Berlitz (Irl.) Ltd.	Dublin	Japan	240	Software localisation

Company Name	Location	Origin	Number of Jobs	Product
Bertelsmann Ag	Dublin	Germany	56	Administration and debt collection
Boston Scientific Corp.	Galway	US	1,000	Medical device company
Citibank	Dublin	US	1,300	Service centre and processing
Dell	Limerick	US	3,000	PCs
Der Ireland	Galway	Germany	175	Shared services and teleservices operation
Deutsche Lufthansa Ag	Dublin	Germany	45	Airline reservation call centre
Digital Equipment Ire	Dublin	US	225	PC technical support centre
Donnelly Mirrors Ltd.	Co. Kildare	US	190	Automotive mirrors
DSC Communications	Louth	US	475	Digital switching equipment for telecommunications
Eastman Kodak	Youghal	US	360	Recordable compact disks
Eastman Kodak	Limerick	US	400	Manufacture of film cassettes for new advanced photo system
Gateway 2000 (Irl.) Ltd.	Dublin	US	1,200	PC production, telemarketing
Guidant Corporation	Tipperary	US	518	Medical devices

Company Name	Location	Origin	Number of Jobs	Product
Hertz Corp.	Dublin	UK	600	Telephone-based service centre
Hertz International Ltd.	Dublin	UK	60	Telemarketing
Hewlett Packard	Co. Kildare	US	1,000	Manufacture of printer pens for inkjet printers
IBM Corp.	Dublin	US	2,850	Project-manufacture of memory storage disks
IBM Ireland	Dublin	US	100	European network centre
KAO Corporation	Dublin	Japan	300	CD-ROMs manufactured
Kostal	Cork	Germany	850	Auto components
Motorola	Cork	US	300	Software development and support
Norsk Data Ire Ltd.	Dublin	Norway	115	Test and logistics centre
Oracle Corp.	Dublin	US	400	Telemarketing centre
Organon (Ire) Ltd.	Dublin	Netherlands	170	Pharmaceuticals
Quintiles	Dublin	US	180	Clinical trials, management and share services

Company Name	Location	Origin	Number of Jobs	Product
Sanmina Corp.	Co. Dublin	US	250	Customised integrated manufacturing
Saturn Solutions	Dublin	Canada	180	CD-ROM
Seagate Technology	Co. Cork	US	1,000	Data storage magnetic disks
Sherwood Medical Industries of Ireland	Offaly	US	102	Medical devices
Shinko Microelectronics	Dublin	Japan	440	Semiconductors
Sitel TMS	Dublin	US	400	Bulk Pharmaceuticals
Smithkline Beecham	Waterford	US	40	Drugs and pharmaceuticals
Wyeth Medica Ireland	Kildare	US	320	Pharmaceuticals
Xerox	Dundalk	US	1,450	Colour toner production

Source: IDA

BIBLIOGRAPHY

Agenda 2000 (1997), Brussels: European Commission.

Bacon, Peter and Brendan Walsh (1996), *Exports and Employment: the Irish Perspective 1985–95*, Dublin: Irish Trade Board.

Bacon, Peter et al. (1998) *An Economic Assessment of Recent House Price Development: Report submitted to the Minister for Housing and Urban Renewal*, Dublin: Government Publications.

Barioch, P. (1981), "The Main Trends in National Economic Disparities since the Industrial Revolution" in P. Barioch and M. Levy-Leboyer (eds.) *Disparities in Economic Development since the Industrial Revolution*, New York: St Martin's Press.

Barry, Frank (ed.) (1999), *Understanding Ireland's Economic Growth*, Hampshire: Macmillan.

Barry, Frank, John Bradley and Eoin O'Malley (1999), "Indigenous and Foreign Industry" in Frank Barry (ed.), *Understanding Ireland's Economic Growth*, Hampshire: Macmillan.

Beckett, J.C. (1977), *A Short History of Ireland*, London: Hutchinson.

Best, Michael H. (1990), *The New Competition: Institutions of Industrial Restructuring*, London: Polity.

Better Local Government: Programme for Change (1996), Dublin: Stationery Office.

Bew, Paul and Henry Patterson (1982), *Sean Lemass and the Making of Modern Ireland, 1945–66*, Dublin: Gill and Macmillan.

Barry, Frank, John Bradley and Aoife Hannon (1999), "The European Dimension" in Frank Barry (ed.), *Understanding Ireland's Economic Growth*, Hampshire: Macmillan.

Bradley J., J. Fitzgerald, I. Kearney, G. Boyle, R. Breen, S. Shorthall, J. Durkan, A. Reynolds-Feighan and E. O'Malley (1992), *The Role of the Structural Funds: Analysis of the Consequences for Ireland in the Context of 1992*, Dublin: ESRI, No 13.

Breathnach, Proinnsias (1998), "Exploring the 'Celtic Tiger' Phenomenon", *European Urban and Regional Studies*, Vol. 5, No. 4, London: Sage.

Breen, Richard, Damian Hannon, David B. Rottman and Christopher T. Whelan (1990), *Understanding Contemporary Ireland: State and Class and Development in the Republic of Ireland*, Dublin: Gill and Macmillan.

Callan, T., B. Nolan, B.J. Whelan, C.T. Whelan and J. Williams (1996), *Poverty in the 1990s*, Dublin: Oak Tree Press, ESRI and Combat Poverty Agency.

Callan, T. and B. Nolan (1999a), "Income Inequality in Ireland in the 1980s and 1990s" in Frank Barry (ed.), *Understanding Ireland's Economic Growth*, Hampshire: Macmillan.

Callan, T., R. Layte, B. Nolan, D. Watson, C. Whelan, J. Williams and B. Maître (1999b), *Monitoring Poverty Trends*, Dublin: Stationery Office and Combat Poverty Agency.

Central Bank of Ireland (1996/99), *Quarterly Reports*, Dublin.

Central Statistics Office (1986–99), Most reports and series.

Commission of Social Welfare (1986), *Report* PL 3851, Dublin: Stationery Office.

Committee on Costs and Competitiveness (1981), Dublin: Stationery Office.

Committee on Industrial Organisation (1965), Dublin: Stationery Office.

Connell, Peter and James C. Stewart (1997), "Demographic Projections and Population Ageing in Ireland", *Conference on Public Service Pensions Policy Issues*, Dublin, 26 September.

Connolly, James (1973), *Labour in Irish History*, Dublin: New Books.

Craig, Maurice (1969), *Dublin 1660–1860*, Dublin: Allen and Figgis.

Crotty, Raymond (1979), "Capitalist Colonialism and Peripheralisation: the Irish Case" in D. Seers, N. Shaffer and M. Kiljunen (eds.) *Underdeveloped Europe: Studies in Core–Periphery Relations*, Hassocks Harvester Press, pp. 225–235.

Crotty, R. (1986), *Ireland in Crisis*, Tralee: Brandon.

Cullen, L.M. (1968), "The Irish Economy in the Eighteenth Century", in L.M. Cullen (ed.), *Formation of the Irish Economy*, Cork: Mercier.

Cullen, L.M, (1972), *An Economic History of Ireland Since 1660*, London: Batsford.

Culliton Report (1992), *A Time for Change: Industrial Policy for the 1990s*, Report of the Industrial Review Group, Dublin: Stationery Office.

Daly, Mary (1992), *Industrial Development and Irish National Identity*, Dublin: Gill and Macmillan.

Department of Enterprise and Employment (1996), *Growing and Sharing our Employment*, Dublin: Stationery Office.

Department of Environment (1998), *Quarterly Bulletin of Housing Statistics*, Dublin.

Drucker, Peter (1946), *Concept of the Corporation*.

Drudy, P.J. (1999), *Report of the Housing Commission*, Labour Party, Dublin.

Dublin Local Authorities (1999), "*Housing in Dublin*", Dublin: Dublin Local Authorities.

Duggan, D., G. Hughes and J.J. Sexton (1997), *Occupational Employment Forecasts 2003*, FAS/ESRI Manpower Forecasting Studies, No. 6, Dublin: ESRI

Durkan, Joe, Doireann Fitzgerald and Colm Harmon (1999), "Education and Growth in the Irish Economy" in Frank Barry (ed.), *Understanding Ireland's Economic Growth*, Hampshire: Macmillan.

Economic Development (1957), (Pr. 4803), Dublin: Stationery Office.

Economic and Social Research Institute (1989), *Poverty, Income and Welfare in Ireland*, Dublin: ESRI.

Economic and Social Research Institute (1996/9), *Quarterly Reports*, Dublin: ESRI.

Economic and Social Research Institute (1997), *Medium Term Review: 1997–2003*, Dublin: ESRI.

Economic and Social Research Institute (1999), *National Investment Priorities for the Period 2000–2006*, Dublin: ESRI.

Economic Review and Outlook (1997), Dublin: Stationery Office.

European Commission (1996), *European Economy*, Brussels: EC.

European Commission (1997a), *European Economy*, Brussels: EC.

European Commission (1997b), *Green Paper: Partnership for a New Organisation of Work*, Brussels: EC.

European Commission (1998), *European Economy*, Brussels: EC.

European Commission (1999), *Employment in Europe, 1998*, Brussels: EC.

Fahey, Tony (1999a), *Housing Data*, paper to Maynooth College.

Fahey, Tony (1999b), *Social Housing in Ireland*, Dublin: Oak Tree Press in association with Combat Poverty Agency and the Katharine Howard Foundation.

Farrell, Brian (1983), *Sean Lemass*, Dublin: Gill and Macmillan.

Foley, Anthony and Michael Mulreany (1990), *The Single Market and the Irish Economy*, Dublin: IPA.

Forfás (1996), *Shaping Our Future*, Dublin: Forfás.

Forfás (1998a), *Annual Survey of Irish Economy Expenditures — Results for 1996*, Dublin: Forfás.

Forfás (1998b), *1997 Employment Survey*, Dublin: Forfás.

Forfás, *Annual Reports*, Dublin, various years.

Foster, Roy (1989), *Modern Ireland 1600–1972*, London: Penguin.

Guiomard, Cathal (1995), *The Irish Disease and How to Cure It*, Dublin: Oak Tree Press.

Healy, Sean and Brigid Reynolds (1997), *Surfing the Income Net*, Dublin: CORI.

Healy, Sean and Brigid Reynolds (1998), *Social Policy in Ireland*, Dublin: Oak Tree Press/CORI.

Hirst, Paul and Grahame Thompson (1996), *Globalisation in Question*, London: Blackwell.

Industrial Development Authority, *Annual Reports*, various years.

Interim Report of the Task Force on Long-Term Unemployment (1995), Office of the Tánaiste, Dublin: Stationery Office.

International Monetary Fund (1997), *World Economic Outlook*, Washington: IMF.

Jacobson, David (1996), "Coping with the Global Economy," *SIPTU South East Region, Biennial Conference*, 17 November.

Jacobson, David and Bernadette Andreosso (1990), "Ireland as a Location for Multinational Investment" in Anthony Foley and Michael Mulreany (eds.), *The Single Market and the Irish Economy*, Dublin: IPA.

Jacobson, David and Bernadette Andreosso (1996*), Industrial Economics and Organisation*, London: McGraw-Hill.

Kearney, Colm (1999), "The Asian Financial Crisis", *ESRI Quarterly*, February, Dublin.

Keating, Bill (1996), "Measuring Growth", *Proceedings of Conference on Measuring Economic Growth*, Dublin: CSO and IEA.

Kennedy K.A. (ed.) (1998), *From Famine to Feast: Economic and Social Change in Ireland, 1947 to 1997*, Dublin: IPA.

Kennedy K.A., Giblin, T. and McHugh, D., (1989), *The Economic Development of Ireland in the Twentieth Century*, London: Routledge.

Keogh, Dermot (1994), *Twentieth Century Ireland*, Dublin: Gill and Macmillan.

Kirby, Peadar (1997), *Poverty amid Plenty*, Dublin: Gill and Macmillan/ Trocaire.

Koedijk, K. and J. Kremers (1996), "Market Opening, Regulation and Growth in Europe", *Economic Policy*.

Krugman, Paul (1995), *Peddling Prosperity*, London: Norton.

Lane, Phillip, (1998), "Profits and Wages in Ireland, 1987–1996", *Journal of the Statistical and Social Enquiry Society of Ireland*, Vol. XXVII, Part V, Dublin.

Lee, George (1994), *The Insider-Outsider Economy*, Dublin: ISME.

Lee, J.J. (1973), *Modernisation of Irish Society, 1848–1918*, Dublin: Gill and Macmillan.

Lee, J.J. (1989), *Ireland 1912–1985: Politics and Society*, Cambridge: CUP.

Leddin, Anthony and Brendan Walsh (1997), "Economic Stabilisation, Recovery and Growth: Ireland 1979–1996" *Irish Banking Review*, Summer.

Leddin, Anthony and Brendan Walsh (1998), *The Macroeconomy of Ireland*, Dublin: Gill and Macmillan.

Lenin, V.I. (1916), *Imperialism: the Highest Stage of Capitalism*, Peking: Foreign Languages Press, 1970 reprint.

Landes, David (1998), *The Wealth and Poverty of Nations*, London: Little, Brown and Co.

Lyons, F.S.L. (1976), *Ireland Since the Famine*, London: Fontana.

Matthews, Alan (1994), *Managing the EU Structural Funds in Ireland*, Cork: Cork University Press.

Moriarty Report (1993), *Employment Through Enterprise*, Response from Government to Moriarty Report, Dublin: Stationery Office.

Murphy, Antoin E. (1994), *The Irish Economy: Celtic Tiger or Tortoise?* Dublin: MMI Stockbrokers.

Murphy, Antoin E. (1996), "The Two-Faced Economy", *Proceedings of Conference on Measuring Economic Growth*, Dublin: CSO and IEA.

National Anti-Poverty Strategy (1996), Dublin: Stationery Office.

National Competitiveness Council (1999), *Annual Competitiveness Report*, Dublin: Forfás.

National Economic and Social Council (1982), *Telesis: A Review of Industrial Policy*, Dublin: NESC, No. 64.

National Economic and Social Council (1986), *Strategy for Development 1986–1990*, Dublin: NESC, No. 83.

National Economic and Social Council (1990), *A Strategy for the Nineties*, Dublin: NESC, No. 89.

National Economic and Social Council (1991), *The Economic and Social Implications of Emigration*, Dublin: NESC, No. 90.

National Economic and Social Council (1992), *The Association between Economic Growth and Employment Growth in Ireland*, Dublin: NESC, No. 94.

National Economic and Social Council (1993a), *Lars Mjoset: The Irish Economy in a Comparative Institutional Perspective*, Dublin: NESC, January, No. 93.

National Economic and Social Council (1993b), *A Strategy for Competitiveness, Growth and Employment*, Dublin: NESC, November, No. 96.

National Economic and Social Council (1996), *Strategy for the Twenty-First Century*, Dublin: NESC, No. 99.

National Economic and Social Forum (1997), *Early School Leavers and Youth Unemployment*, Report No. 11, Dublin: NESF.

O'Brien, George (1921), *The Economic History of Ireland from the Union to the Famine*, Dublin and London: Maunsel.

O'Connell, Phillip J. (1998), *Astonishing Success: Economic Growth and the Labour Market in Ireland*, ILO, Geneva.

OECD (1994), *The OECD Jobs Study*, Paris: OECD.

OECD (1996), *The OECD Jobs Strategy: Enhancing the Effectiveness of Active Labour Market Policies*, Paris: OECD.

OECD (1997a), *Economic Surveys: Ireland, 1997*, Paris: OECD.

OECD (1998), *Revenue Statistics*, Paris: OECD.

OECD (1999), *Economic Surveys: Ireland, 1999*, Paris: OECD.

OECD (1997b), *Economic Outlook, No. 61*, Paris: OECD.

OECD (1998), *Economic Outlook, No. 64*, Paris: OECD.

O'Donnell and O'Reardon (1996), "The Irish Experiment: Social Partnership has Yielded Economic Growth and Social Progress", *European Industrial Relations International*, October.

Ó Gráda, Cormac (1995), *Ireland: A New Economic History 1780–1939*, Oxford: OUP.

Ó Gráda, Cormac (1997), *A Rocky Road: The Irish Economy Since the 1920s*, Manchester: Manchester University Press.

O'Hearn, Denis (1998) *Inside the Celtic Tiger*, London: Pluto Press.

O'Malley, Eoin (1981), "The Decline of Irish Industry in the Nineteenth Century", *Economic and Social Review*, Vol. 13, October.

O'Malley, Eoin (1989), *Industry and Economic Development: the Challenge for the Latecomer*, Dublin: Gill and Macmillan.

O'Sullivan, Mary (1995), "Manufacturing and Global Competition" in J.W. O'Hagan, *The Economy of Ireland*, Dublin: Gill and Macmillan.

O'Toole, Fintan (1994), *Black Hole, Green Card*, Dublin: New Island Books.

O'Toole, Francis (1997), *Tax and PRSI Reform from a Low Income Perspective*, Dublin: Combat Poverty Agency.

Oxfam (1997), *Growth with Equity: An Agenda for Poverty Reduction*, London: Oxfam.

Partnership 2000 for Inclusion, Employment and Competitiveness (1996), Dublin: Stationery Office.

Plunkett, James (1971), *Strumpet City*, London: Panther.

Porter, Michael (1990), *Competitive Advantage of Nations*, Macmillan, London.

Programme for Competitiveness and Work (1994), Dublin: Stationery Office.

Programme for Economic Expansion, 1959–63 (1958), Dublin: Stationery Office.

Programme for National Recovery (1987), Dublin: Stationery Office.

Programme of Economic and Social Progress (1991), Dublin: Stationery Office.

Reicheld, Fredrick F. (1997), *The Loyalty Effect: The Hidden Force Behind Growth, Profits and Lasting Value*, Harvard: Harvard Business School Press.

Roche, W.K. (1995), "The New Competitive Order and the Fragmentation of Industrial Relations in Ireland", *IBEC Employee Relations Conference*, November.

Roche, W.K. and P. Gunnigle (1994), "Competition and the New Industrial Relations Agenda" in Thomas V. Murphy and William K. Roche (eds.), *Irish Industrial Relations in Practice*, Dublin: Oak Tree Press.

Roche, W.K. and J.F. Geary (1998), *Collective Production and the Irish Boom: Work Organisation, Partnership and Direct Involvement in Irish Workplaces*, Dublin: UCD.

Sabel, Charles (1996), *Ireland: Local Partnership and Social Innovation*, Paris: OECD.

Second Programme for Economic Expansion (1964–70), Dublin: Stationery Office.

SIPTU (1996a), "Life after the PCW: Review and Perspectives", Unpublished Research Paper, Dublin: SIPTU, March.

SIPTU (1996b), "Corporate Profits, 1990–1995", Unpublished Research Paper, Dublin: SIPTU.

SIPTU Report, Spring 1999, SIPTU, Dublin.

Socialist Economists (1983), *Jobs and Wages — The True Story of Competitiveness*, Dublin: Socialist Economists.

Socialist Economists (1985), *Jobs and Borrowing — Where the Right is Wrong*, Dublin: Socialist Economists.

Stewart, James C. (1977), "Multinationals and Transfer Pricing" *Journal of Business*, Finance and Accounting, Vol. 4, No. 3.

Stewart, James C. (1987), *Corporate Finance and Fiscal Policy in Ireland*, Aldershot: Gower.

Strategic Management Initiative (1996), Dublin: Stationery Office.

Strobl, E., P. Walsh and F. Barry (1996), "Aggregate Employment Flows in Irish Manufacturing", Paper to Irish Economic Association, TCD working paper, 96/3.

Sweeney, Paul (1990), *The Politics of Public Enterprise and Privatisation*, Dublin: Tomar.

Sweeney, Paul (1992), "Symposium on the Findings of Industrial Policy Review Group", *Journal of the Statistical and Social Enquiry Society of Ireland*, Vol. XXVI, Part VI, Dublin.

Sweeney, Paul (1995), "Employment in Ireland" in Peter Shirlow (ed.), *Development Ireland*, London: Pluto Press.

Tánaiste's Office (1995), *Task Force on Long-Term Unemployment*, Dublin: Stationery Office.

Tansey, Paul (1998), *Ireland at Work: Economic Growth and the Labour Market 1987-1997*, Dublin: Oak Tree Press.

Teague, Paul (1995), "Pay Determination in the Republic of Ireland: Towards Social Corporatism?" *British Journal of Industrial Relations*, Vol. 33, No. 2, June.

UBS (1997), *Prices and Earnings around the Globe*, Zurich: UBS.

United Nations (1997), *Human Development Report*, New York: UN.

INDEX